We Are Family

We Are Family

The Modern Transformation of Parents and Children

Susan Golombok

PUBLICAFFAIRS
New York

PublicAffairs
Hachette Book Group
1290 Avenue of the Americas, New York, NY 10104
www.publicaffairsbooks.com
@Public_Affairs

Printed in the United States of America

Originally published in 2020 by Scribe

First US Edition: October 2020

Published by PublicAffairs, an imprint of Perseus Books, LLC, a subsidiary of Hachette Book Group, Inc. The PublicAffairs name and logo is a trademark of the Hachette Book Group.

The Hachette Speakers Bureau provides a wide range of authors for speaking events. To find out more, go to www.hachettespeakersbureau.com or call (866) 376-6591.

The publisher is not responsible for websites (or their content) that are not owned by the publisher.

Eighty-six (86) words from *The Bastard of Istanbul* by Elif Shafak (Penguin Books 2008, 2019) Copyright © Elif Shafak, 2007

Excerpt from 'WE ARE FAMILY', Words and Music by Bernard Edwards and Nile Rodgers © 1979 Bernard's Other Music (BMI). All rights on behalf of Bernard's Other Music administered by Warner-Tamerlane Publishing Corp. Reproduced by permission of Sony Music Publishing, London W1F 9LD

Susan Golombok, 'Research on Assisted Reproduction Families: A Historical Perspective', ed. Gabor Kovacs, Peter Brinsden, & Alan DeCherney, *In-Vitro Fertilization: the pioneers' history*, 2018, © Cambridge University Press 2018, reprinted with permission

Susan Golombok, *Modern Families: parents and children in new family forms*, 2015, © Susan Golombok 2015, published by Cambridge University Press, reprinted with permission

Excerpt from *Red Dust Road* by Jackie Kay © Jackie Kay 2010, reproduced with permission of the Licensor through PLSclear

Typeset in Fournier MT by Scribe

Library of Congress Control Number: 2020940094

ISBNs: 978-1-5417-5864-3 (hardcover), 978-1-5417-5863-6 (ebook)

LSC-C

10 9 8 7 6 5 4 3 2 1

To John and Jamie, my family

'When you have absolutely no idea what kind of man your father is, your imagination fills in the void. Perhaps I watch him on TV or hear his voice on the radio every day, without knowing it's him. Or I might have come face-to-face with him sometime, someplace. I imagine I might have taken the same bus with him; perhaps he is the professor I talk to after class, the photographer whose exhibition I go to see, or this street vendor here ... You never know.'

ELIF SHAFAK, **THE BASTARD OF ISTANBUL, 2007.**

***

'What is the family? Time was when most people probably thought the answer was not merely clear but obvious. Today it is more complex ... Children live in households where their parents may be married or unmarried. They may be brought up by a single parent, by two parents or even by three parents. Their parents may or may not be their natural parents ... Some children are brought up by two parents of the same sex. Some children are conceived by artificial donor insemination. Some are the result of surrogacy arrangements. The fact is that many adults and children, whether through choice or circumstance, live in families more or less removed from what, until comparatively recently, would have been recognised as the typical nuclear family. This, I stress, is not merely the reality; it is, I believe, a reality which we should welcome and applaud.'

SIR JAMES MUNBY, FORMER PRESIDENT OF THE FAMILY DIVISION OF THE HIGH COURT AND HEAD OF FAMILY JUSTICE FOR ENGLAND AND WALES, 2018.

'We are family

I got all my sisters with me

We are family

Get up everybody and sing'

SISTER SLEDGE

Contents

We Are Family

Preface

It began by chance with a copy of the feminist magazine *Spare Rib,* delivered to my doorstep in Camden, London in September 1976. Recently arrived from my native Scotland, I was beginning a Master's degree in child development at the University of London, and the magazine's cover story caught my eye. It showed a photograph of three women and their three children underneath the headline, 'Out of the closet into the courts: why could one of these women lose custody of her child?' I flipped open the magazine and began to read.

The journalist, Eleanor Stephens, described how, almost without exception, lesbian mothers fighting custody battles against their former husbands were losing the right to live with their children, in stark contrast to the experiences of heterosexual mothers who were practically always awarded custody in those days. At the time the article was published, not a single lesbian woman had been awarded custody of her children by a UK court. There was no actual evidence that lesbian women were poor parents, and yet they were being separated from their children on the grounds that it was against a child's best interests to be raised in a lesbian household. This immediately struck me as unjust and — what's more — unscientific.

The article called for a volunteer to carry out an objective study into the wellbeing of children in lesbian mother families, something that had never been done before. I had been searching for a subject for my Master's dissertation, and felt that it was cruel to break up these families, especially in the absence of any evidence against them. So I responded to the call for help, offering my services as a fledgling researcher. Little did I know that this would be the start of a research project that would continue for the rest of my working life.

I got in touch with 'Action for Lesbian Parents', the group of women mentioned in the article who were dedicated to publicising the unfairness of the legal system and were looking for researchers to investigate children growing up in lesbian mother families. A woman called Berni Humphreys answered my call and invited me to come to her home in Cambridge where the group was based. Berni's house was a large, grey-stoned Victorian villa, with children's drawings on the walls inside. I was nervous throughout the meeting. The women in the group were all mothers, which seemed terribly grown-up to my 22-year-old self, and some were involved in fierce child custody disputes with their ex-husbands. They understandably wanted to make sure that I could be trusted to carry out an independent study, and were especially concerned that I did not hold preconceived ideas about lesbian mother families. They asked me about my background and questioned me in great detail about how I would conduct the research. Some of the women were researchers themselves and gave me a tough grilling. But somehow, I passed their test, and they agreed to put me in touch with organisations that could help me find families who were willing to take part.

Many years later, I moved to Cambridge to become the director of the University's Centre for Family Research. Whenever I pass that grey-stone house I think of the drawings on the walls and wonder where those children are today. I also think about how the families in that house — who had to fight so hard for their existence, let alone acceptance — paved the way for many different types of families, families I could not even imagine in 1976.

***

In the years since then, new reproductive technologies and evolving social norms have radically changed the ways that families are created and structured. The first IVF baby, Louise Brown, was born in 1978, soon followed by children conceived through egg and embryo donation. Sperm donation became much more common, and the first cases of commercial surrogacy, that of 'Baby M' in the US and 'Baby Cotton' in the UK, hit the headlines in the mid-1980s. Today, we have gay fathers with children born through surrogacy and egg donation, single mothers by choice, and lesbian couples sharing parenthood by using one woman's egg to create her partner's pregnancy. There is an increasing trend of much older mothers, a phenomenon that is likely to grow as a result of egg-freezing technologies. And we face the prospect of synthetic eggs and sperm, artificial wombs, and children born with edited genes. Parenthood is becoming accessible in ways we could never have dreamed of just a few years ago. But what impact does this have on children?

Like the judges presiding over lesbian mother custody disputes in the 1970s, many people base their opinions of these new families on assumptions and not evidence. It has always been assumed that the structure of families matters a great deal in child development: the greater the difference from the traditional family, the conventional wisdom goes, the greater the perceived risk of psychological harm to the child. This idea gained prominence in the 20th century, in part through Sigmund Freud's psychoanalytic theory, and remained a cornerstone of later psychological theories.

But is it really true? The results from our first study of lesbian mothers, published in 1983, suggested not: they showed clearly that these children were no more likely to experience psychological problems than children raised by heterosexual mothers, too late for many lesbian women who had already been separated from their children. I suspected this might also be the case for other new family forms, and I wanted to tease apart the effects of family structure from the effects of family relationships through proper scientific research. So I set off on a path that took me, and an outstanding team of researchers — psychologists, sociologists, social anthropologists, bioethicists, and medical doctors — on a fascinating exploration of new family forms as they emerged throughout the twentieth and twenty-first centuries.

I started in London, first at the Institute of Psychiatry and then at City University, and in 2006 moved to the Centre for Family Research at the University of Cambridge, founded by Martin Richards in 1966. We began with lesbian mothers and were the first researchers to follow babies born through IVF and donor insemination from childhood to adult life. Other types of families soon followed.

Around the millennium, we began a new study of families formed through egg donation, donor insemination, and surrogacy, which remains the only study in the world to have investigated children born to surrogate mothers. We have followed these children from infancy to adolescence, and have visited them six times so far, studying how their early experiences affect later development.

More recently, we have been at the forefront of research on gay father families formed through adoption, and have conducted the first study of gay father families created through surrogacy in the United States. Our latest research focuses on co-parents who are raising children together without being romantically involved, children with transgender parents, single fathers by choice, and children born using identifiable egg donors.

We visit these families in their homes to find out about the children's development and wellbeing, and their relationships with their parents. We interview mothers, fathers, and children; observe families interacting with each other; and carry out assessments specifically designed for children, involving stories, games and puppets. We also ask teachers to complete questionnaires on children's behaviour at school

So what have we found? Our research shows clearly that, just as with those pioneering lesbian mother families we studied, children can flourish in all kinds of new family forms. There is no evidence that growing up with lesbian mothers or gay fathers, or that being born through assisted reproductive technologies involving donated eggs, sperm, embryos or surrogacy, will cause psychological harm to children. And yet these families still face enormous prejudice today, even in some of the most progressive countries in the world.

I wrote this book to present the findings of our research, which fly in the face of outdated and biased assumptions about different kinds of families. I ended up mainly telling these families' stories, letting them speak for themselves about what their day-to-day lives are really like. These are the mothers, fathers, donors, surrogates, and children for whom these new family forms do not represent a social or technological revolution, but, rather, their own lives and relationships.

These are stories of parents who have had children against the odds. They are ultimately stories of love.

Chapter 1

Lesbian Mothers: 'Uncharted Waters'

'The homosexuality of the plaintiff as a matter of law constitutes her not a fit or proper person to have the care, custody and control of ... the minor child of the parties hereto.'

JUDGE BABICH, *NADLER V. NADLER*,
SUPERIOR COURT OF CALIFORNIA, (1967).

'I've got two parents who love me. It doesn't matter if they're a boy or a girl.'

ALICE, AGE 7, (2009).

It was 1982 when Anne Hitchins, a 33-year-old mother of three, finally found the courage to leave her husband. She left him a note, closed the door of her seafront home in a holiday resort in the north of England, collected her unsuspecting children from school, and, thanks to a friend's offer of a house to rent, stepped fearfully into the unknown. Anne had never been employed, never paid a bill on her own, never so much as kissed anyone other than her husband, and she had very little money. But she was desperate for a different life. For years she had endured her husband's drinking, gambling, and bullying; it was time to break free.

The years that followed were challenging. Anne's children reacted badly to the separation; the youngest became angry and disruptive, and longed for her parents to reunite. Her husband promised to change if she returned, although she knew that he would not. Her parents riled against her for bringing shame upon the family. The authorities encouraged her to go back home.

Anne had been just 16 when she met her husband, a 19-year-old philosophy student who frequented her parents' pub near the local university. To Anne — who had grown up on a working-class housing estate, left her low-achieving school with no qualifications, and was now expected to look after her five younger siblings — he offered escape, and the promise of a new life. She fell in love and, to the disapproval of her parents, soon became pregnant with the couple's first child. The swinging sixties hadn't quite reached their northern town; unmarried mothers brought disgrace upon their families. The pregnancy was covered up and a wedding hastily arranged at the local Registry Office. She was 18 and it was 1968.

Despite her shotgun wedding, Anne was content. Now married, she could leave her parents' home and build her own life. The couple moved to her husband's birthplace on the south coast, and their daughter was born. Anne quickly settled into motherhood, and had three children within five years. In the mid-1970s, when the youngest child was a toddler, the family returned to the north of England for her husband's new job in local government. He was the breadwinner and Anne raised the children. 'I wouldn't have been allowed to work! Not in those days. Who else would look after the children? I willingly put myself in that situation and carried on being quite happy with it for a fair time.' She kept a spotless house, and made sure her children were well fed, but soon her husband's late-night gambling, drinking, and smoking with his friends began to take its toll on their relationship.

It was a neighbour who first opened Anne's eyes. She gave Anne a copy of the feminist magazine, *Spare Rib*, where Anne read with fascination about local women who were setting up a refuge for victims of domestic abuse. Anne wanted to help. She knew how to care for children, so she offered to run the crèche. But when her husband found out, he forbade her from being involved. He wanted her to stay at home, even though their children were now in school. So she carried on in secret. Here, among these enterprising women, Anne discovered a sense of purpose. She also realised that she wasn't happy in her marriage. On learning of a friend's divorce, Anne realised that she too could escape, but it would not be easy. She thought about it for months. It took a particularly vicious row with her husband over her finding part-time work to give her the strength to walk out. As she recollected to me 40 years later, 'I realised I wasn't fulfilled. I realised I was unhappy. And I realised I was a victim of mental battering.'

It was not until after she had left her husband that Anne fell in love with Rita, another friend who had supported her along the way. But the relationship was too dangerous. 'I knew if there was evidence, he could have taken the children,' said Anne. 'I desperately wanted to keep the children, so I made the decision to split up with Rita. I knew I would have lost them. It was cut and dried in those days. It was not until my children were all over eighteen that I could relax. It was only then that I knew he couldn't come along at any time and take them away.'

Anne's fears were justified, as she would soon learn. Following her divorce, she moved to Birmingham and was offered a job at a newly established Women's Advice Centre where she helped women, especially those who had lost custody of their children because of their sexuality.

'They were deemed unfit mothers,' she told me. 'I supported more than thirty lesbian mothers who were fighting for custody of their children. Not one got their children back. They were completely destroyed.'

***

Long before the 1970s there were, of course, lesbian women who were married to men and bringing up children. Women who were aware of their sexuality but felt they had to conform to society's expectations of a heterosexual marriage, or who had fallen in love with another woman after becoming a wife and mother. But these women were usually forced to keep their sexuality secret. It was not until the 1970s, inspired by the growth of the women's and gay liberation movements, that lesbian women with children began to live their lives more openly. For many, this would result in acrimonious custody battles that they were bound to lose.

While Anne was counselling desperate lesbian mothers through their custody disputes in the UK, in the United States, a similar situation was unfolding. In October 1975, in Dallas, Texas, Mary Jo Risher's life was turned upside down when she opened the door of the home she shared with her partner, Ann Foreman, and their three children — Mary Jo's two sons and Ann's daughter — and was served with a writ. Mary Jo's former husband, who had recently remarried, was seeking custody of their boys on the grounds that she was living with Ann 'in a homosexual relationship as man and wife'. The document expressed his wish that the children 'should be removed from this immoral and undesirable environment' as soon as possible. Mary Jo was distraught.

The ensuing trial, which took place in a Dallas court and lasted for more than a week, centred on the speculated effects of Mary Jo's lesbian relationship on her younger son, Richard, then aged eight. Her other son, Jimmy, aged 17, was already living with his father. The jury of ten men and two women heard evidence from almost 20 expert witnesses, many of whom claimed that Mary Jo's sexual orientation would cause her son harm; in particular, that he would find it difficult to acquire a masculine identity and would possibly grow up to be gay, an outcome that was considered highly undesirable at the time. It was just two years since the American Psychiatric Association had removed homosexuality from their list of psychiatric disorders, and homophobia was rife. The jury deliberated for a day and a half before deciding that Richard should live with his father. On hearing that she had lost custody of her son, Mary Jo broke down in anguish. Just a few days later, she was required to hand over her young son, who she had raised from birth, to her ex-husband and his new wife. She was permitted to see him only every other weekend.

Speaking to Sandra Elkin, the creator and presenter of *Woman*, the first American television programme on women's issues, in 1977, Mary Jo said, 'Doctors went on the stand, educators, babysitters, relatives, friends, psychologists and a psychiatrist, and at no time did they prove that I was an unfit mother.' The foreman of the jury, Tony Liscio, a former Dallas Cowboys American football player, who was one of the two members of the jury who voted in favour of Mary Jo, told the press afterwards that the jury could not let go of the issue of Mary Jo's sexuality. Her extremely conventional lifestyle didn't help her; the fact that she was a lesbian trumped everything.

'I was president of the Dallas County Council of Parents and Teachers Association, an active member of the Southern Baptist Church, and a past Sunday School teacher. My life has revolved around children, working for the betterment of all our boys and girls,' said Mary Jo. 'My children were evaluated by a psychiatrist. Both came out as well-balanced, age appropriate, normal, healthy, and happy. I think that's probably what parents should strive for.'

Mary Jo was asked in court whether she would give up her homosexuality if she knew she could keep her son. To her, it was an unfair question, as members of the jury were unlikely to be asked to choose between their husband and their child. In the end, it all boiled down to one key issue: 'Some of the jurors were afraid that if my son remained with me, he would become a homosexual.'

In the rare cases during the 1970s where lesbian mothers were allowed to retain custody of their children, they were often not permitted to live with their female partners. In December 1972, the case of Schuster vs. Isaacson came to court in Washington State. Sandy Schuster and Madeleine Isaacson, both deeply religious, had met through their church the previous year and fallen in love. Between them they had six children. When they fled to progressive California to live as a family, their husbands pursued them and abducted one of Sandy's children and both of Madeleine's. Although both the social worker and the psychiatrist appointed by the court declared the children to be well adjusted, loved, and perfectly happy with their new family circumstances, the judge would only award custody to the mothers on the condition that they lived apart. To avoid being separated, while complying with the court's order, Sandy and Madeleine moved out of their joint home into adjacent apartments. When their former husbands found out about their new living arrangement, they were enraged and took the women back to court. The battle continued for a further six years. It was not until the case reached the Washington Supreme Court in 1978 that Sandy and Madeleine won the right to live together with their children.

This practice did not end in the 1970s. One of the most shocking cases in which a lesbian woman lost custody of her child took place in Florida in 1995. Mary Ward, who was raising her 11-year-old daughter with her female partner, lost custody to her ex-husband, a convicted murderer who had killed his first wife during a custody dispute. Newspaper-headline writers had a field day: 'Lesbian mum vs. killer dad', 'Custody given to killer', and 'Gay mom battles killer dad for kid'. In a television interview, the father callously described the killing: 'I shot her three times in the upper left shoulder. She told me not to kill her, she would give me the baby and a divorce. I fired three times into the heart ... And I reloaded and I shot her six more times point blank.' A documentary about the case, *Unfit: Ward vs. Ward*, released in 2012, asked the question, 'Who is more fit to raise a child? A convicted killer? Or a lesbian?' In this case, the judge ruled that a convicted murderer who knew little about his daughter's life, including which school she attended and what grade she was in, offered a more suitable home for the child than the lesbian couple. Placing far greater weight on the mother's sexual orientation than on her qualities as a parent, the judge summed up, 'I believe that this child should be given the opportunity and the option to live in a non-lesbian world.'

***

While Mary Jo Risher and the women Anne Hitchins counselled in Birmingham were fighting for custody of their existing children in the 1970s, other lesbian women were taking motherhood into their own hands.

Times were changing, and the growth of feminism had led to new ways of living and new ways of creating families. Carol Wiltshire and her female partner Hilary Jackson were part of a vibrant community of feminists and left-wing activists living collectively and sharing child-care while also conserving Georgian and Victorian terraced streets in north London that were threatened with destruction. Consciousness-raising groups were the bedrock of feminism in the 1970s, and Carol and Hilary spent hours sitting around kitchen tables with like-minded women, talking intensely about women's lives, the function of families, their relationships with their mothers, and how best to live both ethically and politically as lesbians and as feminists. They wanted to understand women's roles and relationships, and to create alternative family structures free from oppression based on sex, gender, or sexual orientation. For many young feminists, it was a time of optimism and high ideals.

Carol and Hilary both loved children. They were involved in caring for the children in their community and had always assumed that one day they too would be mothers. They chose self-insemination as their means of conceiving a baby, the do-it-yourself 'turkey-baster' method, in which insemination with sperm from a donor was carried out at home with a syringe. As the older of the two, they decided that Hilary would become pregnant first. She conceived using the sperm of a friend of a friend. Gay men in their wider social circle were happy to donate sperm in those days; they felt it was a positive and supportive thing to do for lesbian women. Carol and Hilary's first daughter, Daisy, was born in 1983, but the AIDS crisis changed everything. The man who had provided the sperm used to conceive Daisy was happy to do so again, but he was not willing to take an HIV test. So, like many other lesbian women, they advertised for a donor in the alternative London weekly politics and events magazine, *City Limits*. Their chosen respondent was an altruistic young man who wanted to help lesbian couples have children but also wished to remain anonymous. Carol gave birth to the couple's second daughter, Rowan, in 1986.

For Carol, her community was her sanctuary. She had grown up in a small rural town in England in a very traditional family, the oldest of three children, and had first realised that she was a lesbian in the 1960s when she was 14. It was a lonely experience. It was not until she left home to go to university that she came out. Her parents disowned her. They were ashamed of her. And they didn't want her anywhere near her younger siblings. When Carol gave birth to Rowan, her mother didn't come to visit. 'It was always, "What would the neighbours think?" What could she say to the priest?' she remembered. 'I found out that my mother had gone all the way to a family event only a few miles away from where I lived, but she hadn't come to see me and my baby. It was absolutely awful. She couldn't tell her friends about me. She just wished I didn't exist. When I had a child, it was the last straw.' While Carol's siblings were supportive and welcomed her children, she felt very hurt at being rejected by her mother. As she put it, 'Even though we had lots of friends, we didn't have our own mothers. We were motherless mothers. We felt bereft.'

Despite this, life was generally happy for the young family. They lived in a housing cooperative that they were both actively involved with, and were part of a network of other lesbian mothers and their children. It was a warm and convivial time. But this utopia could not last. A clause in the Local Government Act, known as Section 28, introduced by the British prime minister, Margaret Thatcher, in 1988, was to have a devastating effect on the lives of lesbian mother families and all gay men and lesbian women living in the UK.

Section 28 banned the promotion of homosexuality, making it illegal to 'intentionally promote homosexuality or publish material with the intention of promoting homosexuality', or promote the teaching of homosexuality as 'a pretended family relationship'. It would not be repealed until 2003. Carol, having witnessed the struggles of lesbian mother friends fighting custody battles in the 1970s, feared that Rowan would be taken from her: 'I was very deeply terrified that I would lose her. I was anxious that she would be taken into care. That we would be seen as unfit parents. That we would not be considered to be a proper family. That we would be seen as a "pretend" family.'

One particularly worrying question was where could the couple's children go to school? If teachers were forbidden from talking about lesbian mother families, how would this affect how Daisy and Rowan were treated? Hilary and Carol's priority was to protect their girls, and there was only one school that they could trust to do this, which already had a good track record for supporting children with lesbian mothers. The problem was, they didn't live within its catchment area.

Section 28 caused other difficulties for the family and their community. It emboldened their homophobic neighbours across the street to begin a campaign of harassment towards them. The neighbours shouted abuse at them and made threats until the situation became so bad that Carol, Hilary and the children had to vacate their home at weekends. Today, such behaviour would be classed as a hate crime; in 1988, no one did anything about it. The family were under siege.

Thanks to Carol's determination and the unflinching support of a senior housing officer, they made their escape and transferred to a housing association property near their preferred school. 'We were very, very lucky,' recalled Carol. 'There were other lesbian families at that school. We met together regularly. We'd go on walks and picnics with the children. There were always events. The children knew that there were other families with two mummies. They didn't feel alone.'

***

In 1976, when I began to plan my first study of lesbian mother families, not a single lesbian woman who had fought for custody of her children in the UK had won. Three grounds for denying custody to lesbian mothers were repeatedly voiced in court: that their children would be teased and bullied at school, and would develop psychological problems as a result; that their children would be unsure of whether they were boys or girls, and would behave inappropriately for their gender, with boys, in particular, preferring the toys, games, and activities usually associated with girls; and that lesbian women lacked the capacity to be good mothers.

One particular case stands out in my mind. It took place in London in the summer of that year and was the subject of the *Spare Rib* article by Eleanor Stephens that had first brought this issue to my attention. Five-year-old John had been living with his mother, Sue, and her female partner, Mary, for two years in the idyllic English countryside. Their home was set in acres of woodland with streams running all around, and they were surrounded by relatives and friends. At first, Sue's ex-husband had agreed to John living with Sue and Mary, and they were all on friendly terms. But when he remarried, he decided that John should live with him and his new wife in a traditional family unit. His relationship with Sue turned sour, and before long they ended up in court.

Sue thought she had a watertight case. Welfare workers and character witnesses gave glowing reports on her mothering. The judge agreed that John had an excellent relationship with his mother, but was concerned about the effects of Sue's sexual orientation on her son's development. Both Sue and her former husband produced psychiatric reports that addressed this issue. Sue's psychiatrist emphasised the quality of her relationship with John, and argued that this was what mattered most for his future wellbeing. But the psychiatrist on her ex-husband's side claimed, 'John's mother practices statistically abnormal sexual acts which can be looked upon either as a deviation from normal or frankly perverted. I have no evidence before me to state that this environment will not affect John's future emotional and psychosexual development.' This psychiatrist went on to assert that the absence of a father in the home would prevent John from identifying as male, and that he would feel ashamed and embarrassed about having a lesbian mother when he reached adolescence. The judge sided with Sue's ex-husband, awarding him custody. He capped off his judgment with the statement: 'These are uncharted waters which I'm not prepared to sail on.'

John was removed from his home with Sue and Mary, where he was happy, and placed with his father and new stepmother. Sue was granted access once a fortnight and for part of the school holidays. The judge ruled that when John visited, Sue and Mary had to sleep in separate rooms.

Speaking to Eleanor Stephens soon after losing her son, a devastated Sue highlighted the need for research into the children of lesbian mothers: 'We desperately need some research on all of this. I believe this would have had a tremendous effect. It would undermine some of the statements they made which are based on nothing but prejudice and ridiculous myths about homosexuals.'

It seemed to me that the opinion of the psychiatrist retained on behalf of the father, and acted on by the judge, was rooted in a very narrow view of the processes involved in a child's psychological development. Although some theories of child development that were prominent at the time did predict the outcomes described by this psychiatrist, others did not. In the absence of any specific research on the topic, we simply didn't know. This custody case brought home to me the pressing need for evidence on the experiences of children in lesbian mother families.

I very much wanted to carry out a study on the children of lesbian mothers for my Master's thesis, but not one of my lecturers was willing to supervise me; some thought the topic wasn't interesting, others that it was too controversial. Fortunately, the expert who had been called on behalf of Sue, the eminent child psychiatrist, Sir Michael Rutter, head of the Department of Child Psychiatry at the Institute of Psychiatry in London, was a strong advocate of the importance of empirical data in this field. He knew that no such research existed, and that the statement by the opposing expert had been based on speculation rather than fact. Through a chance encounter with a member of his research team when he came to give a lecture to my Master's class, Michael Rutter heard about my study and offered his support.

The aim of our research was to address the questions that had arisen in the child custody cases being fought in the UK and the US: Were lesbian mothers less capable as parents? Were their children more likely to experience emotional and behavioural problems? And were their sons less masculine, and their daughters less feminine, than boys and girls from heterosexual homes? (At the time, children who did not conform to behaviour that was typical of their gender were considered to have a psychological disorder. Today, this is not the case; differences in gender-related behaviours are seen simply as variation between people, and not unusual.) We decided to compare lesbian mother families where the children had been born into a heterosexual marriage to families with single heterosexual mothers. Both types of family were headed by mothers, so any differences found between them were likely to result from the difference in the mothers' sexual orientation rather than the presence of fathers in one group of families and not the other.

I planned to interview the mothers about their experiences — their previous marriages, their day-to-day lives as lesbian couples bringing up children together, and the reactions of their children to their new family circumstances. I knew that not only had the children been separated from their fathers, but many had also gained a stepmother — a relationship that can be difficult at the best of times. I wanted to find out whether having a stepmother was more difficult for children of divorced lesbian mothers than having a stepfather was for children of divorced heterosexual mothers, whether the children lost contact with their fathers, and how their non-traditional family set-ups affected them at school.

A major focus of the study was to assess the quality of the relationship between each mother and her child. We would do this using a procedure designed at the Institute of Psychiatry specifically for this purpose that assessed not just what the parents said but how they said it, taking account of their facial expressions, gestures and mannerisms, and tone of voice when speaking about their children. Most importantly, I examined the children's psychological adjustment. I asked detailed questions about their emotions and behaviour, and transcripts of the mothers' responses were independently examined by a child psychiatrist who was unaware of the child's family background. Teachers would participate too by completing questionnaires about the children's behaviour at school. The teachers' reports were important in case the mothers underplayed their children's problems, or were accused of doing so. The children's gender development was explored through interviews with the mothers and the children about their favourite toys, games and activities.

The assessments that I conducted involved a high level of training to administer and analyse. A colleague and I were video-recorded carrying out practice interviews and given feedback by experts at the Institute of Psychiatry until we could do them well. It took several weeks of intensive coaching for us to be deemed ready to be sent out on the road.

Buoyed by a £2,000 grant from the Nuffield Foundation, with the use of the Department of Child Psychiatry's bright red Mini, and armed with my weighty reel-to-reel tape recorder, I began my research in the spring of 1977. It took me all over England, Scotland, and Wales. I visited suburban streets, council estates, country villages, seaside towns, central London, northern cities, and the remotest countryside. I travelled alone, never quite sure of where I would end up, relying on my map-reading skills and the kindness of the families who had agreed to be interviewed. It was often nerve-wracking. Each time I rang a new doorbell, the same questions would arise in my mind: Who would answer the door? Would they be friendly? Would they have a scary dog? And would the children want to speak to me?

I felt privileged to hear the mothers' very intimate stories. Many had been faced with unbearable choices, like Anne Hitchins. Did they remain in an unsatisfactory marriage for the sake of their families? Or did they follow their hearts and take a giant leap into unknown territory where they were likely to lose not only family and friends but also their children?

Abby Curtis, a teacher who took part in my study, found herself faced with this dilemma when her sons, James and Stephen, were nine and six. Although Abby had first become attracted to girls when she was 15, she'd passed these feelings off as teenage crushes. She didn't know that women could be gay. After she left school, her feelings towards women intensified, but she didn't do anything about it. When she was 24, she married her boyfriend of three years and soon became a mother. The marriage didn't last. When she eventually confided in her husband about her sexuality, he wanted to try to live with it. But they argued a lot and Abby was unhappy. She was 33 when she met Sadie, a local nurse. They moved in together with Abby's children one year later. It was the most difficult decision of her life. Abby lost many of her friends when she set up home with Sadie. Although they claimed to accept her new situation, all but one stopped visiting, and some no longer allowed her to babysit their children.

Rachel Benton, like Abby, had ignored her teenage attraction to women and married young. She had met her future husband when she was 16, married him at 19, and had been unhappily married for 14 years when she fell in love with Mabel. In August 1977, when Rachel, Mabel, and Rachel's daughter Nadia, then aged seven, took part in my research, they had been living together as a family for three years. Although Rachel had been worried about losing custody of Nadia, it turned out that her biggest problem was keeping her former husband involved in his daughter's life. Often, he would not see Nadia for weeks or even months, and sometimes when he did arrange to take her out, he didn't turn up, leaving his young daughter distraught.

At the end of the study we found that, contrary to the beliefs of many psychiatrists, and judgments in UK and US courts, lesbian mothers were just as warm, involved, and committed to their children as heterosexual mothers. Their children were no more likely to show emotional and behavioural problems, and the boys were no less masculine and girls no less feminine. Two other studies carried out by child psychiatrists in the United States around that time, one by Martha Kirkpatrick at the University of California, Los Angeles, and the other by Richard Green at the State University of New York at Stony Brook, each adopting a similar approach, came to exactly the same conclusions.

These findings flew in the face of those who claimed that children raised in lesbian mother families would be psychologically damaged, and, not surprisingly, were subjected to the deepest scrutiny in courts. In one case in the mid-1980s in which I was called as an expert witness by Gill Butler, the leading British solicitor acting for lesbian mothers, the psychiatrist commissioned as an expert witness on behalf of the father waved our scientific article in the air and pronounced that the research was not worth the paper it was written on.

Gill remembers repeatedly coming up against the ingrained attitude of mostly older, male judges, who had little understanding of the issues. Even seemingly clear-cut cases came down to the wire. 'One of the first cases in which a lesbian mother won custody in the United Kingdom involved a seven-year-old boy,' she told me over lunch at NOPI restaurant in London. The mother had formed a relationship with a woman from her neighbourhood. When her husband found out, he was furious. He left the family home and began custody proceedings, arguing that the child would be teased and ostracised, and would grow up to be gay. However, he was unable to look after the child himself as his work took him away for long periods of time. He proposed that his ex-wife's mother would look after the child when he was away from home. Gill Butler argued in court that the child had a perfectly good, willing, and able mother already, who could look after him. After hearing the evidence from all of the parties, the judge awarded custody to the mother. 'What sticks in my mind is that he said it was "a finely balanced case",' she recalled. 'So you had a husband who was away three weeks out of six, a wife who was not working and was able to look after the child, and that was "finely balanced"! It was extraordinary. Had she been heterosexual there would not have been an issue.'

In another case, the following year, I was cross-examined by the barrister acting for the father in a similar custody dispute on every single detail of our research in an attempt to discredit it. His criticisms seemed endless: the numbers of families investigated were too small. The mothers were all volunteers. Mothers whose children were experiencing problems would have been unlikely to take part, producing over-positive findings that did not reflect the true difficulties experienced by the children. The mothers would have presented their families in the best possible light, as they knew that negative findings might harm their cause. The children were still young. They would experience psychological problems and difficulties in forming romantic relationships when they grew up. And the million-dollar question that came up in every custody case: If the children were raised by lesbian mothers, would they themselves grow up to be gay? Because of the ingrained homophobia in society at this time, even the smallest likelihood of this happening was sufficient for a judge to remove a child from their lesbian mother and award custody to their father.

The limitations of our research were often exaggerated by the father's counsels in custody disputes. However, some of the criticisms were valid. Research on families cannot be carried out with the same precision as research in the basic sciences, as families cannot be experimented on in the same way. It is simply not possible to randomly allocate some children to have lesbian mothers and others to have heterosexual mothers to discover what happens, in the way that some patients may randomly be given a new drug, and others an older drug, to test differences in outcomes. Family researchers have to work in alternative ways, slowly building up a picture based on a series of investigations that focus on different questions, and repeating these investigations with new groups of families to find out whether the findings remain the same. It is only when several studies, ideally by different research groups, produce similar findings that confidence can be placed in the results. The question raised in these early court cases — was it detrimental for the long-term development of children to be raised in lesbian mother families — could not be answered straight away.

I wanted to follow up with the boys and girls from our study as adults. By this time, public concern about lesbian mother families had shifted from custody disputes to the issue of whether lesbian women should be allowed to foster or adopt children, or have access to assisted reproduction. There was still an assumption that growing up in a lesbian household would be damaging to children in the long term, and I hoped that further research would shed light on whether this was true. The challenge facing me now was to secure funding. Against the advice of my senior colleagues, who told me I didn't have the slightest chance of success with such a controversial topic, I applied to the Wellcome Trust, the largest funder of medical research in the United Kingdom. Fortunately, the Wellcome Trust has always been a forward-thinking organisation, and the committee that assessed my application could see the point of my proposed study, considered it to be scientifically sound, and awarded me a grant that enabled me to re-visit the families from my original study in 1991, almost 15 years after they had first been seen. By that time, the children were in their mid-20s.

Fiona Tasker, a psychologist who had recently completed her PhD on young people with divorced parents at the Centre for Family Research in Cambridge, came to work with me. We interviewed more than 60 per cent of the people who had taken part as children. This was quite an achievement, given that we had not intended to see them again at the time of the original study and had not kept in touch. When we tried to find the mothers, we discovered that three-quarters had a different address, rather more than we had hoped for. The only way we could trace them was through the UK National Health Service Register. We were not allowed to request the mothers' addresses, but we could ask for the names of their family doctors and depend on these doctors' goodwill to pass a letter on. With no way of telling whether our letters had been forwarded or not, we waited anxiously. Gradually, the mothers began to contact us and put us in touch with their grown-up children.

It was fascinating speaking to these young adults, who we had not seen since they were children, and hearing their thoughts on their families now. We discovered that those with lesbian mothers had more positive relationships with their mother's new female partner than those with heterosexual mothers who had acquired a stepfather. This was because the mother's involvement with a new partner affected the child's relationship with their biological father differently in the two family types. In lesbian mother families, the mother's female partner was viewed as an additional parent, and most of the children had also maintained a relationship with their father. In contrast, when the heterosexual mothers remarried, the children often lost contact with their biological fathers. Their stepfather was seen as a replacement for their biological father, and generally did not match up.

Stephen Curtis, Abby's son, described a warm relationship with his mother's partner, Sadie, whom he had lived with from the age of seven. He was 21 and studying science at university when we caught up with him in 1992. 'I got on well with Sadie. I don't remember having problems with her,' he told us. 'I can remember having fun and doing things with Sadie that I enjoyed; playing games and playing tennis. We went on holidays to the beach and to Bible weekends as a family. I remember doing the garden together. It was nice. Home was a happy environment.' But Stephen wasn't as close to Sadie as he was to his mum or dad. 'I don't think I was ever as close to Sadie as I was to my natural parents. We were close. It was like a step-parent would be, I suppose. We all got on.'

Nadia Benton felt differently. She adored her mother's new partner, Mabel, and considered Mabel, and not her father, to be her second parent. When we tracked Nadia down in 1991, she was 21, had recently married her long-term boyfriend, and was training to be a social worker. She told us that she had lost touch with her father when she was a child because he wasn't interested in her. One of her most vivid memories was waiting for him to visit one Saturday morning: 'I was sitting on the stairs and waited there all day with my little hat on for him and he didn't come. I sat on the stairs crying, "My daddy's coming and I'm not taking my coat off."' When Nadia was growing up, her mother Rachel worked long hours, so Mabel looked after her. Nadia remembers Mabel being great with children. She would cook special meals for Nadia and play silly games with her. 'My mum's soppy with children, but she's very business-like. Mabel is very cuddly,' Nadia told us. 'If I fell over, Mabel would say, "Come and have a hug", whereas my mum would rub it better and say, "Be a soldier."' Nadia's friends loved Mabel, too. They would tell Mabel their problems and all about the boys they fancied. Her friends accepted Mabel because she was nice to them: 'Me and my friends were in the school athletics team and Mabel used to help us with that because she had been a physical training instructor in the army. She used to take us out into the back garden and teach us athletics. If there was any prejudice, it would be gone by the time the children went home because Mabel was such good fun.' Reflecting on her relationship with Mabel now that she was an adult, Nadia said: 'I love Mabel for her merits, because of the way she is. She's not my biological parent so I love her for herself because she's special.'

A question that had come up time and time again in custody disputes was whether children who had grown up in lesbian mother families would develop mental-health problems in adulthood, but the young adults we spoke to were no more likely to have suffered from anxiety or depression, or to have sought help from professionals in connection with mental-health issues, than other adults of the same age.

As the future sexual orientation of the children of lesbian mothers had been central to child custody judgments in the 1970s, and remained a deciding factor in some cases in the 1990s, we asked the young adults in our study about their sexuality. Although similar proportions of young adults had had teenage crushes on people of the same sex, girls with lesbian mothers were more likely to act on these crushes, probably because they didn't fear parental disapproval. But as adults, the children of lesbian mothers were no more likely to identify as lesbian, gay, or bisexual than the children of heterosexual mothers. Ninety-two per cent said that they were heterosexual, a proportion that is similar to the population at large. The remaining 8 per cent were women who identified as lesbian. None of the men identified as gay. The claim that the children of lesbian mothers would themselves grow up to be gay turned out to be untrue.

One criticism of our research that arose time and time again was that the original study in the 1970s had been conducted using volunteers. Mothers whose children were experiencing problems may have decided against taking part, claimed our detractors, which could have produced an overly positive impression of how well the children were doing. It had not been possible to recruit lesbian mother families from the population at large. Instead, we had depended on lesbian women's magazines, social groups, and word-of-mouth. But that changed in the 1990s. One day, out of the blue, I received a phone call from the director of the Avon Longitudinal Study of Parents and Children, a large community study of mothers and their children living in the west of England, to ask whether I could help with the assessment of children's play. I enquired whether I would also be able to investigate the 7-year-old children of lesbian mothers in the study, alongside the children of single mothers and children with a mother and a father in the home, and she agreed. In the United States, the psychologist Charlotte Patterson and her team at the University of Virginia conducted a similar study of 14-year-olds with lesbian mothers in collaboration with the National Longitudinal Study of Adolescent Health, which examined a large, national sample of adolescents who were recruited through schools. Even with these general population samples, the findings were the same.

Slowly but surely, our research began to influence the outcome of child custody disputes, and by the new millennium few lesbian women were losing custody of their children because of their sexuality. Today, hardly any cases go to court. In those that do, judges usually focus on whether there is evidence that the children in question are at risk of specific harm, and no longer simply assume that being a lesbian makes a woman an unfit parent. It's a great pity that this change of opinion came too late for lesbian mothers from the 1970s like Anne and Mary Jo.

***

As attitudes were slowly beginning to shift, the increasing use of donor insemination as a treatment for infertile married couples also changed the way that lesbian woman were able to become parents. Donor insemination, known in the 1970s as artificial insemination by donor, or AID, refers to the insemination of a woman with sperm from a man who is not her partner. The main differences between donor insemination and the self-insemination practiced by Carol and Hilary are that donor insemination is carried out at a clinic and, until a change in the UK law in 2005, involved anonymous sperm donors.

In the mid-1970s, in most cases, lesbian mothers raised their children below the radar of the general public. That all changed on 5 January 1978, when one woman's story hit the headlines. Although she was anonymous at the time, her name was Gillian Hanscombe. Gillian had grown up in Melbourne, Australia and moved to the United Kingdom with her female partner in 1969. She had wanted to have a baby for some time, she told me, when I met with her almost 40 years later. While out canvassing for an election, Gillian met the ebullient television presenter, Jackie Forster, who told her about her escapades transporting semen across London from a doctor who was willing to give lesbian women donor insemination. Gillian immediately knew that this was what she wanted to do. She consulted the doctor, a respected gynaecologist, and quickly became pregnant, becoming the second lesbian mother in the country to have a baby by AID.

Gillian had no notion of the press storm that was about to break. It came to a head when a journalist, posing as one half of a lesbian couple, asked Jackie Forster for advice on AID, and Jackie introduced her to the doctor. Shortly afterwards, one of the sperm donors realised that he had been photographed going into the clinic and warned the doctor that the press was sniffing around. On the night the story of Gillian's insemination broke, press from 17 countries lay siege to the headquarters of Sappho, a lesbian social group founded by Jackie Forster, of which Gillian was a member. A last-minute injunction prevented her name from being published, and blocked her face in the photos surreptitiously taken by journalists, but the negative and sensational nature of the press took a toll on both Gillian's life and the lives of lesbian mothers across the country.

Headlines such as 'Dr Strange Love' and 'Ban these babies' in the London newspaper the *Evening News* triggered a national outcry against lesbian women raising children. The MP Rhodes Boyson asserted: 'This evil must stop for the sake of the potential children and society, which both have enough problems without the extension of this horrific practice.' Another MP, Jill Knight, claimed: 'A child needs above all a normal and natural family environment. I cannot imagine that it is in the best interest of children to be born in such circumstances. The "Brave New World" should not lose sight of the fact that they are not little nuts and bolts but living, feeling, and breathing children.'

As I sat with Gillian in April 2017 in her picturesque cottage in the Devon countryside, enjoying one of her delicious cream teas, it was hard to recollect the strength of public outrage that she had provoked all these years ago. The baby who had caused the scandal was now a highly successful 41-year-old director in a large marketing company, about to have a baby of his own. Not one of the claims about the damage that Gillian would cause to his future wellbeing had turned out to be true. Back then, she had helped recruit families to my study through Sappho. 'Did you know it was me?' she asked. I admitted that I'd had an inkling, but had never been sure.

After the news broke, Gillian didn't tell anyone that she was the anonymous mother, desperate to protect her son. It was his story, too. 'I thought that when he was old enough to have a vote, I would ask him what he thought about the scandal,' she told me. When he turned 30, she gave him all the newspaper clippings. I told her I was curious to know what he thinks about it now. 'He thinks I was very brave, which is nice of him,' Gillian replied. I asked what she would say to all the people who questioned her competence as a mother. 'The proof of the pudding is in the eating,' she replied. A very apt response from a woman who makes the perfect cream tea.

***

Much has changed in the last 40 years. Joanna Lawrence from the United States comes from today's generation of lesbian women, who routinely turn to donor insemination to have a baby. Joanna's experience was the polar opposite of Gillian's. She likened ordering sperm to ordering a pizza: 'You call in and you give them your client number, and then you tell them the number of the donor that you want, and then you talk shipping, and then it magically arrives at your door within 24 hours.'

As a child, Joanna always assumed that one day she would be a mother. But she could never have imagined how that would come about. Joanna had grown up in the 1980s in a small town in rural northeast Kansas. There were no skyscrapers or even stop-lights, the population reached 800 at its height, and there were only 21 students in her high school graduating class. It was a tight-knit community of mostly blue-collar workers where everyone knew everyone. Joanna came from a large, close family. Her mother and father each had six siblings, all married with children. Joanna had eight cousins on her father's side and 12 on her mother's. Family get-togethers were like a big party.

When the time came for Joanna to go to university, she wanted to meet new people. She chose a university that was three hours' drive away rather than the one attended by her family and friends only 45 minutes down the road.

Joanna was almost 30, employed as a project manager in health care, and had recently divorced her husband of 12 years when she met Kate. They worked in the same office, quickly became friends, and ultimately fell in love. Family was important to both of them and they wanted to have children together. As the younger of the two, they decided that Joanna would be the one to carry their baby.

The couple was astonished by the number of male friends and family members who offered them their sperm. But they declined them all. They decided to use a sperm bank, deliberately opting for an anonymous donor to protect themselves from the possibility of the biological father claiming paternity of their child. This was particularly important to them because same-sex marriage was not legal in Kansas at that time, and the law prohibited non-biological mothers in lesbian couples from becoming legal parents through second-parent adoption. Although they had married in the state of Massachusetts, in Kansas only Joanna, as the biological mother, could be the legal mother of their child.

Their first task was to choose their donor from the sperm bank's extensive online catalogue. It was overwhelming. What skin colour did they want? Eye colour? Hair colour? Eye shape? Religion? They could also search for more esoteric characteristics such as attached or unattached earlobes, should they wish to. Joanna and Kate spent hours refining their search and trying to find the right match. They paid extra to hear the donor's voice and find out about his personality. The donor they finally settled on, from the many thousands available, matched Joanna's ethnic background and Kate's hair, eye, and skin colouring. But what really swung it for them in the end was that his favourite colours, orange and red, were the same as Kate's. After hours and hours of searching, they went with their gut feeling. The process took six months.

When the vial of sperm arrived, it was in an enormous package. 'Inside a giant box was what I always lovingly refer to as my "alien baby" canister,' Joanna described to me. 'It was a stainless-steel container with fog rolling out of it. That's exactly how it arrived! And there were warning labels about wearing safety glasses and safety gloves! It was a huge canister that came up to your knees and inside was a little vial two centimetres high.' Handling the vial was stressful. The instructions stated that it should be placed in water at body temperature within 30 seconds or it would explode, and then left to thaw for 10 to 15 minutes. It was essential to maintain a consistent temperature to avoid damaging the sperm. Once thawed, the sperm had to be transferred to a syringe ready for insemination.

It took several attempts for Joanna to fall pregnant, and then she was faced with the task of telling her parents. 'I didn't really know how to start the conversation,' Joanna told me, 'so I just said, "You know what? Here's the deal: I'm pregnant."' She will never forget their reactions. Her mother, who she thought would be ecstatic, pushed her coffee cup away, folded her hands on the counter, looked at Joanna very seriously, and said, 'Well I thought that ship had sailed.' Her father was bewildered. 'My dad, I could see the wheels turning,' Joanna said. 'There was practically steam coming out of his ears, he was thinking so hard about this and I could tell he didn't know which question to ask. So finally he turned to me and said, "Well how did *that* happen?" After the initial shock, they were very happy.'

In 2009, Joanna gave birth to Ricky, a beautiful baby boy.

Unlike the children of divorced lesbian mothers, who spend their early years in a traditional heterosexual family, children born to lesbian couples by donor insemination only ever have two mothers. This was the basis of a further challenge from proponents of the traditional family. Because psychologists know that the first few years of life are important in shaping later development, it was suggested that children raised for their whole lives by lesbian mothers, without fathers, would be more likely to experience psychological problems and show non-conventional gender development.

The increased use of donor insemination by lesbian women in the 1980s and 1990s sparked a new wave of research, and the first studies of children born to lesbian couples by donor insemination were published in the late 1990s by psychologists such as Charlotte Patterson in the United States and Henny Bos in Europe, and my own research team in the United Kingdom. We compared donor-conceived children with two mothers to donor-conceived children with a mother and a father, focusing on the quality of family relationships and the psychological adjustment of the children using a similar approach to our earlier research. There were few differences between the two family types, apart from greater involvement in the day-to-day care of the children by co-mothers in lesbian mother families than by fathers in traditional families. Most importantly, children who had been raised by lesbian mothers from birth were doing just as well as children with both a mother and a father.

A key study of lesbian mother families created by donor insemination was initiated in 1986 in the United States by the psychiatrist Nanette Gartrell from Harvard Medical School. The families were recruited during pregnancy, and followed up with when the children were aged two, five, ten, 17, and 25. Their scores on a widely used screening instrument to detect behavioural and emotional problems were compared with those of American children in general. When the children of lesbian mothers were aged ten and 17, they showed fewer emotional and behavioural problems on this measure than other children of the same age. When they were 25, they were as psychologically healthy as their peers.

This is still the only study beginning in childhood, other than our own study in the UK, to have investigated the children's sexual identity. At age 17, 5.4 per cent of the boys examined by Nanette Gartrell identified as gay, a proportion that is similar to that of young men generally. None of the girls identified as lesbian. When compared with children from a large survey of families in the United States, the children of lesbian mothers were no more likely to have engaged in same-sex relationships than their peers. By the time they were 25, both the sons and daughters of lesbian mothers were more likely than their peers to report same-sex attraction, identity, and experience, which the researchers put down to either the non-judgemental attitudes of their parents, the young adults being more attuned to their own same-sex feelings, their genetic linkage to sexual minority parents, or a mixture of all three. They also pointed out that most of the young women and men identified as heterosexual. This pattern of results is similar to our own study. The higher proportion of young adults in the US study who reported same-sex relationships most likely reflects the shift towards more positive attitudes to same-sex relationships since the 1990s, when the UK study of young adults took place. Coming out as lesbian or gay today is less problematic for many young people than it was back then, although there are still barriers.

***

It is clear from the past forty years of research that children raised in lesbian mother families are just as well adjusted and loved as those raised by a mother and father. But one concern still remains — the stigmatisation they suffer from their peers. Anna, who took part in my first study in the 1970s, remembered being too frightened to tell her classmates about her family; she lived in constant fear of being outed. When she was 13, her best friend, Kathy, used to regularly come for sleepovers at her house. One day, Kathy asked where Anna's mother's female partner slept. Anna told her that she slept with her mum. The consequences were devastating. Kathy told everyone at school. When we re-visited Anna 15 years later, she remembered, 'I wasn't allowed to go to Kathy's house any more. Her mum and dad forbade me from going anywhere near, and that hurt me because she had been my best friend for a long, long time. I lost that friend. And then, of course, there was a chain reaction. Everybody found out. They said, "Don't go near her, she'll turn out like her mum."' Not long after this, Anna met Hugh, her first boyfriend: 'Once I started going out with Hugh, they looked at me differently. They must have thought, "Well, she's not like we were saying because she's got a boyfriend."'

Between October 2009 and February 2010, members of my team at the Centre for Family Research in Cambridge worked with the LGBTQ+ organisation Stonewall on a study of the school experiences of 82 British children with same-sex parents, to find out whether attitudes had changed since the time of our original research. Speaking to children as young as four, we explored what growing up with lesbian mothers was like for them. Mark, aged eight, explained that when class-mates use the phrase 'that's so gay' as an insult he feels upset. Other children are shunned because of their lesbian mothers. Hannah was 16 when she spoke to us. She lived with her mother, Sarah, her mother's partner, Jo, and her sister, Alice, aged seven, who was born to Sarah and Jo through donor insemination. Hannah described an unpleasant incident when she started college: 'A girl said, "I know I don't know you very well, but a couple of girls have been saying that your mum's a lesbian." When I replied that mum *is* a lesbian, she said, "Oh, my God, that's sick."'

One problem that many children mentioned was having to explain about their family over and over again because no one else in school talked about same-sex parents, which had been one of the fears Carol and Hilary had experienced more than 30 years ago, in the 1980s. Hannah said, 'When people find out my mum's gay [they ask] well how are you here? Then I have to explain that my mum was married to my dad, and now she's not, and then they ask, what about your sister? And then I say well she was donor insemination. They just accept it, but sometimes people don't understand, they're a bit confused, and I have to explain.'

Decades of research has shown that the problems faced by children with lesbian mothers come from outside their families, and not from within. One reason for the prejudice these children experience is other people's lack of familiarity with families like theirs. The children we spoke to in our study with Stonewall repeatedly told us that they never see families like their own in the books that they read or the films that they see, something that's perhaps not surprising given that the children's book *Jenny Lives With Eric and Martin* was one of the catalysts for the introduction of Section 28, and *Heather has Two Mommies* was the American Library Association's ninth most banned book in the 1990s. Many children in our study gave instances of teachers assuming they had a mum and a dad. While there has been a huge shift in attitudes since lesbian mothers first became visible in the 1970s, stigmatisation is present in our schools to this day.

What the British children told us is backed up by the findings of research from other countries. Even in the Netherlands, which is known for its liberal attitudes towards homosexuality, and was the first country to introduce same-sex marriage in 2001, the psychologist Henny Bos and sociologist Frank van Balen found that teenagers with lesbian mothers encountered prejudice and stigmatisation at school. In Nanette Gartrell's study in the United States, almost half of the children at early adolescence had experienced teasing or rejection at school because of their family.

These studies examined not only the extent, but also the effects, of stigmatisation on the children. In the Dutch study, children who had been stigmatised showed greater emotional problems in their early school years, and at early adolescence boys showed more disruptive behaviour and girls reported lower self-esteem. The same was true in the American study; greater emotional and behavioural problems were found among early adolescents who had been stigmatised because of their lesbian mother family, and by late adolescence, those who had experienced stigmatisation reported greater anxiety, depression, and behavioural problems. The researchers also wanted to discover what might protect children against the negative effects of homophobia. The findings were the same in both the Netherlands and the United States. As well as strong, supportive relationships with their mothers, contact with other children with same-sex parents and, in particular, a school environment that was friendly towards lesbian and gay people made a positive difference to children's mental health.

***

The research on lesbian mother families has not only helped bring about legislative change, but also has challenged two widespread assumptions about the family: that fathers are essential and that heterosexual parents are essential in order for children to thrive. More than 40 years of research has shown that neither is true. What matters most for children is the same in lesbian mother families as it is in traditional families: warm, sensitive, and involved parents, whatever their gender and sexual orientation, as well as supportive communities and enlightened schools.

This knowledge has helped bring about sweeping changes in recent years. Today, depending on where they live, lesbian couples may marry, adopt children jointly, and become the joint legal parents of children born through assisted reproduction. In a growing number of countries, single lesbian women may also adopt children or have children through donor insemination. There are still many battles against homophobia, stigmatisation, and discrimination to fight, but in stark contrast to previous generations, for whom being a lesbian meant closing the door on motherhood or the risk of losing existing children, many young lesbian women now see motherhood as a possibility for them.

Today's children and teenagers, too, have a very different life from that of young people raised by lesbian mothers in the latter part of the twentieth century. Sophie was 17, and living in San Francisco, when she took part in our US study of teenagers born to lesbian mothers through donor insemination. We wanted to find out how teenagers today feel about their lesbian mother families and their thoughts about the method of their conception. Sophie's mothers — Annika, who she calls Mommy, and Leila, who she calls Momma — have always been open with her about her conception. They talked to Sophie about it as soon as she began to ask where babies came from, explaining in greater detail as she grew up. One of my research team interviewed Sophie in the family's San Francisco home in 2015. Like many children who are told about the circumstances of their birth from when they are young, Sophie is comfortable with having been donor conceived: 'It's something I've always known. There was never *a* moment. I didn't think it was something weird. I have a bunch of friends who have the same situation so I never thought anything of it.'

***

Anne Hitchins has witnessed a huge transformation in attitudes towards lesbian mothers that was beyond her wildest imagination in the 1980s and 90s when she worked at the Women's Advice Centre. Her experiences there inspired her to go to a further education college to catch up on the schooling that she had missed out on as a teenager. She went on to take a university degree in environmental science, funding her way by being a live-in carer, and was then employed to work on environmental projects with local communities. Anne is close to all three of her grown-up children and is a loving great-grandmother. She is particularly proud that her youngest daughter, who reacted the most negatively of all her children to her divorce, is now in a high-powered position in social services, and has been recognised for her outstanding work with children in care. Anne and her partner, Bea, had a civil partnership in 2013, on International Women's Day, the eighteenth anniversary of when they met. Anne is astounded by how quickly change has happened: 'Bea and I were brought up in an era when it was dangerous to draw attention to yourself,' she told me when we met in her east London home. 'The other day I watched a young, married lesbian couple with their baby walk down the street holding hands. It's incredible that we've seen such acceptance in our lifetime.'

Chapter 2

Donor Conception Families: 'Made Out of Love'

'Never expect me to think of them as my grandchildren.'

JANE, GRANDMOTHER OF MIA,
A CHILD CONCEIVED BY SPERM DONATION, (1993).

'My dad is still my dad.'

JASON, AGE 14, BORN THROUGH DONOR INSEMINATION, (2014).

In 2004, when she was 13, Louise McLoughlin's parents sat her down at the kitchen table in their family home in Ireland and told her something that would forever change who she thought she was: that she had been conceived using the sperm of an anonymous donor. Unlike some donor-conceived children, it had never crossed Louise's mind that her dad was not her biological father. The revelation came as a bolt from the blue.

'That night, I slept between the two of them,' she recalled, 'and I remember looking at their wedding photos crying my eyes out and thinking, "Who are these people? I don't know who I am, I don't know who these people are." It was absolutely terrible. All of a sudden, I felt like a stranger in the family.'

Her parents asked her not to talk about it outside of the house as they hadn't told anyone and it would upset her dad. They didn't discuss it with her again for more than a year.

For Louise, the secrecy and sense of shame that this revelation engendered was the worst part. She thought about her donor conception all the time, and, like others in her situation, spent hours looking in the mirror trying to work out which of her features were from her mum and, by default, which came from her biological father. As she described it when she called me about an article she was writing for *Vice* magazine, her reflection changed; she didn't recognise herself, she became a stranger to herself. Because her donor was anonymous, there was no way of tracking him down, so she tried to work out what he was like through a process of deduction. 'I used to imagine what he was like and think, "Oh well, I'm creative and my parents aren't so obviously that's from him."' Louise wrote her donor letters that she could never send. She wondered whether he had children that he loved. And she wondered why he couldn't love her, since she was his child too.

When Louise was conceived, her father's sperm was mixed with the donor's sperm so that her parents would never be sure that she was not his biological child, a practice that was common at the time. When she was 15, just a couple of years after she learned about her conception, they took a DNA test to find out. As expected, because they didn't look alike, the test proved that her dad was not her biological father. In spite of everything, Louise loves and admires her dad: 'My dad is an incredible person. He's very generous, selfless, and softly spoken. He's just lovely. But we're very, very different. He's very quiet and he doesn't talk about his emotions. I've only seen him cry three times in his life — when he told me I wasn't his kid, when his father died, and when we got the result of the DNA test.' Louise is close to her mother too, despite a rocky patch in her teens after finding out about her donor conception: 'I have very fond relationships with my parents. I was definitely a very wanted child, there's no denying that.'

My research on lesbian mothers had made me interested in how other kinds of new family forms, such as Louise's family, affect the children who grow up in them. As happened with lesbian mother families, concerns were raised by the media and proponents of the traditional family about the children born through assisted reproduction. Would children born by *in vitro* fertilisation (IVF) be psychologically different from other children? Would their mothers and fathers, who had often endured years of stressful fertility treatment, set themselves unattainably high standards of parenting, or be over-protective of their much-wanted children? Would non-genetic parents in families formed through egg, sperm, or embryo donation be more distant from, or even hostile towards, their children? And might this have a negative impact on the children's emotional wellbeing? I was fascinated by these questions, so I extended my research to include families created by assisted reproduction.

***

Nineteen seventy-eight was a big year for new family forms in the United Kingdom, and the rest of the world. Not only did the British public learn about lesbian mothers through the media frenzy surrounding Gillian Hanscombe's donor-conceived child, but it was also the year that Louise Brown was born through IVF in Oldham, Lancashire — the first baby in the world conceived outside the human body, and an international sensation. *The Economist* vividly described the scene outside Oldham General Hospital on the day of Louise's birth: 'The world's press was camped outside; the front doors locked and staff forced to sneak in and out via a side entrance. Patrick Steptoe and Robert Edwards, the obstetrician and physiologist who had, nine months before, taken an egg from one of Mrs Brown's ovaries under anaesthetic and fertilised it *in vitro* with her husband's sperm, were in hiding.' *Time* magazine hailed it, 'The most awaited birth in perhaps 2,000 years.'

In IVF, a woman's eggs are removed from her ovaries and fertilised by sperm in the laboratory, and the resulting embryo(s) are transferred to her womb to develop. It's hard to imagine today — now that millions of IVF babies have been born worldwide, and Louise Brown has two children of her own — but many people were bitterly opposed to this new reproductive technology. Although Louise Brown's birth was celebrated as a scientific breakthrough by most of the world's media, religious leaders were against it — procreation without sex was seen as unnatural and immoral, and scientists were accused of 'playing God'. The Catholic Church, in particular, was opposed to IVF, based on the belief that life begins at conception, and that it is a sin to create embryos outside the body; this continues to be its stance today. Some people went as far as to claim that IVF children would be born without a soul. Other concerns focused on whether the children might be born with physical disabilities, with allusions made to 'Frankenstein' babies. I met women who had become mothers in the early days of IVF, who told me they had been shunned, or had been on the receiving end of hostile remarks, because of their 'test-tube' babies. Even close relatives were sometimes wary of the new addition to their family. As one of the first IVF mothers said to me, 'I think my mother-in-law thought he was going to come out with two heads. She does love him, I'm sure he does, but there's always been that little something. Even when she came to the hospital after he was born, she didn't pick him up.' Louise Brown, in her autobiography, published in 2015, described the sack-loads of hate-mail that her parents received. As the reproductive biologist, Martin Johnson, one of Robert Edwards' first PhD students, recounted in 2010, 42 years later, there was such antagonism to IVF in the early days, even among Steptoe and Edwards' medical and scientific colleagues, that they could not attract the necessary funding to pursue their work. The Medical Research Council, the government body responsible for funding medical research in the United Kingdom, turned them down. It was only thanks to an injection of cash from an anonymous donor — the American philanthropist and television executive, Lillian Lincoln Howell, whose identity was not discovered until 2010 — that they were able to continue their ground-breaking research.

In the early years of IVF, doctors and embryologists were focused on achieving successful pregnancies followed by the birth of healthy babies. The longer-term psychological outcomes for the children conceived was of little interest. But that was not the case with Robert Edwards, who friends and colleagues knew as Bob. He was interested in the children right from the start, and believed that social science research was crucial to the overall endeavour of creating healthy families through IVF.

I first met Bob at a conference in Paris in 1991 where I was presenting the findings of a small pilot study of IVF children. He was in the audience and, with his irrepressible enthusiasm, strongly and publicly supported our research. He was not only a vocal advocate of our work, but also made sure that it was discussed by ethics committees and at conferences on the social and ethical aspects of assisted reproduction. Caught up by his boundless energy, I found myself attending meetings on ethics and law; meetings that were well out of my comfort zone as a young developmental psychologist. But Bob wouldn't take no for an answer. In 2004, as I was preparing to spend my sabbatical leave as a Visiting Professor at Columbia University in New York, he invited me to speak at a conference he was holding on the Ethics, Science, and Moral Philosophy of Assisted Reproduction at the Royal Society in London. I agreed on the condition that I would not have to produce a written paper. 'Don't worry,' said Bob. 'I shall have your talk recorded and transcribed. All you will need to do is look it over.' What he didn't say was that the person he had in mind for the job had newly arrived in the United Kingdom and spoke very little English. I spent the first week of my sabbatical cursing Bob and trying to undo the mess. But you couldn't be angry with Bob for long. He was the warmest, kindest person you could ever hope to know. He was the first person to invite me to lunch when I moved to Cambridge many years later, and one of the first to arrive at my housewarming party. He went out of his way to welcome a newcomer and I think that says it all.

IVF paved the way for other family forms that had not previously been possible, including families in which mothers give birth to genetically unrelated children using donated eggs, families formed through embryo donation in which children lack a genetic connection to both their mothers and their fathers, and families like Louise McLoughlin's, with children conceived using donated sperm who are genetically unrelated to their fathers. Although donor insemination, a relatively straightforward procedure involving the insemination of a woman with the sperm of a man who is not her partner, was neither new — the first case was reported in 1884, and tens of thousands of children had been born through donor insemination in the United States by the mid-1950s — nor required the use of IVF, it became much more widely used as a treatment for male infertility following this breakthrough. At that time, opponents saw the involvement of a third party in the conception of a child as a threat to marriage and family relationships. In 1984, summarising the arguments against donor insemination, the report of the Warnock Committee, set up by the British government to consider the implications of new developments in assisted reproduction, stated, 'AID children may feel obscurely that they are being deceived by their parents, that they are in some way different from their peers, and that the men whom they regard as their fathers are not their real fathers.'

***

Sometimes scientific research results from serendipity rather than careful planning, and that was the case with my first study of families formed through assisted reproduction. One afternoon in 1986, when I was working as a research assistant at the Institute of Psychiatry in London, I was interviewing patients in the gynaecology ward of King's

College Hospital across the road for an unrelated project when I spotted the IVF doctor John Parsons. Here was my chance to ask whether he might be willing to put me in touch with the families created through his clinic. But would he be annoyed at being accosted by someone he barely knew while busy with his patients? It was a split-second decision. He could leave at any moment and my opportunity would be lost. I plucked up the courage to approach him, and he responded with enthusiasm. John Parsons was keen to know how the families would fare as the children grew up, and lent his support to the pilot study that became the launch-pad for our future research. Robert Winston, now Lord Winston, who headed another prominent IVF clinic at the Hammersmith hospital in London, also backed the research, and Tony Rutherford, one of the doctors at the clinic, collaborated on our study.

In the late eighties, once a substantial number of IVF children had been born, I submitted a funding proposal to the UK's Medical Research Council and, in the early nineties, now at City University, London, I, along with colleagues from research institutions across Europe, applied to the European Commission's Biomedical Research Programme. We wanted to conduct an international, in-depth study of parents and children in families formed by assisted reproduction. Both applications were successful, and so we began the marathon task of visiting hundreds of families in their homes in Italy, Spain, the Netherlands, and the UK. We saw families with children conceived by IVF using their mothers' eggs and fathers' sperm, and families formed through donor insemination in which the children had been conceived using sperm from anonymous donors, as well as comparison groups of families with children who had been adopted in infancy (who also lacked a genetic connection to their parents, in this case both parents), and families with naturally conceived children. We visited the families twice, first when the children were around six, and again when they were 12.

In direct contrast to the concerns of health professionals that the stress of infertility and its treatment would put a strain on couples' marriages and take its toll on their relationships with their children, and the suggestion of the Warnock Committee that a missing genetic link between the child and their parent might threaten the relationship, it turned out that the children conceived through assisted reproduction — including those born through donor insemination — were well adjusted, and the parents actually had stronger relationships with their six-year-olds than the parents who had conceived their children naturally. The adoptive families fell somewhere between. We also examined family relationships from the children's perspectives with specially designed tests using stories and family figures, and found that the children born through assisted reproduction were close to both their mothers and their fathers. There were no differences between the IVF and donor insemination children. When the children were 12, all four family types continued to thrive. Where differences were found, the families created through assisted reproduction were again doing even better than the other families, and the fathers of children born through donor insemination were no less affectionate, and no more hostile towards their adolescent children than the biological fathers.

Some of our findings were startling. None of the 111 sets of parents who had used donor insemination had told their children about their conception by the time they were six, less than 10 per cent had done so by age 12, and, among the British parents, who we saw again when their children were 18, not one additional set of parents had disclosed this information in the intervening years. This was in spite of more than half of the parents confiding in a friend, a sister, or a parent, risking the possibility that their child would find out by accident from someone else. We were surprised by the extent of the secrecy surrounding donor insemination, especially as the parents of adopted children were generally open with them about their origins. When we asked parents why they had decided not to tell their children that they were donor conceived, their overwhelming response was fear: they were afraid of upsetting their children and disrupting their loving relationships with their fathers, and they worried that their children would not be fully accepted by their families, especially the paternal grandparents who lacked a genetic connection to them. Claire, the mother of seven-year-old Debbie, said, 'My husband doesn't want her not to love him. I know it wouldn't make any difference, but he doesn't want her to know, in case it would change her feelings towards him.' The couple were also worried about the reaction of the father's parents: 'They might treat our child differently from their other grandchildren. It was a chance we couldn't afford to take.' The parents of donor-conceived children also wanted to protect the fathers from the stigma of male infertility, which was widely misunderstood at the time; often men who could not have children were assumed to have sexual problems or be lacking in masculinity. What's more, parents didn't know when, what or how to tell their children about their conception, and because donors were anonymous at that time, they would not have been able to answer their children's inevitable questions about who the donor was. Some parents also felt that by the time their child was six they had lost their chance. As Cindy put it, 'We've left it too late. I think if you're going to tell them, we'd have to have done it when they were very young. It's too late now.'

Susie, a teacher, and Andrew, an engineer, found themselves in this situation. They had tried for ten years to have children, undergoing different kinds of fertility treatment, before their daughter Emily was finally born through sperm donation after eight unsuccessful attempts. They told their parents and siblings about Emily's conception, but decided against telling anyone else, including Emily. One day, Susie let slip to a colleague that her daughter had been born by donor insemination. She has regretted it ever since: 'I felt absolutely awful … I had this overwhelming feeling of betrayal, that I had completely betrayed my husband and my child. This woman knows something about my daughter that my daughter will never know.'

Susie and Andrew hadn't told Emily about her donor conception because they didn't want her to be treated differently from other children, or to upset her, and they wanted to preserve the special relationship that existed between Emily and her dad. They were worried that Emily might love him less if she found out that he was not her genetic father. 'I would hate for her to retaliate and say to her dad in an argument "You're not my real father",' said Susie. 'I would be mortified if she said that.' On top of that, the sperm donor was anonymous so it would not have been possible for Emily to know his identity. This worried Susie: 'I've tried to put myself in her situation, never knowing, and it's like having a huge weight on your shoulders.'

Emily's parents wanted to protect her from the trauma that Louise McLoughlin went through when she discovered she was donor-conceived and couldn't find out anything about her donor. Although Susie and Andrew believe that they have made the right decision, they worry that Emily might find out by accident, which could be extremely upsetting for her. Unlike lesbian couples, who are compelled to answer questions about their children's origins because they have two mothers, heterosexual couples like Susie and Andrew do not have to disclose this information, and are faced with the dilemma of whether or not to keep their children's origins secret.

***

The children in our European study had been born in the mid-1980s, when parents were still being advised by doctors to keep their use of donor insemination to themselves to avoid stigma. But there was growing disquiet about this practice among infertility counsellors and social workers. It was clear that adopted children were happier when they had information about their birth families, and there was a growing body of opinion that openness about their biological origins would be beneficial for donor-conceived children too. Some proponents of openness believe that keeping donor conception a secret will undermine family relationships, creating barriers between those who know (the parents) and those who do not (the child). Research has shown that children can sense when they are not being told something — they pick up on their parents' facial expressions, tones of voice, or avoidance of certain topics of conversation. Families love to talk about who resembles who, but in the case of donor-conceived children, parents sometimes try to avoid this subject, and the children might notice this. Some people feel that secrecy about biological parentage is morally wrong, whatever the effects on the children; they believe that children have a right to know. Since the early 2000s, both the American Fertility Society and the Human Fertilisation and Embryology Authority, the government body that regulates the practice of assisted reproduction in the United Kingdom, have recommended that parents should tell children about their donor conception, although in neither country is it mandatory for them to do so.

Although our first study provided important insights into the experiences of families formed through assisted reproduction, it didn't tell us how the children themselves felt about their conception because so few had been told. So, in 2000, when donor conception had become more widespread, and parents of donor-conceived children were starting to be more open with them about their origins, we began a new study.

A driving force behind this new research was Vasanti Jadva, one of my undergraduate students in London in the late 1990s, who joined the project at the start, accompanied me to Cambridge in 2006, and is a key member of the Centre for Family Research to this day. In addition to the many other projects that Vasanti is involved in, she continues to lead this one, still going strong now that the children are young adults.

We got off to a bad start. On the evening of 22 May 2001, I was at home watching the ten o'clock news when an item came up that put my heart in my mouth; the listed Victorian building where we worked was on fire. I could see flames coming out of the roof! I had never made it so quickly from my home in the City of London to my office in Clerkenwell as I did that night. When I arrived, fire engines with 60 firefighters were at work, and the Vice-Chancellor and Dean of Social Sciences were looking on in shock. The building had been safely evacuated, including students sitting a psychology exam, but it had been badly damaged and was in danger of collapse. It seemed as if the interviews from all of the research that I had carried out since the 1970s were about to be destroyed forever. The fire crew fought the blaze throughout the night. It turned out I was lucky, although some of my colleagues were not. The worst we experienced was water damage from the hose pipes.

Feeling very relieved that 25 years' work had not been lost, we began our new study. We wanted to find out how children who knew that they had been conceived through sperm donation were affected. By this time, egg donation had become an established treatment for female infertility, following the birth of the first egg donor baby in Australia in 1984 — the very first time a woman had given birth to a child who was genetically unrelated to her — so we also included a group of egg donation families. With the help of a generous research grant from the Wellcome Trust, and the support of nine fertility clinics up and down the United Kingdom, we recruited 50 families created through sperm donation, 51 egg donation families, and a comparison group of 80 families formed by natural conception, all with babies born at the millennium, and visited them six times from infancy to adolescence.

As in our earlier study, the families flourished when the children were in their pre-school years. We visited them in their homes when the children were one, two, and three, and saw more positive relationships between parents and their children in the assisted reproduction families. This gave us greater confidence that the findings of our earlier European study were correct. By the time of this new study, parents seemed more inclined to tell their children about their donor conception; when the children were one, 56 per cent of the egg donation parents and 46 per cent of the donor insemination parents planned to be open with them about their conception.

We saw the families again when the children were seven and ten. Seven is an important age for children who lack a biological connection to their parents as, by then, they have acquired a deeper understanding of what this means. Children have usually grasped the concept of genetic inheritance by this age, and adopted children — most of whom will have been told about their adoption — understand that being adopted means losing a birth family as well as gaining an adoptive family. In spite of the parents' initial intentions to be open with their children, when the time came, many found it hard. Only 41 per cent of the egg donation parents and 21 per cent of the donor insemination parents had told their children about their conception by the time they were seven. Some of the egg donation parents were open about their use of IVF because their family and friends knew about it, but not about their use of donor eggs. As Claudia, mother of a seven-year-old son conceived using egg donation described it, 'He's asking all the questions. He knows the basic facts. I think soon we should explain that his egg was fertilised outside the body, and wait a little longer to explain I'm not the genetic mother.' The majority of the children in our study were growing up not knowing that their mum or dad was not their genetic parent. Parents who had told their child had usually begun to do so by the time they were four.

One advantage of visiting families multiple times is that it's possible to examine the effects of events that happened early in children's lives on their later development; in this case, the disclosure of donor conception in early childhood on the children's adjustment in middle childhood and adolescence, although we can never be completely sure that one causes the other. We found that openness is generally best. Instead of the scenario parents had been dreading — in which they imagined themselves being rejected or, at best, having to console a very upset child — they were surprised to find that children who were told about their conception in their pre-school years accepted this information. Some showed little interest and others were curious, but not one child was distressed.

When the children were seven and ten, the families were still doing well, but the parents had better mental health and more positive relationships with their children in families where they had been open about the donor conception, although these parents may have been more communicative generally, not just about their children's conception. We found long-lasting benefits of early disclosure. Children who were first told about their conception when they were very young had better relationships with their mothers at age 14 than those who found out later on. This was particularly striking as both the mothers and the teenagers independently voiced this. As the research showed that young children are not upset by finding out about their conception, and there may be harmful effects of secrecy, we concluded that it is generally better for parents to tell their children from an early age, although this may not be true in cultures where the use of donated eggs or sperm is prohibited or taboo.

Gabby, who works in Human Resources, and Steve, an office manager, were the parents in one family who took part in our research. When she was just 16, Gabby was told by doctors that she was going through menopause early and would never have children naturally. When she met Steve five years later and they started dating, she was upfront with him about her inability to have children and also about her desire to become a mother through different means. Today, Gabby and Steve have three children born through egg donation. Their daughter, Anja, and their younger twins, Martin and Nick, were conceived using two different egg donors.

Gabby and Steve's children have always known about their conception. 'It was never a secret with us,' said Gabby. 'Our families and friends know. At some point somebody's going to say something and I didn't want that to be the way they found out. I just always wanted them to know. I'd hate to sit them down when they're 18 and suddenly tell them.'

Gabby began to tell her children fairy stories about their conception when they were little, such as: 'Once upon a time there was a lady who couldn't have any children, so another lady helped her, and — *whoosh* — she had a beautiful baby, and that baby was you!' It wasn't until the children started school that they began to ask questions. Gabby described a conversation with Anja when she was seven, 'She asked if she came out of my tummy, and I said, "You came out of my tummy but the doctor had to help me put you in my tummy because I didn't have any eggs, so another lady, who I don't know, gave some to the doctor and he gave them to me," and she became quite interested in that point and said, "Did the eggs come in a box?" and I said, "No darling, not those kind of eggs." She wanted to know how big the eggs were, she said, "This big?", "No", I said, "You couldn't even see them, they were so tiny," and she said, "Oh, right," and went off to play.'

Gabby and Steve's children were comfortable with their origins, most probably because they had never known differently, unlike Louise McLoughlin whose whole identity was thrown into question when she found out that her dad was not her biological father. This was the same for the 14-year-olds from our study who had been told about their conception when they were younger. Most said that it wasn't a big issue for them, although some were curious about their donor and wished to know more.

***

The prospect of having a genetically unrelated child can be daunting for parents. Susan Imrie, a psychologist who had become interested in family research through her previous position as a parliamentary researcher, and Vasanti Jadva, explored the thoughts and feelings of 85 new mothers of babies conceived by egg donation in a study that began in 2013. Many said that they had worried during pregnancy about whether they would bond with their babies and whether the babies would feel like their own. Florence said, 'My only concerns were how was I going to feel about him when he arrived and whether I would feel that he was mine', and Amy explained, 'That's all I thought about before he arrived, what if we don't bond?'. Some, like Lottie, were concerned that their baby would not bond with them: 'That was my whole preoccupation — would I bond with this baby, would this baby bond with me? My biggest fear was that this baby would think — who the hell are you?'

When their babies arrived, most mothers discovered that their fears were unfounded. As Nina described it, 'I just loved him unconditionally as soon as he was born.' Georgia said, 'I don't think I could love him more if he was completely my genetic material.' For others, it took longer, and some struggled with the idea that their child was not genetically related to them: 'I couldn't give myself a hundred per cent to her, emotionally. I took care of her, I did what I needed to do, but I didn't feel that she was my child really. It took a while for that feeling to come in.' Although this also happens to mothers who are genetically related to their babies, the mothers in our study whose children were conceived using donor eggs attributed their feelings to the absence of a genetic link with their child. A few continued to struggle with these feelings throughout the first year, such as Wendy, the mother of twins: 'Biologically they're not my children, even though I was pregnant with them and I gave birth to them, and that's still quite a hard thing for me to square in my own mind.' But the majority of the 85 mothers in our study had bonded with their babies by the time they were one.

Jess, a curator in a local museum, and her husband, Sam, a software developer, who lived in a pretty suburb of Sheffield, had been together for 14 years, and had been trying to conceive for eight years, before their baby, Jack, was born through egg donation. Jess had always imagined that she would be a mother, and that her children would be genetically related to her and her husband. 'At the back of your mind you imagine what the babies might look like,' she said when she took part in our study when Jack was one. 'You wonder whether you'll see parts of other members of your family in your child. My dad died when I was in my 20s, and I had an idea that perhaps there'd be a part of him, in a look or in the handwriting, or just some shadow that's passed down.' When Jess was informed by her doctor that egg donation was her only option — after six rounds of insemination with her husband's sperm and four IVF cycles using her own eggs, two of which ended in miscarriage — she found the idea hard to accept, but once she'd made the decision to proceed, she became pregnant on the first attempt. 'It was very, very difficult for the first 20 odd weeks because I was angry that I'd managed to get pregnant so easily with someone else's egg, but not with my own. It wasn't until the baby was moving and kicking that I began to look forward to being a mother. He would kick in the night and I would poke him and he'd kick back … so you'd have this little game, and that's when I thought "this is my baby". The first few months of Jack's life were difficult for Jess. She explained, 'People said, "you'll never experience a feeling of love like it", but I didn't in the first few months. It's a relationship that's grown over the last year. We've got to know each other. When I catch his eye and we both share a little smile, it's just that little precious moment of knowing and understanding each other.' Jess has mixed feelings about the prospect of Jack meeting the egg donor when he grows up, but she'd like to do that. When asked why, she replied, 'Just to say thank you. And for her to meet Jack because he's cracking, he's absolutely lovely!'

Another question that Susan and Vasanti set out to answer was whether knowing that their child could potentially meet their egg donor when they grew up — as was the case with the children in this study, all of whom were born following the removal of donor anonymity in the United Kingdom in 2005 — would interfere with mothers' relationships with their children. Although parents are not required by law to disclose the donor conception to their children, many planned to do so, and there is always the risk that children will find out in other ways. If the mothers felt threatened by the prospect of their children forming a relationship with their egg donor in the future, might this affect their confidence, and consequently, the relationship with their children? To examine this, they compared the egg donation mothers' thoughts and feelings about their infants with the thoughts and feelings of mothers whose babies had been conceived through IVF with their parents' own eggs and sperm. They also video-recorded mothers and babies playing together to examine their behaviour towards each other. They found that the egg donation and IVF mothers were very similar; both were warm towards their babies, and experienced few negative feelings towards them.

***

In families created by embryo donation, which usually happens when couples donate surplus embryos from their own IVF treatment to another couple, the children lack a genetic connection to both of their parents, like adopted children, except that the parents experience the pregnancy and birth, and the children are not separated from their birth parents. Today, many children who are put up for adoption have suffered trauma in their early years — physical, sexual, or emotional abuse, or neglect — which makes them more at risk for mental health problems than children born through embryo donation. But does the absence of a genetic link to both parents, even when children are raised by their non-genetic parents from birth, adversely affect family relationships, as suggested by some critics? In the early 2000s, Fiona MacCallum, a psychologist who worked with me in London at the time, set out to find out.

Like other kinds of assisted reproduction families, Fiona found that those formed through embryo donation were doing well. But they stood out in one way — the parents were even less likely to tell their children about their conception. Their reasons were similar to those of parents of donor-conceived children. Some wished to protect their children from the distress of discovering that they are not genetically related to their parents. Janice, mother of five-year-old Jason, said, 'I think it would cause a lot of insecurity in Jason, a lot of upheaval, and a lot of upset.' And some were worried that their children would reject them if they found out. Amelia said, 'Possibly, you'd get "you're not really my parents, what right have you got?"' Others, like Isabel, whose daughter was born in the days of anonymous donors, were concerned that their children would be disturbed by not being able to find out who either of their genetic parents is: 'He's not going to be able to find out, so why make him think Daddy and I aren't his real parents?' A further consideration was how the children would be treated by other members of the family. As Maria explained, 'I don't want him to feel left out. I want him to know he has a family that will look after him. I want him inside the family rather than outside.'

It seems that embryo donation is shrouded in even greater secrecy than egg or sperm donation because the children lack a genetic connection to two parents instead of one; parents fear that both of them will be rejected if the children find out, and the children may never be able to discover the identity of either of their genetic parents. But just as there is greater openness today about sperm and egg donation, the same seems to be true of embryo donation.

Maya Grobel, a therapist, and her husband, Noah Moskin, a film-maker, who live in California, arrived at embryo donation after three years of unsuccessful fertility treatment. Their trials and tribulations, and eventual jubilation at the birth of their daughter in 2015, are movingly documented in their film, *One More Shot*.

'Embryo donation isn't something that you just decide to do one day,' Maya told me when we met on a slightly chilly morning in Los Angeles in the spring of 2019, sipping coffee under the palm trees to keep warm. 'We went from IVF to multiple intrauterine inseminations to IVF with donor eggs, and then you get to the point where you look at what you have left — what resources you have left, emotionally, physically, relationally, financially. Embryo donation wasn't something we knew much about. Once we did, we had to wrap our heads around what it meant to give birth to a child who's not genetically related to us.'

Being able to carry a pregnancy and give birth was important to Maya. 'The idea of being able to grow and carry and nurse and have that connection with a child, regardless of genetics, felt good to me,' she said. 'We really felt strongly that it was love not genetics that was going to inform our family, and that the parenting process was most important.' It's often assumed that couples who become parents through embryo donation will have trouble bonding with their children because they lack a genetic relationship with them, but that was not the case for Maya. She said, 'I'm this child's mother. She's a part of my heart and we love each other. My husband feels the same way. They're so connected and they love each other so much. I've no doubt that we're her parents.'

But Maya and Noah don't know the identity of the egg donor used to create the embryos, or of the couple who donated the embryo that became their daughter. As Maya explained, 'In the United States, if an individual or couple relinquish their remaining embryos to their clinic, recipients are often not allowed to know who they are.' This worries Maya. She would like her daughter to be able to know the people she's genetically connected to. 'I'm not comfortable with the lack of information, and I'm even less comfortable that there's a gate-keeper at a clinic, a donor coordinator or a nurse who has access to my daughter's information, such as how many half-siblings she has, yet we're not privy to any of that information.' Maya believes that children have the right to know where they come from, and that parents should do the best that they can to provide this information. She has already explained to her daughter that she had donor helpers — special people who gave a part of themselves to help Mommy and Daddy have a baby.

And she plans to explain to her daughter that she has one full genetic brother and several half-siblings in an age-appropriate way. As things stand, she's unable to tell her more than that.

There is a more troubling side to embryo donation. In 2012, a company in California began to sell embryos that they had created in the laboratory from the sperm of a male donor and the eggs of a female donor. What will the impact be on children who lack a genetic link to their parents of discovering that they had been produced from two people who had never met? We don't yet have the answer, but from what we know about the importance to many donor-conceived people of finding out about their origins, this information may well be unwelcome and upsetting. As Jackie Kay, the Scottish poet, put it in her acclaimed memoir about being adopted, 'Nobody wants to have been created out of hate, or boredom, or foolishness or ignorance. I prefer to believe that I've been made out of love.'

***

The use of donated eggs or sperm to create children becomes even more complicated when a family member is the donor, a practice known as intra-family donation. This most frequently happens when women donate eggs to a sister or sister-in-law who is unable to conceive a baby herself, or when brothers of infertile men donate their sperm. Less commonly, eggs or sperm may be donated across generations, from daughters to mothers, or from fathers to sons. Although this kind of donation means there's a family connection between the donor and the child, and a genetic connection between the non-genetic parent and the child if the donor comes from their side of the family, this practice has raised concerns about the undue pressure that may be placed on a family member to donate, and the future fall-out on family dynamics. Relatives who offer to donate their eggs or sperm wish to help members of their family overcome the heartbreak of infertility, but might they be coerced into doing this, either because they feel they can't say no when asked directly, or because they feel under an obligation to assist? Will they interfere in the child's upbringing because they are the child's genetic parent? And when eggs or sperm are donated by a sister or brother, or sister- or brother-in-law, how will children respond to the discovery that their aunt or uncle is actually their genetic parent, and their cousins their half-siblings? Or, when a daughter donates eggs to her mother, that their sister is their genetic mother, and their mother their genetic grandmother?

Very little is known about the outcomes of intra-family donation, so we looked again at the nine families from our longitudinal study of children born at the millennium whose children had been conceived using a sister or sister-in-law's eggs. It was a small number, but we thought that it would give us some insight into these families as the children grew up, something that no one had explored before. We focused on the first ten years of the children's lives and found no evidence that the egg donors felt maternal towards them; the donors saw themselves as aunts. As Jean, mother of ten-year-old Sharon, described her family, 'She's my sister, so she's my daughter's auntie, and she is very much her auntie, and that is her role.' The mothers did not appear to be threatened by their relative's genetic link to their child, and all but one remained close to her. But notably, most of the parents had not told their children about their conception to avoid complications in the family. Some mothers were concerned that similarities in appearance between their child and the egg donor, or her children, would give the game away. Physical resemblance can be a particular problem when the donor is a sister-in-law and lacks a genetic connection to the child.

I met Rina and her husband, Kamal, in their home in Leicester, England, when they first took part in our study. The couple both came from large Indian families and had planned to have three children, so finding out that Rina could not conceive because of early menopause was deeply upsetting for them. Rina's sister-in-law, Anita, realising how much it meant to Rina, offered to donate her eggs so that the couple could have a child. The two women had grown up together and were very close. Rina and Kamal gratefully accepted the offer, but decided not to tell Kamal's parents in case they disapproved; they told them about the IVF but not about the egg donation. But Rina thinks that her mother-in-law suspects the truth. 'Yesterday, I went to my mother-in-law's and she looked at my baby and said, "She looks like your nephew,"' Rina told us. 'She taunts me whenever she sees me. It's hard to swallow.' Rina and Kamal love their baby daughter, Dayna: 'Even though my sister-in-law donated her eggs, Dayna is part of us. Both of us. She's our child now. We don't see her any differently.' When we re-visited the family when Dayna was seven, Rina and Kamal had still not told Kamal's side of the family about Dayna's conception. They hadn't told Dayna either, but they intended to do so when they thought she was old enough to understand.

We don't yet know how children born through intra-family donation who are told about, or uncover, their origins later in life will feel when they discover that their donor is a relative, and the donor's children are their half-siblings. This may depend on how well they got on with each other before they found out. They may feel especially wanted and loved because of the lengths their family went to in order to have them, or, as suggested by some critics, they may feel deceived not just by their parents but by their entire family.

***

Until relatively recently, most donors were anonymous, like Louise McLoughlin's donor. This has meant that even when parents were open with their children about their conception, donor-conceived children and adults could not find out who their donors were or anything about them. Sometimes their parents had information about the donor's physical characteristics, such as their height, weight, eye and hair colour, but often they knew little beyond that.

Changing attitudes towards telling children about their donor conception has resulted in an increasing number of donor-conceived children and adults who know about their origins, and who wish to trace their donor and donor siblings — genetically related half-siblings born from the same donor who have grown up in different families. This became possible in the United States in 2000 when Ryan Kramer, an 11-year-old donor-conceived boy, and his mother, Wendy, founded the Donor Sibling Registry, a website that enables contact between families who share the same donor. If the family have the donor's unique identification number, they can enter it to connect with others born from that donor. Since its inception, 67,000 people have registered with the website and 18,000 matches have been made between donor-conceived children and their half-siblings and/or donors.

I first came across the Donor Sibling Registry in 2007 while reading the newspapers at home one Sunday morning. By this time, I had moved to the Centre for Family Research in Cambridge where much of our research focused on families formed through donor conception. *The Sunday Times* ran an article about the Registry that included an interview with Wendy Kramer. The idea of genetic half-siblings who had grown up in different families making contact with each other was fascinating to me; it was something that was not possible in the United Kingdom yet because anonymous sperm donation had only recently been banned and the oldest children who were eligible to discover the identity of their donors were still only two. The following morning, I showed the article to Vasanti and Tabitha Freeman, a sociologist who specialised in family relationships, and they too were intrigued. We were all keen to discover why some parents and children search for their sperm donor and donor siblings, and what the outcome is. I contacted Wendy Kramer to find out whether she might be willing to collaborate with us on a study to find out. To our delight, she agreed, and, in 2007, we joined forces with the Donor Sibling Registry to conduct a survey.

The mothers and donor-conceived children and adults who took part in our survey were curious about similarities in appearance and personality with their donor and donor siblings, and also wanted to gain a greater understanding of their ancestry and of themselves. The questions the children most wanted answers to were: Do I look like him? Is my personality like his? And what is his family background? To our amazement, we uncovered a new phenomenon. Some donor relations who were finding each other over the Internet were forming close emotional bonds. In many cases, the children were more interested in their donor siblings than they were in the donors themselves; they wanted to find out about their donor, and some wanted to meet him, but they didn't usually see him as their father, and they were more likely to develop close and enduring connections with their donor siblings. On reflection, that's not surprising. Many were only children who were pleased to find brothers and sisters, especially as they were often of a similar age. Through the Donor Sibling Registry, lesbian mother families, single heterosexual mother families and traditional two-parent families are finding themselves related to each other through their children. Sometimes, they come to view each other not as new acquaintances, but as family. As Jenny, who was surprised by the strength of her feelings put it, 'I felt very maternal toward my son's brother and sister. I know that genetically I have no relationship to them, but they are my family, they are a part of me, they mean the world to me.' Pamela said, 'I was actually just curious about what the siblings might be like — personalities, looks, etc. After connecting with the other moms it turned out to be a more wonderful experience than I'd ever imagined. We've become a family of sorts of our own and share a special bond. It wasn't why I sought the siblings but it was a completely wonderful surprise.'

There were clear differences in the reactions of children and adults to discovering they were donor-conceived depending on the age at which they found out. Those who had been told as young children were much more likely to accept this information. As Elena, a 13-year-old girl who was told during childhood explained, 'I was so young I don't remember feeling much more than interested and curious', and Kiera, a 15-year-old girl said, 'I've always been accepting of it because I never knew any different.' In contrast, those who found out later in life, like Louise McLoughlin, were more likely to feel upset, angry at being lied to and deceived by their parents. Mandy, a 19-year-old woman who found out as a teenager described it as, 'One of the most shocking and upsetting moments of my life', and another young woman said, 'I felt alone.' Some donor-conceived people claimed they had always felt that something was amiss. A woman who didn't discover she was donor-conceived until she was middle-aged told us, 'I asked about being adopted several times throughout my childhood and adolescence and was told that I was being foolish. I knew.' Far fewer people with heterosexual parents had told their fathers about their search for donor relations than those with lesbian parents had told their non-genetic mothers, most probably because they didn't want to upset them.

Although there has been a huge shift in opinion away from the recommendation of fertility doctors in the 1980s and 90s that parents should keep their use of donor conception secret from their children, the introduction of legislation to give donor-conceived people the right to find out the identity of their donor is relatively recent. The first country to do this was Sweden in 1985, long before any other country. Today, in addition to the United Kingdom, donor anonymity has been abolished in several countries including Austria, Germany, Norway, Iceland, Finland, Switzerland, the Netherlands, New Zealand, and the Australian States of Victoria, New South Wales, and Western Australia. In these jurisdictions, donor-conceived people who are aware of their origins — those born from egg and embryo donation, as well as sperm donation — can find out who their donor is, usually when they are 18, and try to contact their donor directly if they wish to do so. As parents are not required by law to tell their children that they are donor-conceived, only those who are aware of their donor conception, or perhaps suspect it, know that there's anything to find out.

The most radical and controversial legislation on the disclosure of donor conception has been enacted in the State of Victoria in Australia, where donor-conceived people and their parents can not only contact their donors through the Victorian Assisted Reproductive Treatment Authority (VARTA), the government body that regulates assisted reproduction, but they can do this even in cases where the donors had donated sperm decades earlier on the understanding that they would always be anonymous. The justification given for this contentious change in legislation is that children have a right to know their genetic origins, and this right is considered to trump donors' rights to anonymity.

Louise Lane, who grew up in Melbourne, benefitted from this law. 'Don't worry darling, he's not your father.' These were the words that changed Louise's life shortly after her parents divorced. In March 2015, following a breast cancer scare, Louise's mother, Elizabeth, told her 31-year-old daughter that she had been conceived by donor insemination. She said, 'I want you to know that you were conceived in love, and very much wanted, but this is how you came to be.' Elizabeth had intended that Louise would eventually find out through a note in her will. Louise is relieved that it didn't come to that: 'I'm really glad she told me because if I'd found out in her will, I would've been so angry! It's not the right way to do it. You lose one parent and then all of a sudden you find out that you weren't related to the other one.'

Following 15 rounds of donor insemination over a period of two years, Elizabeth had given birth to twins in 1981, followed by Louise two years later using the same sperm donor. Like many couples going through donor insemination at that time, they were advised to go home, have sex, and pretend that the donor insemination had never happened. They didn't tell anyone, not even their closest family. As time went on, Elizabeth became increasingly uncomfortable about keeping this secret from her children, and felt they should be told. She worried that if they should need blood donation and turned to a cousin for help, only to find out they weren't biologically related, it would be an awful shock. It preyed on her mind. But her husband was against it. He thought there was no need to tell them, and that it would be opening Pandora's box. Growing up, Louise suspected that she may have been adopted, and even asked to see her birth certificate when she was a teenager, but her dad was named as her birth father which didn't enlighten her. Louise looked a bit like her dad and got on well with him, but she felt that something didn't quite add up.

Elizabeth felt hugely relieved when she eventually told Louise the truth. On a video for VARTA, she said, 'As a parent you wonder how your child will take this information. Will they be cross with you? Will they run away from it all because you've completely destroyed their vision of what their life was all about? Was it all a big lie?' But she need not have worried. Louise's first reaction was simply, 'Wow!' and since that day, Elizabeth has never felt any negativity from her daughter about the circumstances of her birth.

Within hours of finding out about her conception, Louise called the fertility clinic in Melbourne where she had been conceived and found to her joy that her records still existed. The clinic administrator put her in touch with VARTA, and following a counselling session, she began to search for her donor. Just one week later, Louise received the phone call she had been waiting for. Her donor had been found, and not only that, she had nine half-siblings in eight different families who had been born from his donations, and two half-siblings who were his own children! She was amazed: 'I remember when I first found out, I went and looked at myself in the mirror and I thought, who is the other half of me? Who is the other half of the person looking back at me? What type of person is my donor? What is he like?' Louise yearned to meet her donor and donor siblings, but couldn't begin to search for them because her older brother and sister didn't know. 'It was twelve months before my mum told them,' she explained. 'I put together a whole pack for them — the books, the research material from VARTA, and the non-identifying information — so that when Mum told them, they had it. And then I went searching.'

As part of the process, Louise was required to produce a statement of her reasons for wishing to contact her donor. She wrote, 'I learned that I was donor conceived in 2015 at the age of 31 and my initial response was one of awe and amazement! Awe in that the generosity of a person whom my parents had never met enabled me to exist, and amazement in the decade-long perseverance of my parents to create a family. With me in my wallet I carry a piece of paper with the basic information you completed on the donor form in 1980. "FE" — the donor code allocated to you — lists your height, weight, build, eye colour, religion, and family status at the time of donation. Some of these I share with you; I am 175cm, blue eyed and medium build too. I wonder what other traits and/or characteristics I may have inherited from you? For example, my initial university degree was Engineering/Law. Your occupation was listed as "Professional Engineer". What are the chances! I truly hope that I get the chance one day to meet you, but should that not happen, I would like you to know that your conscious decision in donating meant that others could experience the joy of having their own family. And I, in turn, will one day have the joy of starting my own family. I hope that I have given you some sense of what your contribution has meant to my parents, myself, and my siblings, and no doubt to the other families too. I sometimes imagine that you and your wife had experienced the joy of creating your own family, and wanted others to experience that miracle too. Thank you.'

Louise first met her donor, Ross, on 18 July 2016 in a meeting room at a sports club in a leafy district of Melbourne. Her mother Elizabeth, Ross's wife Carolyn, and Kate Bourne, VARTA's Donor Registers Service Manager, were there too. Elizabeth was nervous to meet the man who had enabled her to become a parent. She was worried how her children would feel if he wasn't a good person. But Louise was excited. 'It was easy really,' said Louise. 'He walked in and I thought, "Oh yes, that's my biological father."' Kate took a picture of Elizabeth and Ross, and turned to Louise and said, 'That's the first photograph of your two biological parents.'

An even more contentious aspect of the Victorian legislation is that, as well as donor-conceived people now being able to contact their donors, even those who donated anonymously, the donors themselves are also allowed to search for the children they helped create, some of whom have no idea that they were donor-conceived. For families where parents have not told their children, being contacted by the donor can be a bombshell that blows the family apart. When Ross asked Louise if she would like to meet her half-siblings, her answer was an unequivocal 'yes', but it has not been easy. By law, only he could make the first move. He was required to contact VARTA, who would approach anybody conceived using his sperm on his behalf. But he would have preferred to reach out to their parents in the first instance. It has been traumatic for some to find out as adults that they were donor-conceived, and for their parents to have the secret they had kept for decades exposed. It is what Susie and Andrew feared might happen if Emily ever found out about her donor conception. Some of the genetic half-siblings did not want to meet. But once the dust settled, others came round and were pleased to have found out. It validated their feelings growing up that something was amiss. Louise feels very fortunate: 'I'm proud to be donor-conceived and I'm amazed about the way my case has unfolded, from the records existing, having VARTA and the amazing services there, being able to track down my donor and become friends with him, and finding out his reason for donating. I just really loved that. And then meeting the other half-siblings, and finding more and more of them. I just got lucky. I really did.'

But there are not always happy endings. In 2018, Australia's leading fertility doctor, Professor Gab Kovacs, received a letter from one of his patients from the early 1980s: 'She told me that her 36-year-old daughter had received a letter from VARTA informing her that a sperm donor wanted to contact her. As was common practice at the time, the parents had not disclosed to their daughter that she was donor-conceived. You can imagine the shock their daughter received when reading the letter. Her mother was also shocked and upset when her daughter called to tell her about it,' said Gab. 'The mother did not deny her daughter's right to know, but she was upset by the way she was informed. She described it as "cruel and unkind". She was upset that she, as her mother, was not contacted before her daughter, giving her the opportunity to speak to her daughter first. She said that she was thankful every single day for the gift of her daughter, but she wanted to prevent other parents of donor-conceived children having to go through what happened to her family.'

***

Before donor conception became widely practised in the 1980s and 90s, it was taken for granted that it takes two to make a family — a mother and a father who conceive genetically related children. It was also assumed that children who are not the genetic progeny of their parents are less likely to thrive. This is partially because research on other kinds of families in which children lack a genetic connection to their parents, such as adoptive families and stepfamilies, has found these children to show an increased likelihood of developing psychological problems, which has sometimes been put down to the absence of a biological link. But this was not the case in the donor-conceived families we studied; genetic relatedness is less important than previously thought for raising happy and well-adjusted children. The problems experienced by adopted and stepchildren appear to spring from the difficult family situations in which they often find themselves before being adopted, or before and after moving into a stepfamily. Adopted children have often suffered neglect or abuse before being placed with their adoptive parents, sometimes for many years, and many have been moved from one foster family to another before being adopted, making it hard for them to put down roots. Children in stepfamilies have often been separated from a parent who they were close to, and must form new relationships with their step-parents, which is not always easy, and sometimes with stepbrothers and stepsisters too.

Just because donor-conceived children are well adjusted does not mean that their donor is unimportant to them. Some donor-conceived people have no interest in finding out about, or searching for, their donor, just as some adopted people have no interest in their birth parents. But others search for their donor over the Internet, using websites such as the Donor Sibling Registry, something that is likely to become easier as technology becomes more advanced, our lives more digitised, and more donors are open to revealing their identities. Both donor conception and adoption leave some children curious about their biological parents, and sometimes uncertain of their identity, a phenomenon known as 'genealogical bewilderment', first described in the 1960s in relation to adoption by the psychologist, H. J. Sants. The question of whether donor-conceived children should be told about their genetic origins remains one of the most hotly contested issues in assisted reproduction today. In 2012, the Nuffield Council on Bioethics in the United Kingdom established an eight-person Working Party, of which I was a member, to consider this issue. We acknowledged that each family will have their own set of circumstances to weigh up when making their decision, depending on their cultural, ethnic, and religious background, but concluded that, ideally, children should be told about their origins, and told as early as possible, so that they will grow up always knowing this fact about themselves.

***

In November 2017, Louise McLoughlin found her donor-conceived half-sister, Jess, online, 13 years after the revelation that tore her world apart. At first, Louise focused on searching for her donor, but when she met with a group of other donor-conceived people, she noticed that everyone else was more interested in finding donor siblings. Four months after signing up to *Ancestry.com*, Louise received a message that said, 'I don't want to alarm you, because you may not be donor-conceived, but I am, and I'm very sorry if this is a shock to you but we've matched as very close so I'd just be interested in finding out more.' At first the two women thought they might be cousins, but after messaging each other back and forth for an hour, they realised that they were probably genetic half-siblings. 'She messaged me on WhatsApp and her photo came up. Seeing my donor sister's face for the first time was absolutely incredible,' Louise told me. 'I can't put how I felt into words. I just cried. I was shaking. It was completely overwhelming.'

They met two months later at a busy London railway station: 'It was completely terrifying,' Louise remembered. 'We were meant to meet under the big clock in the centre. It's the busiest station in the world, everyone looks like they're coming towards you, and if you don't know the face of the person you're looking out for, it's very intimidating. So I ended up putting my back against the wall and hiding, and of course, that's the second she saw me, when I was crouching behind a sign! And bless her, she pretended she hadn't seen me and did a loop and then said hello normally. Then, a few hours in, she said, "I saw you hiding behind the sign." I said, "You'd never guess I was hiding." And she replied, "I absolutely saw that!"'

On that first meeting, in a station restaurant, Louise and Jess talked for hours about their lives. Jess had two mums and had always known that she had been born with the help of a sperm donor. But she too wished to find her donor siblings. Like Louise, she was curious to meet others with whom she shared a genetic link. Now, they talk to each other every day, and try to see each other once a month. Meeting

Jess has brought Louise unexpected joy: 'It was never really a hole that I felt I had in my life, because I had had such a loving childhood. But we're both absolutely on the same page, and I'm very thankful to have met her.'

Chapter 3

Sperm, Egg, and Embryo Donors: 'Missing Branches'

'I had started to think, 'Who will remember me when I'm gone? Who will talk about me? Who will be my heir? ... What if I had 100 [children]... or even more?'

'LOUIS', A PROLIFIC DUTCH SPERM DONOR, SPEAKING TO *THE GUARDIAN*, (2018).

'It's the best thing I've ever done. I'm thrilled with the relationship I have with my new daughter. I'm best friends with her mother. My parents are thrilled with their new granddaughter. This has only been a positive, win-win experience.'

SPERM DONOR, ADRIAN, WHO WAS CONTACTED BY HIS DONOR DAUGHTER, CINDY, (2007).

In 1981, Ole Schou had a dream. It was a dream about sperm. But this was not just ordinary sperm: it was a vivid, startling, and surreal dream about sperm frozen in time — completely still — under ice. 'I knew it was a strange dream, a peculiar dream, because there was nothing happening in the dream. There was no movement. Just a still picture. But because it was so strange, I didn't forget it,' Ole told me when

I visited him 36 years later in Aarhus, Denmark. At the time of the dream, Ole was studying business management at Aarhus Business School and restoring a farmhouse in the countryside. He knew nothing about sperm. His interests were hang-gliding, skiing, motorcycling, climbing mountains, and deep-sea diving — the more extreme the sport, the better.

But this dream was to change the course of Ole's life. The image of frozen sperm did not leave him; he was curious to find out more. 'I remember going to the library and asking the woman there if she had some literature about frozen sperm. It was a little awkward, but she took it very professionally and produced a list of 168 articles. They were about reproduction, fertility and infertility, and also about cryobiology — it was the first time I had heard about that. I didn't know anything about sperm or fertility treatment at all. I became more and more curious — captivated and obsessed — and wanted to read more and more about the beginning of life. A whole new world opened up for me. It was then that I had the fantastic idea of opening a sperm bank.'

First, Ole had to learn about sperm. With a children's microscope, a gift from his parents when he was 13, he studied his own sperm. He would sit up late at night in his farmhouse with his microscope, his books and his primitive computer learning how sperm worked and carrying out experiments on different freezing methods. He had no experts to consult. All of his knowledge came from books and scientific papers. 'I was studying each night until 4 am because everything was calm. I had my Italian espresso machine, and smoked cigarettes to boost my concentration. It was a wonderful time. I was so focused.'

In February 1986, Ole made the decision to open a sperm bank, and on 1 November 1987, with the help of a small loan from his mother, Cryos — named from the Ancient Greek word *cryo*, meaning frost — opened its doors for business. It was not an immediate success, and, within a year, was closed due to insufficient income. 'But then the first Danish private fertility clinic opened — the *Mermaid Clinic* in Ebeltoft,'

Ole recalled. 'I went to see them and left with a large order. I re-established the company. I couldn't afford a car so I went around the city on my bicycle putting up posters advertising for donors. That was 1990. After one week, there was a pregnancy; after two weeks, there were five pregnancies. Doctors from other clinics called me. I said I can deliver today — I can send a helicopter or a courier. They were amazed.'

Today, Cryos is the world's largest sperm bank, delivering frozen sperm to more than 100 countries and responsible for the birth of more than 65,000 babies. A painting depicting Ole's transcendental dream about sperm, by a donor who is an artist, adorns the lobby, a reminder of both the origins of the sperm bank and the role of sperm in the origins of life. When I visited in 2017, I was struck by the ordinariness of the building; it is bright, airy, and stylish, and looks like any other successful organisation. It was only when we entered the laboratory that the enormity and significance of what happens at Cryos hit home. Inside were gleaming, steaming, stainless-steel containers filled with thousands of vials of frozen sperm — millions of potential people — standing to attention, as if to say, 'Pick me! Pick me! Pick me!'

***

Who are the men who donate their sperm to enable childless couples and single and lesbian women to become parents? And why do they do it? Although sperm donation has been used by doctors as a treatment for infertility since the 1940s and the first child conceived using frozen sperm was born in the United States in 1953, sperm donation remained cloaked in secrecy until the 1990s, when social workers and fertility counsellors began to campaign for an end to donor anonymity. Before this, young men heard about the need for sperm donors from adverts on student notice boards, or through word-of-mouth. As most donors were recruited from universities, often from medical schools, it was assumed that they were impoverished students doing it for so-called 'beer money'. But was that really true?

In 1993, the UK's Human Fertilisation and Embryology Authority (HFEA) asked me to carry out a study of the attitudes and experiences of sperm donors, who in those days were all anonymous. I was coming to the end of my first study of children born by donor insemination, and was curious to find out more about the men who made these families possible. The HFEA was concerned about the shortage of donors, especially in light of an increasing demand for donated sperm as infertility treatment became more accessible. There was also growing pressure to remove donor anonymity, which they believed would result in an even greater shortfall. They wanted to learn about the motivations of sperm donors to help them find ways of encouraging more men to donate in the future.

We discovered that money was only part of the story — altruism also played a part. Although almost two-thirds of the men stated that they would not donate sperm if they were not paid, most said that they also wanted to help other people have children. They were not particularly interested in the children they helped create, however: half didn't want to know whether any children had been born from their donation, and two-thirds said that they would not donate if there was a chance they could be identified by any future offspring. In Denmark, a survey by Bjorn Bay, a doctor specialising in fertility treatment, and his colleagues, of men who had donated sperm anonymously at Cryos in 1992, 2002, and 2012, produced similar findings. But over the three decades, an increasing number of men were willing to disclose non-identifying information about themselves, such as their education, occupation, personality, and interests, a trend that Bay put down to the growing understanding that this information may be important to those born from their donation.

As more countries banned anonymous donation, there were increasing concerns that men would no longer donate sperm, but these turned out to be unwarranted. Although there was an initial reduction in the number of young, single men who were willing to be sperm donors, attempts to recruit a different type of sperm donor — older, married men who already had children of their own, and who were less concerned about anonymity — proved successful. Sperm banks have proliferated since Ole Schou founded Cryos. Today, couples and single women can select donors online from extensive catalogues, and, at the touch of a button, sperm from a chosen donor can be shipped around the world. At the millennium, 80 per cent of the sperm procured from Cryos was destined for heterosexual couples. Just 15 years later, in 2015, only 20 per cent went to heterosexual couples; 30 per cent went to lesbian couples, and half to single women. This is partly due to the increasing number of lesbian couples and single women forming families through donor insemination, but also because of the introduction of intra-cytoplasmic sperm injection (ICSI) in the 1990s, which enabled infertile men with abnormal sperm or low sperm counts to become fathers through the injection of a single sperm into their partner's egg to fertilise it when previously their only option to have a child would have been by using donor sperm.

The first time Benjamin Jensen applied to Cryos to become a sperm donor in 2012, he was turned down because his sperm count didn't meet the required standard. He was 18, and an elite footballer with an active social life. When he was 22, by then himself a father of a one-year-old daughter, Christina, he tried again. This time, he passed the stringent screening procedure, which involved a detailed medical examination, including blood, sperm, and urine analysis, to ensure that he was healthy and unlikely to pass on any genetic disorders to any donor children. Benjamin became a donor partly for financial reasons — he was a student training to become a teacher at the time — but also because a friend's baby boy had been conceived by sperm donation and Benjamin and his wife, Maj, could see the joy the child had brought his mother.

Benjamin knows that at least one child has been born from his donation, but not the actual number. 'Maj and I have discussed it a lot,' he told me when I met him at the Head Office of Cryos in Aarhus in May, 2019, 'We feel that fatherhood is more than genes. It's the role that you fulfil and the care that you give your children that makes you a father. I don't see them as my children.' The couple now have three young children of their own, and haven't yet decided whether to tell them about their donor siblings. Benjamin opted for anonymous donation, which means that Cryos will not release his identity, and his sperm will only be used in countries where anonymous sperm donation is permitted. His main worry is that a large number of children might have been born from his donation in countries that don't have legal limits. 'That's the thing I'm most concerned about,' he told me. 'I know that a maximum of twelve families can be formed from a single donor in Denmark. But might I have many more children in other parts of the world? And might these children try to find me through the Internet one day?'

In countries that no longer allow anonymous donation, men who become sperm donors do so with the understanding that they may be contacted in the future by the children they helped create. James Cooper is one such donor. James donated sperm in 2017 at the age of 40. He had a happy childhood, growing up with his two parents and older sister in the southwest of England. He did well at school and attended a top university where he studied politics and economics, later becoming a lawyer. But James had one regret. His past relationships hadn't worked out, and he was now unlikely to have children of his own. 'What set me thinking about becoming a sperm donor was that I had reached the age where my friends were having children, or not. Some were having difficulties in conceiving, and others faced different barriers because they were gay or didn't have a long-term partner. I would have liked to have kids, but didn't. So I thought that being a sperm donor would be a nice thing to do.'

Following a thorough screening procedure, James was accepted as a sperm donor at the London Sperm Bank, and donated sperm weekly over a period of several months. He hasn't yet inquired whether any children have resulted from his donation, although he is legally entitled to find out the sex and year of birth of any children born. He plans to do so in ten years' time as that's closer to the date when any children born from his donation may try to contact him. According to UK law, anyone conceived with the help of a donor since April 1st, 2005 may ask for their donor's name, date of birth, and last known address when they turn 18. So the earliest date at which James may receive the proverbial 'knock on the door' is 2035.

I asked James how he felt about being a donor when I met him at the London Sperm Bank two years on. He said, 'I would like it if children have been born. If that has happened, I hope that they're happy, and the parents are happy. If they get in touch in the future, I would welcome it. By that time, they know who their real parents are, and they're probably just curious to see whether you've got the same interests.'

But James did have some concerns: 'I'd worry that things hadn't turned out so well for them. There are families that are unhappy, and kids that are unhappy, and I'd hate to think I'd created something like that. I'd worry that they didn't think that my donation was a good idea, or that they didn't think their parents should have had children, or they'd been unhappy in their lives, or they'd been unhealthy because of something I'd unwittingly passed on.'

James found the counselling session that he attended as part of the process of becoming a donor helpful. It made him aware that his motivations were more complicated than he had previously acknowledged. As he described it, 'I was slightly kidding myself that it was entirely about doing something good. Speaking to the counsellor, I did admit that there was an aspect of selfishness about it, and sadness that I'd not had children myself. It made me think about it more, and realise that, as a donor, you're not the real parent. It was useful to have that discussion. It helped me come to a sensible conclusion about it.'

***

In the United States, where there is practically no legislation on the identification of sperm or egg donors, and the use of identifiable donors is at the discretion of the egg or sperm bank, many children and adults born through anonymous sperm donation try to find their donors through the Donor Sibling Registry founded by Ryan Kramer and his mother Wendy. For some, this is a hugely positive experience. But what about the donors themselves? How do they feel when contacted by their genetic children many years, or even decades, after they donated sperm?

Alongside our 2007 survey on families who share the same sperm donor, we conducted a parallel survey of anonymous donors who had, at a later date, made their identity available through the Donor Sibling Registry website. Most of these donors wished to know how many children had been born from their donation, and some wanted to know who the children were. Those who had been contacted by their donor children were usually happy about it and intended to keep in touch. Phil, who heard from his biological daughter, Caroline, after making his identity available on the Donor Sibling Registry website, said, 'It was more emotional than I expected, even though it was just via emails and a couple of letters and photos. My donor daughter actually looks a good deal more like me than my sons do. We have the same interests of music, dance, art, reading, and so on, without any contact prior to a year or so. It's quite fun really.'

But it doesn't always work out so well. Neil, who described his initial contact with his biological daughter, Julie, as being very welcome and positive, was later cut off by Julie's mother which he found very difficult. And many men worry about having been a sperm donor; they feel that they didn't properly consider the implications of what they were doing at the time. Mark said, 'It took me quite some time to realise that the children created by my donation were just that — they were children created by my donation. I feel terrible that somewhere there is someone that has absolutely no idea who I am, or they might think that they were abandoned.' Paul expressed a similar worry, 'Years later I came to regret the experience somewhat when I realised that there could be children out there who have absolutely no way of tracing me.'

Often men who donate sperm when they are young and single do not grasp the significance of their donation until they enter into a committed relationship and have children of their own — children who are genetic half-siblings of the children born from their donation. This presents a challenge for some donors, such as Ron, who told us, 'My wife seems to feel threatened by it, and hit the roof when she found out I had told my kids about their half-brothers and sisters.' But for others, like Ken, it's not a problem, 'The basis for making contact was not so much for me personally to meet my donor child and for her to know me as her genetic father, but rather for my 10-year-old daughter to one day meet her donor half-sibling.' Donors' parents are affected too. Some are shocked and distressed to find out that they have genetic grandchildren who they don't know. Others welcome the news, especially if they don't have grandchildren of their own. Freddie said, 'My mom, who otherwise has no grandchildren, is thrilled with these additions to the family. My sister enjoys being an aunt. I am very happy to know these kids and consider myself very fortunate.'

***

The day after I met Louise Lane to talk about her experiences of discovering that she had been conceived by sperm donation, I met her donor, Ross, and his wife, Carolyn, who lived just a few miles away from Louise's home in Melbourne. I wondered how likely it was that they had passed on the street, or had sat next to each other in a café, or at the cinema, without knowing. It seemed surreal for me to go so easily from one to the other when it had taken them more than 30 years to do the same.

In 1979, on hearing a radio campaign advertising for sperm donors, Ross and Carolyn made a joint decision that Ross should volunteer. The couple had two young sons of their own, and wanted to help those who were not so fortunate. 'We had some friends who'd been trying for a while to start a family and nothing had happened,' said Carolyn. 'We knew what they were feeling. How painful it was for them.' Ross passed the screening process and donated sperm in 1980. He was assured that he would always be anonymous. Any children born from his donation would never be able to find out that Ross was their genetic father.

The couple got on with their busy lives, and with raising their boys. They didn't think much more about Ross's sperm donation. That is, not until 2009, when they heard that the law in Victoria had changed to give donor-conceived people access to the identity of their 'anonymous' donors. 'We were a bit shocked by that. What would we do if there was contact? How should we handle that?' said Carolyn. 'We hadn't told our children, they were tiny at the time, and Ross had donated sperm anonymously. We didn't expect there would be any comeback from the donor-conceived children. I was nervous about it, and what these children might be expecting.'

Nothing happened at first. And then, one day in 2015, the phone rang. Carolyn took the call. It was someone from the office of Births, Deaths, and Marriages, asking to speak to Ross. With some trepidation, Ross called back. 'I was asked whether I would share some information with a donor-conceived child. I thought, "If a child has found out that their dad isn't their dad, I've got to fill in the gaps." I was happy to do that. I immediately said "yes".' Soon afterwards, Ross received a letter from a person he had helped conceive. 'She wrote a personal letter. Just talking about herself and how she came to be. And she made it clear that she had no personal expectations of us. It was Louise!'

Louise struck lucky with the missing branches of her family tree. Ross was an amateur genealogist and sent her a long list of ancestors — more than 2,000. And Louise informed Ross that 12 children had been born from his donation, including two sets of twins. Ross and Louise continued to correspond. But Ross and Carolyn's own children, who were all adults by then, remained in the dark. The situation was unsustainable. They had to be told. 'We decided that we should get them all in and tell them at the same time,' said Ross. 'We said, 'You've got to come to a family meeting'. That threw the cat among the pigeons because they didn't know what it was about. Were we going to divorce? Had we won the lottery? We told them together. And we told them that they had 12 half-brothers and sisters.'

I was, of course, intrigued to know how their family had responded. 'The eldest boy was very quiet. He didn't say much then. The youngest was very happy. He said, "Oh, you've found a sister for me! I've never had a sister." He was fine. It didn't worry him at all, and his wife was quite comfortable with it. A few days later we heard from our eldest who said that he didn't mind what we did, but he didn't want to be part of it all.'

Once Ross and Carolyn had spoken to their family, it cleared the way for them to meet Louise. 'We wondered what we would say. Whether we would all be struck dumb and say nothing, but it's not what happened,' recollected Carolyn. 'It was hugs all round, the first time we met.'

But it has not all been plain sailing. 'The next sibling contacted by VARTA went down like a lead balloon,' recalled Ross. 'She was told over the telephone while she was sitting in a car park at lunchtime. She didn't know she had been conceived by sperm donation.' In another family, one brother, conceived using a different donor, was given an AncestryDNA kit as a present, which forced their mother to tell both of her sons about their donor conception. When Louise attended a social event organised by VARTA, she recognised the brother who was her genetic half-sibling straight away. That turned out well. But another donor sibling was distraught when she found out about her donor conception. It turned her family upside down.

***

Although sperm donors have traditionally donated through sperm banks and fertility clinics, and been unaware of who the recipients of their sperm are, today an increasing number of donors are being recruited through connection websites that enable direct contact between donors and recipients, should they wish it. Women look for donors on these websites for a number of reasons including the possibility of contact with the donor before and/or after their child is born; the wish to find an anonymous donor, which is no longer possible in countries where donor anonymity has been banned; and the lower cost.

In 2014, my colleagues Tabitha Freeman and Vasanti Jadva carried out a survey with Pride Angel, one of the largest and most well-known global connection websites. Tabitha had met the Director of Pride Angel through a committee they both sat on, set up by the Human Fertilisation and Embryology Authority to examine the practice of egg, sperm, and embryo donation in the United Kingdom, and was interested to learn more. Who are these men? What are their motivations? Why are they using a website instead of more traditional methods? And how does it turn out? Like sperm bank donors, the overriding reason men gave for joining Pride Angel was to help people have children. Other motivations included having biological children, knowing people who had experienced infertility, and confirming their own fertility. Again, payment was not the biggest factor, although it is not known how much money changes hands as connection websites are not subject to the same restrictions as licensed sperm banks and fertility clinics. On a more sordid note, when asked about their preferred method of donation, almost half of the heterosexual donors favoured so-called 'natural insemination'. But in line with the website's advice, most women opted for self-insemination, rejecting the men who seemed not to be acting in good faith.

The possibility of lifelong contact with children born from their donation is appealing to many prospective Pride Angel donors, especially gay men, who might never have children of their own. Many of the gay donors we heard from said that this was one of the reasons they had registered with a website rather than a sperm bank, and more than half of the gay men whose donation had resulted in a baby were in touch with the family.

Frank, 44, is in a civil partnership and works in the hospitality industry. When he became a donor for a lesbian couple, they agreed that he would receive email updates and photographs of the child twice a year, and that he would visit the family once a year. He said, 'I wanted to spend some time at their house so that the child can know me, and know they have a father, or a male figure, in their life, to prevent problems when they ask, "Who is my dad?".' Frank's donation resulted in the birth of twin girls. One year on, he spends more time with the family than he had originally planned: 'I can see them grow up, know what they look like, be there in the background, and come forward if required. If they needed a kidney, they would know who to ask.'

Jon, 32, a single gay man who works in health care, is more involved than Frank in the life of his donor baby. He visits regularly, helps with childcare, and provides general support. When asked how he sees his relationship with the baby's lesbian mothers, he said, 'We describe ourselves as a "little family", so family I guess.' Like Frank, Jon thinks it's important that his donor child knows who he is. 'It's not just about making babies,' said Jon. 'Children are only children for a fraction of their lives. As adults, they deserve to know where they came from.'

This sentiment was echoed by other Pride Angel donors. Bill said, 'It is, in my opinion, better that a child knows who their father is, and as the child becomes older they can have honest answers to their questions.' Jim saw it as mutually beneficial, 'I think that the child should have the right to know who their biological father is when they hit a certain age. It's also interesting from the donor's point of view to see how the person turned out.'

Connection websites are not without their risks for donors. Unlike men who donate through sperm banks or fertility clinics, who have no legal or financial responsibilities towards any children born from their donation, men who make their own arrangements with women they meet online do not have this protection. Also, sperm donors and the mothers of their biological children may fall out, and men who had hoped to play a part in their children's lives may be denied access to them. There are also risks for the women who buy sperm online, in particular, that there is no requirement for donors to be screened for medical conditions, and donors who they may know little about are their children's legal fathers. We don't yet know how relationships between those who use connection websites turn out over time, either for donors or the recipients of their sperm. More importantly, we don't yet know the consequences for children of this method of sperm donation.

***

A serious concern about sperm donation is the large number of children that may be born from a single donor, a situation that has arisen in countries that have no regulation on this. This is problematic for a number of reasons, not least because donor siblings may inadvertently begin a romantic relationship with each other which could result in accidental incest. In the United States, the guidelines of the American Society for Reproductive Medicine recommend limiting the number of children born to each donor to 25 per population of 850,000, but there is no legal requirement to do so. We know from our own research, and from the research of others, that the actual number is often much higher.

In our 2007 survey with the Donor Sibling Registry, we found a group of 55 siblings born from the same donor, and since that time, sibling groups of more than 100 have been identified. In the United Kingdom, the maximum number of children that may be born from each donor is ten, unless parents wish to have further children from the same donor, but it is only possible to keep track of men who donate through sperm banks and fertility clinics; those who donate via connection websites, or to people they know, are not monitored or regulated.

In one of the most extreme examples, a Dutch donor known as 'Louis', who donated sperm at three sperm banks in the Netherlands over a period of 20 years, has been responsible for the births of at least 200 children. Some estimates put the figure at closer to 1,000. The donor, now 68, realised in his thirties that he would never have children of his own, and worried that when he died, no one would remember him. He lived alone, and believed that he had autism, which prevented him from sustaining romantic relationships. In an interview with *The Guardian* in 2018, he spoke of his plan to create large numbers of children through sperm donation in the hope that one day some of them would track him down. He found the first children in 2011 through the Dutch TV show *Who is my father?* Within seven years, he had identified 57. Although Louis has embraced his donor children, it's not always that way. Many donors feel overwhelmed when they are contacted by large numbers of their genetic children. They may be happy to connect with the first few who get in touch, but as we found in our research with the Donor Sibling Registry, the more the number goes up, the more likely it is that donors will remove themselves from the website or simply won't respond.

***

Since the 1980s, with the advent of IVF technology, it has been possible not only for men to donate sperm, but also for women to donate eggs.

In the early days, only fresh eggs could be used, as freezing eggs for later use produced poor results, but in 2005, the introduction of vitrification, a rapid freezing technique, proved to be a game-changer. Today, egg freezing has become so reliable that the chance of achieving a pregnancy is similar to using fresh eggs, and egg banks — repositories for frozen eggs available for donation — are being established around the world.

There has been a sharp rise in demand for donated eggs, partly because women are starting their families later, often in their late thirties or forties, by which time the quality of their own eggs has deteriorated. Women who experience early menopause, or who have medical conditions that cause infertility, and gay couples and single men, may also turn to donated eggs to help them create a family.

Egg donation is a more complicated and invasive procedure than sperm donation. For this reason, women receive higher levels of compensation for donating eggs than men receive for donating sperm. In countries where commercial egg donation is permitted, such as the United States, it's not unusual for women to be paid $5,000–$10,000 for their eggs, and some may even be paid more, depending on their appearance and qualifications. In the United Kingdom, the compensation is £750 per donation, and all egg donors receive the same amount.

Egg donors are required to take hormones to maximise the number of eggs they produce, and their eggs are collected via a needle that is passed through the woman's vagina and inserted into her ovaries. Susanna Graham, a medical doctor with a background in anthropology and bioethics, who joined the Centre for Family Research in 2010, interviewed egg donors attending a London fertility clinic in 2014, to explore their motivations and experiences. She found that egg donors are primarily motivated by the desire to help infertile women have their own children rather than by financial compensation.

Priya was 23 when she volunteered to donate her eggs. She first heard about it on the radio. Like many egg donors, she knew people who had been personally affected by infertility. 'It's all down to having seen first-hand both my aunties' struggles to conceive,' she said. 'And being someone who has always wanted to have children, the thought of being told that you couldn't have children must be soul destroying.' Priya didn't want her own children at that time, but she did want to give another woman who was faced with infertility the chance to become a mother.

Priya says she would have donated her eggs even if she did not receive financial compensation. 'When I first heard about it on the radio and started doing research about egg donation, I didn't know you received any money. So it was quite a shock! But, yes, I guess it was nice to be paid for something that you were more than willing to do for free.'

Claire was single and training to be a midwife when she learned about egg donation. 'Patients were coming in and having scans and operations to look at their ovaries. These women had been trying for years to have a baby. That just made me think, "I'm single, I'm thirty, I'm not using my eggs, and I want to help someone. I'll give it a go."' Claire decided not to discuss her decision with her friends in case they put her off, but she did tell her immediate family. Her sister and father were supportive, but her mother was shocked: 'I think in her head my mother was thinking, "Are there going to be lots of little babies like you running around?" Eventually she came round to the idea and thought it was a good thing to do.'

At her initial appointment, Claire was asked to fill in many forms, and then she was invited back for a full screening which involved more forms, blood tests, and a consultation with a doctor who explained the egg donation procedure and the medication that she would need to take, including the injections that she would administer herself. When the scans showed that the time was right, Claire went back to the clinic for her eggs to be collected. Because she was sedated, she can't remember much about it. Her impression was that it was over quickly and didn't hurt. She produced 14 eggs.

Egg donors, like sperm donors, are not allowed to know who receives their eggs — they may only find out the sex and year of birth of any children born — but Claire was curious: 'I wanted to know what they are like, what they look like, what they do, whether they have other kids. I don't know where my eggs are. It would be nice to know.' Although Claire would have preferred to meet the couple who received her eggs, she doesn't feel a connection to the children who may have be born from her donation. As she put it, 'I believe that the connection will be with the mum who has given birth. Motherhood is when an egg becomes a person and you are looking after that person and love that person. If I didn't donate my eggs, I would have lost them anyway. An egg to me is nothing big.'

Like Priya, Claire wasn't expecting to be paid, and would have donated without any financial compensation. For her, the reward was more personal, 'I think it's an amazing thing to do, and I found it fascinating. Instead of wasting my eggs, I gave them to someone else. It made me feel like I was a good person.'

Claire is an identifiable donor because she donated her eggs following the removal of donor anonymity in the United Kingdom in 2005, which means that any children born from her eggs may search for her when they become adults. When asked how she feels about the prospect of being contacted in the future, Claire replied, 'I would love to have a discussion with them about it. I think it would be a bit weird, but it doesn't concern me. I'd just meet them and explain my story and that would be it. Just answer their questions rather than developing a friendship or relationship.'

Because egg donation is such a demanding procedure, egg donors are in short supply, especially in countries such as the United Kingdom where there is little financial incentive. In 1998, the London Women's Clinic introduced a novel scheme to increase the supply of donor eggs while at the same time helping women in need of IVF. The idea was simple: women who were undergoing IVF were asked to donate some of their eggs in exchange for a reduction in the cost of their fertility treatment. It was called 'egg sharing'. It seemed like a mutually beneficial situation, but critics disagreed. The British Medical Association came out against it on the grounds that poorer women who desperately wanted children would be providing eggs for wealthier women because it would be the only way they could afford IVF.

Of even greater concern was that some women who donated their eggs would themselves be unsuccessful in their attempt to conceive. Might they have had a better chance had they not given away some of their eggs? And if the recipient of their eggs was to give birth to a child when they had not, would donors suffer emotionally from the knowledge that their genetic children were being raised by someone else? Figures from the Human Fertilisation and Embryology Authority revealed that this happened to around 20 per cent of women who shared their eggs. In 2008, *The Sunday Times* reported: 'Hundreds of women who have given away half their eggs in exchange for cut-price fertility treatment have been left childless while other women have given birth to their genetic offspring.' A fertility doctor was quoted in the article as saying, 'In 18 years' time some of these women will still be barren and they could have their biological children, born to other women, knocking on their doors. I believe these women who have been left childless will suffer psychological problems as a result of giving half their eggs away.'

To find out how donors actually feel about their involvement in egg sharing, a practice that is still permitted in the United Kingdom, Zeynep Gurtin, then a social scientist at the Centre for Family Research, collaborated with the London Women's Clinic on a survey of donors who had shared their eggs between 2007 and 2009. As UK donors were no longer anonymous by that time, the women knew that any children born from their donation might contact them once they turned 18.

Forty-eight egg donors participated in the survey, of whom two-thirds had given birth to their own children. It turned out that the donors' motivations for participating in egg sharing were not simply to obtain cheaper treatment; they also wanted to help those in a similar situation to themselves. Vivienne echoed many of the others when she said, 'Egg sharing was the best option for me for two reasons. The first being that I realised someone who could not even produce their own eggs would be suffering more than I. The second, it would also help with the costs of this treatment.' Compassion for the women who received their eggs was apparent from the comments of many of the donors, such as Jane: 'I can empathise completely with my recipient. We both shared a longing to be a mother, and I was more than happy to help another woman realise her dream of having a child.'

Not all of the donors, whether successful or unsuccessful in their own treatment, wished to find out whether their recipient had conceived a baby. In spite of this, most were open to future contact by any children who resulted from their donation. In direct contrast to the assumption that there would be a large gap in income and social status between the (poorer) egg sharing donors and (wealthier) egg sharing recipients, we found that they generally had similar levels of education and were in professional occupations.

We were particularly interested in the women whose own treatment had been unsuccessful but who knew that the woman who had received their eggs had conceived a child. There were only five women in this situation in our study, as not all knew the outcome of their donation. Not one felt negatively towards the woman who received her eggs, and three were explicitly magnanimous towards her despite their own failure to conceive. As one woman put it, 'I was upset at first, but now I know that I have done something amazing for someone else,' and another said, 'Although my treatment was unsuccessful due to medical complications, I was very pleased for her and her family.'

Although this is the first study of its kind, and donors who declined to participate may have had more negative opinions, 92 per cent of the 48 donors who took part said that they were glad they had taken part in egg sharing. We don't yet know what will happen when the children grow up — whether they will contact their donors, and how the donors will feel about it, especially if they haven't had children of their own — but our study suggests that most women who participate in an egg sharing programme do not regret their decision in the years immediately following their donation.

***

Today, an increasing number of egg donors in the United States are known to the families they helped create, and are part of the children's lives. This new trend raises complex questions about how the relationship between egg donors and their genetic children will evolve over time, whether conflicts will arise with the children's parents, and how the children will feel once they understand the true nature of the connection.

In 2013, when Kelley Hageman, 28, decided to become a donor, she didn't think very deeply about how she would feel about any children born from her eggs. She lived in San Diego, where she was training to be a nurse, and responded to one of the many adverts she had seen as she went about her daily life. One of her friends had been a donor so Kelley knew something about it, and she was attracted by the payment of $6,000. 'They have signs everywhere in San Diego for egg donors,' she told me. 'I thought, I'll give it a shot and if it works then maybe it's meant to be and if it doesn't, then it's not.'

Kelley submitted an application form to an egg donation agency with details of her education, family background, medical history, and a photo — and waited. Within just two weeks, the agency called to say that she had been chosen by a gay couple from Italy. The next stage involved comprehensive screening including genetic testing. Did she wish to proceed? Kelley agreed. She passed the screening process, and after synchronising her menstrual cycle with that of the surrogate who would carry the pregnancy, she injected herself with hormones for 12 days. On the 13th day, her eggs were retrieved. The egg collection was easier than Kelley had expected, but she suffered complications. Her ovaries had become overstimulated, and her abdomen filled up with fluid. She recalled, 'It got pretty serious quickly. It was frightening. They put me under anaesthesia immediately and they drained the fluid. I was back to normal within 48 hours.'

Kelley knew very little about the couple who had chosen her as their egg donor, other than their nationality and sexual orientation. She would have liked to meet them for her own peace of mind, but they didn't offer, so she assumed that she never would. Although she was told that her donation had resulted in a pregnancy with twins, she wasn't informed when they were born. But two weeks later, a card arrived in the mail: 'It was a card from the dads thanking me, and telling me the names of the twins — a boy and a girl — and the date that they were born. They asked if I wanted to come to meet them.' Kelley booked a flight that same day, and two weeks later she visited the family in San Diego where they were still living. 'I spent two days with them. It was over a weekend. Then a year later, I went out to Italy to visit them. And last year we met in Paris, so I've gotten to see them every year. We keep in touch on Facebook and we connect through WhatsApp.' Kelley feels very close to the twins and hopes to stay in touch with them as they grow up: 'I just adore them! I love them very deeply. They are a big part of my heart.'

A few months later, Kelley received another call from the agency. She had been chosen again, this time by Adam, a single heterosexual man. Would she be willing to donate her eggs once more? Kelley was unsure. She was worried about a re-occurrence of ovarian hyper-stimulation, a potentially fatal condition. She also wanted to meet the prospective father before making a decision. He agreed, and she spent a day with him in Los Angeles, where he lived, learning about his background and getting a sense of what he was like. 'He had been married once and his wife didn't want children. It was a dream of his to be a dad. It was something that he really wanted,' said Kelley, 'I thought, well, he seems okay, so why not give it a chance?'

Once again, Kelley's donation resulted in the birth of boy and girl twins, who are now four. This time, she was in contact with the father from the beginning, and she sees the twins four times a year, although they don't know who she is: 'They know me as Kelley. The boy just does his own thing. But the girl, I feel like she knows that I'm different. That I love her differently. We have a very strong connection, even without her knowing who I am. She always asks for me to come, and when am I going, she asks when I'm coming back. She's going to figure out who I am sooner or later.'

Five years on from first donating her eggs, Kelley, now 32, has no regrets, but she acknowledges that being with her genetic children can trigger complicated emotions: 'I wouldn't take it back. I'm very glad that I did it. But sometimes it's a little bit hard just because we are connected. Part of me wants to be with them, but the bigger part is just pleased that they're here, and pleased that I get to know them and watch them grow. They're happy and healthy, and that makes me very happy.' Kelley feels that knowing the families she helped create was the right decision for her. 'Otherwise, I would have wondered who they were, where they were, what they were. I would have always wondered,' she said. 'I think it would have hurt because there's a longing to know who they are.' I asked whether she would like to have children of her own one day. 'I definitely would. Maybe one, just because I'm getting older now, but I definitely would like to be able to keep one of them! For my own!'

***

When people donate sperm or eggs, their donations are used to conceive a child with the eggs or sperm of an unknown person, or with the eggs or sperm of a person they know, but who is not their partner. Embryo donation is different. This is when a couple who plan a family together through IVF produce more embryos than they need, and decide to donate their embryos to someone else. Any children born from their donation could have been their own.

On a cold and snowy night in January 2017, Jennifer Vesbit lay in bed in Portland, Oregon, next to her sleeping husband, Tom, while 3,000 miles away in New York City, Alisa was giving birth to Jennifer and Tom's genetic child, a full-sibling of the couple's four-year-old twins. 'I got a text from Alisa at 10 pm, which was the middle of the night in New York,' Jennifer recalled. 'A snowstorm meant that the people who had planned to support Alisa through the birth couldn't reach her. She was alone in a hospital bed in New York City and I was lying awake in my bed in Portland. I texted back to let her know I was with her in spirit. It felt surreal.'

The next morning, Jennifer received a photo of Alisa's son on her phone, 'He looked exactly like my son looked on the day of his birth,' said Jennifer, 'but the photo arrived on a group text, so all these people were writing, "He's so beautiful", and, "He's perfect", and I had to read all of that. It's not that I wasn't happy for her — I was — but I felt that I was just this invisible person and she was getting all the congratulations. It was hard to see everybody talking about how beautiful and perfect he was. I just wanted somebody to acknowledge me. I wouldn't change a thing, but it was much more difficult than I thought it would be.'

The journey to becoming embryo donors began for Jennifer and Tom after the birth of their twins in 2012. They had gone through five years of trying for a baby, including a devastating miscarriage in 2010. 'It was the worst day of my life,' Jennifer told me. 'I'll never forget it. I didn't know I had that kind of grief inside me.' After much soul-searching, the couple decided to give IVF one more try. This time, they produced three embryos. Two were transferred to Jennifer's womb which resulted in the twins. They froze the third.

Each year, a letter arrived from the clinic asking what they wanted to do with their frozen embryo — have it destroyed, donate it to medical research, donate it to someone else, or continue to pay for it to be stored? Jennifer was so busy caring for her twins that she couldn't decide. They carried on paying for storage. It wasn't until the twins turned four that the couple began to think about what to do. Tom didn't want to have more children. His preference was to donate the embryo to medical research. Jennifer wasn't so sure. Because there was only one embryo, it was a difficult decision for her: 'I think when there's one, it makes it a little harder to decide what to do. It seems like more of a person. And it seems like this person needs to have a chance. So it's either going to be me, or it's going to be somebody else.' Jennifer worried that the person born from their embryo might feel out of place in the family they grow up in, and might feel unwanted by Jennifer and her family. But she was also aware of the joy their gift could bring to someone else, were the embryo to become a person. After deep consideration, Jennifer and Tom decided not to have another baby nor to donate the embryo to science. They decided to give it to someone else.

The couple cared a great deal about choosing the right recipient for their precious embryo. When Jennifer came across the website Miracles Waiting, designed to connect embryo donors and prospective parents, it felt right. They posted a photo, information about themselves, and a statement about what they were looking for in a recipient, and waited. Whenever someone expressed an interest, they sent a list of questions that they had composed themselves and asked them to respond. 'A couple in Minnesota were the first ones to get back to us,' said Jen. 'It's weird because it's almost like dating when you're trying to figure out where your embryo should go. They were into hunting and I just couldn't see my embryo living in Minnesota hunting!'

Then they heard from Alisa, a single woman in New York City. 'When I read her answers to our questions, standing in my kitchen, I just started to cry. I'll never forget it,' said Jennifer. 'I thought, "It's going to be her. It's going to work." It was a total gut reaction. I just saw a future of the embryo becoming a human and being able to have some contact with this human but also having the distance as well, which felt like a perfect scenario. It felt serendipitous.' Jennifer and Tom continued with the selection process, meeting with Alisa on Skype and following up references. It took just three weeks from the day they posted their profile on Miracles Waiting to the day they told Alisa, 'It's you!'

Jennifer was at Listen to Your Mother, a story-telling event in Portland in celebration of Mother's Day, when she found out that Alisa was pregnant. 'That's another day I'll never forget!' she told me. 'People were on stage telling their stories of motherhood. It was a really emotional day for me to find out.' Jennifer felt a mix of emotions when she heard the news: 'It was happiness; it was also fear; it was also a little bit of jealousy, if I'm honest. I think a little part of me wanted to do the right thing by donating, but then if it didn't work out we'd think, "Well, we tried to help somebody, but now we get on with our lives." Once you find out that she's pregnant, it becomes very real. You start to think, "We decided this person's life. We decided who was going to be this person's mom. We decided where this person was going to live. This is the start of a lifetime of having this person in the world."'

✳✳✳

Since the time of Ole Schou's dream, the ability to freeze not just sperm, but also eggs and embryos, has changed the landscape of reproductive donation beyond recognition. In the intervening years, we have seen a shift from the disinterested sperm donor to sperm, egg, and embryo donors who are open to contact with their genetic children, and donors who actively embrace it. Many countries don't regulate donation, and even in countries that do, the growth of connection websites mean that there is little control over how many children can be born from any one donor, who the donors are, and whether donor children can access information about them. The absence of regulation also leads to malpractice, such as the case of the fertility doctor who secretly used his own sperm to father 49 children in the 1970s and 80s, and possibly many more. In 2019, another fertility doctor lost his license in Canada for using his own sperm, and the sperm of unknown donors, to impregnate his patients. This deception has had far-reaching and damaging effects on the families. There is an urgent need for regulation of sperm, egg, and embryo donation, not only to prevent unacceptable numbers of donor siblings, but also to protect parents, and donors themselves.

Jennifer Vesbit and her family met up with Alisa and her son for the first time in July 2017, when the baby was six months old. Jennifer had been preparing for the day and imagining how it might be: 'I was worried. Will he feel like mine? When I hold him, is there going to be an undeniable bond? Will we have regrets? I was expecting to feel so much emotion, and then we got there — we met them at the park — and I just felt that he was hers. My biggest take-away from that day was a feeling of peace.'

Two years on, the families have reached a comfortable arrangement for staying in touch. Alisa sends Jennifer a monthly email with pictures of her son and an update. On top of that, they meet up twice a year. 'Me and my kids and husband baby-sat Alisa's son a few months ago, a scenario that could have been our life,' said Jennifer. 'When Alisa came to pick him up, he was so happy to see her, and I was content to put him back in her arms. It's so clear that she's his mom.'

Chapter 4

Surrogates:
'Tummy Mummies'

'It is inconsistent with human dignity that a woman should use her uterus for financial profit and treat it as an incubator for someone else's child.'

WARNOCK REPORT ON HUMAN FERTILISATION AND EMBRYOLOGY, (1984).

'I think it's amazing. It's difficult for a woman to give away a child she's given birth to and I just think it's fantastic that my mum can, and make people so happy.'

KATE, DAUGHTER OF TRADITIONAL SURROGATE, AGE 16, (2013).

On 4 January 1985, in labour with the United Kingdom's first surrogacy baby, 28-year-old Kim Cotton was under siege. Outside the north London hospital where she was giving birth, the press was gathering in ever increasing numbers. Inside, between contractions, Kim was being subjected to a barrage of questions from a social worker about the identity of the baby's parents and the operations of the American agency that had brokered the surrogacy arrangement. Kim didn't know the answers. She hadn't been given the names or whereabouts of the couple who had travelled to the United Kingdom to await the birth of their baby, conceived through artificial insemination using Kim's egg and the sperm of the intended father, who she had never met. She had trusted the agency to deal with the practicalities. Now, both Kim and the European couple had been abandoned by the agency, left to sort out the legal complications by themselves.

The social worker's insistent questioning was so stressful that Kim lost control of the labour and the pain became unbearable. As she remembered when we spoke in 2018: 'What upset me was that the social workers had known, right back from August, that I was the surrogate and they had all that time to come and question me and ask me what the plan was. But they waited until I was in labour to interrogate me. In the end I just got up and locked myself in the bathroom to try to get the labour back on track.'

When Baby Cotton entered the world that evening, Kim was overwhelmed by relief and joy that she had given birth to a healthy baby girl. She did not feel an emotional bond with the baby. She did not see her as her own. But unknown to Kim, while she was in labour, Baby Cotton had been placed under a 'place of safety' order which meant that the child couldn't leave the hospital or be given to her intended parents. Kim was devastated when she found out. After all she had gone through, the baby might not end up with the couple who so desperately wanted her. Kim and her husband, Geoff, spent the night with Baby Cotton. The following morning, Kim left hospital through a back door, driven away on the floor of a car covered by a blanket to avoid the throng of reporters waiting outside: 'I left the baby there which was the hardest thing ever, not knowing what would happen to her or if she would go to her rightful parents.'

From her home in London, Kim watched as Baby Cotton's fate played out in the media. On Tuesday 8 January, four days after the birth, Baby Cotton was made a ward of court. The only way the intended parents could claim her as their daughter was to fight for her in the High Court. Three days later, the judge, Mr Justice Latey, declared the intended parents to be a 'warm, caring, sensible couple', and granted them custody. That weekend, unbeknown to the hoard of waiting journalists, Baby Cotton flew out of the country with her mother and father to her new home in Europe. To this day, Kim doesn't know what became of Baby Cotton or even who she is. All these years later, she still feels sad about being denied the opportunity to hand her to the intended parents: 'I didn't get any of that joy, or feeling of job well done, you've done something really special. It just wasn't like that at all, it was quite miserable and traumatic.'

Kim had had a happy childhood, growing up in north London with her two older brothers and a younger sister. Her passion was ballet. She had trained as a classical ballerina until she was 17, but gave it up when she just missed being accepted by the prestigious Royal Ballet School. At 18, she became engaged to Geoff, her boyfriend of three years. She married him at 19, and by 24 she was a stay-at-home mother of two children. It was a television programme about an American commercial surrogacy agency that was opening a branch in the UK that sparked Kim's interest in becoming a surrogate. She thought it would be a good way of earning money while being able to stay at home to look after her young children, and helping a couple who couldn't have children. It seemed like a win-win situation. She would receive £6,500, and having a baby for a childless couple seemed like a good thing to do. Kim assumed that no one outside her immediate social circle needed to know.

That all changed when the head of the agency went public, announcing to the media that the first surrogacy baby in Britain was on its way. Headlines such as, 'Rent a womb' and 'Buy a baby' triggered a public outcry. How could a woman give away her baby for money? And should agencies be allowed to profit from this? A full-scale search for the surrogate kicked off. Kim knew that the likelihood of her remaining anonymous was slim, so she took the advice of a neighbour who had contacts in the media and signed a deal for exclusive rights to her story with the *Daily Star* newspaper in return for their protection and a fee of £15,000. The *Daily Star* stayed true to its word. It was the staff of the newspaper who orchestrated Kim's escape from hospital after the birth.

In 1986, not long after the Baby Cotton scandal in the United Kingdom, the case of Baby M produced a similar furore in the United States when the child's surrogate mother, Mary Beth Whitehead, refused to give Baby M to William and Elizabeth Stern, a couple who had paid her $10,000 to be a surrogate for them. Although Mary Beth had signed a legal contract stating that she would relinquish the baby, she'd had a change of heart and felt unable to let her go, which resulted in a high-profile legal battle between Mary Beth Whitehead and the Sterns. This was the first surrogacy dispute in the United States and it centred on who should have custody of the child. Like Kim Cotton, Mary Beth had conceived Baby M through artificial insemination using her own egg and the intended father's sperm, and a key argument of her legal team was that it was not in the child's best interest to be separated from her biological mother. On the Sterns' side, the argument focused on whether or not a surrogacy contract was enforceable by law.

Custody was awarded initially to William and Elizabeth in a New Jersey lower court. The judge ruled that Mary Beth must stand by her arrangement with the Sterns and hand the child over. On appeal, however, the New Jersey Supreme Court ruled that the surrogacy contract was invalid on the grounds that payment to a surrogate was 'illegal, perhaps criminal, and potentially degrading to women', and that Mary Beth Whitehead and William Stern were the legal parents of the child. Although custody was awarded to the Sterns, as this was considered to be in the best interest of Baby M, Mary Beth was awarded visitation rights as the child's legal mother. When Baby M, whose real name is Melissa Stern, turned 18, she began the process of terminating Mary Beth Whitehead's parental rights and making Elizabeth Stern her legal mother. Speaking to a journalist from the *New Jersey Monthly* in 2007, shortly before her twenty-first birthday, she said, 'I love my family very much and am very happy to be with them. I'm very happy I ended up with them. They're my best friends in the whole world, and that's all I have to say about it.'

These two highly contentious court cases resulted in an international backlash against surrogacy. A key concern was the poor treatment of surrogate mothers (who generally prefer to be known as surrogates, as they don't see themselves as mothers of the children they give birth to for other people). They were portrayed as poverty-stricken, socially disadvantaged, vulnerable women exploited by wealthy childless couples, and receiving money for carrying a child was seen as tantamount to baby selling. This view was almost universal, voiced by academic commentators across the spectrum — some, feminists; others, proponents of the traditional family — and in all sectors of the media, with the exception of a small group of feminist scholars, mainly from the United States, who believed that women should have autonomy to decide whether or not to carry a pregnancy for someone else. The influential Warnock Committee came out against surrogacy in its 1984 report, mainly on the grounds that it exploited the women: 'Even in compelling medical circumstances the danger of exploitation of one human being by another appears to the majority of us far to outweigh the potential benefits ... Such treatment of one person by another becomes positively exploitative when financial interests are involved.' Surrogacy was considered to be more objectionable than sperm donation as the contribution of the surrogate was seen as 'greater, more intimate and personal'.

Newspapers were similarly emphatic that surrogacy was a dangerous and undesirable way of creating families. In 1985, the *Mail on Sunday* published an article with the headline, 'Someone Else's Baby', which presented surrogates as the ultimate 'other woman' who would threaten the marriage of the intended couple. Opponents of surrogacy argued that surrogates were likely to regret their decision when the time came to relinquish the baby they had nurtured for nine months, and that the intended parents would reject the surrogates once they had their baby.

In reaction to the Baby M dispute, some American states outlawed surrogacy completely and others banned commercial surrogacy. Only a few, including California, continued to permit surrogates and surrogacy agencies to be paid. In the United Kingdom, the Surrogacy Arrangements Act, which prohibited commercial surrogacy but allowed the payment of genuine expenses to surrogates, was rushed through parliament in 1985 following the Baby Cotton debacle, earning the United Kingdom the epithet, 'the surrogacy capital of Europe', for instituting the most lenient legislation on surrogacy in Western Europe. This is still the case today.

As Kim Cotton and Mary Beth Whitehead had conceived their surrogacy babies using their own eggs, they were the genetic mothers of Baby Cotton and Baby M, respectively. This type of surrogacy is called 'traditional surrogacy', but is also known as 'genetic surrogacy', 'straight surrogacy', and 'partial surrogacy'. Following the introduction of IVF, it became possible for embryos to be created in the laboratory using the eggs and sperm of the intended parents, or donor eggs and/or sperm, and then transferred to the surrogate's womb, a procedure commonly known as 'gestational surrogacy', but also referred to as 'host surrogacy' and 'full surrogacy'.

Despite having had her fingers badly burnt, Kim Cotton did not give up on surrogacy. After Baby Cotton's birth, she was inundated with letters from infertile couples who wanted to have children through surrogacy, and from fertile women who wanted to be surrogates. In 1988, she set up the organisation Childlessness Overcome Through Surrogacy — known as COTS — to introduce couples who wished to find surrogates to women who wanted to become surrogates. Three years later, Kim became a surrogate for the second time, a spur of the moment decision when another surrogate pulled out. She gave birth to twins, Alice and Oliver, in 1991. This time, her experience was very different. The twins were conceived through gestational surrogacy which she found much easier; she knew the couple and remained close to them all through the pregnancy, and she was able to hand the twins to their intended parents.

'It was completely different,' Kim told me. 'When the twins were born, the joy in the room was unbelievable. The parents' faces when they held their twins for the first time is imprinted in my heart forever. It was a magic moment. This time I could complete the circle, witness first-hand the rewards of our extraordinary journey together. It was incredible.'

***

In June 1997, soon after we had published the findings of the second phase of our European study of families created by assisted reproduction, I was invited by the United Kingdom government to join a three-person team tasked with reviewing the law on surrogacy. The Chairperson was Margaret Brazier, Professor of Law at the University of Manchester, and the other member was Alastair Campbell, Professor of Ethics in Medicine at the University of Bristol. Prompted by recent cases where surrogacy arrangements had broken down or had caused controversy, including cases involving a mother carrying a child for her daughter and a daughter carrying a child for her mother, as well as disquiet about the increasing levels of payment being offered to surrogates under the guise of 'expenses', we were asked to consider whether the existing law continued to meet public concerns.

The legislation introduced in 1985 to ban commercial surrogacy had been designed to discourage people from embarking on surrogacy. Instead, we found that the opposite had happened — surrogacy had increased in the United Kingdom in the intervening years. Rather than feeling exploited, many of the surrogates we spoke to felt proud to have helped childless couples. A small minority saw surrogacy simply as a solution to their financial problems, but many told us that they found surrogacy a rewarding experience. In the United States, the practice of surrogacy had also grown by the late 1990s, although it was legal in only some states. By that time, almost all US surrogacy arrangements involved gestational surrogacy using the intended mother's egg and the intended father's sperm, as this was thought to reduce the likelihood of surrogates wishing to keep the baby, or of being permitted to do so if challenged in court.

My experience on the surrogacy review committee, especially speaking to women about their reasons for becoming surrogates and their feelings about it, made me see surrogacy in a new light. Was it really the case that surrogates were always vulnerable women forced into surrogacy as a last resort to solve their financial problems? Did they find it hard to relinquish the baby? And were they at risk of developing psychological problems once the baby was born and had been handed over to its intended parents? Led by Vasanti Jadva, my team decided to carry out a study of surrogates to answer these questions. We had already begun an investigation of families formed through surrogacy at the millennium, alongside our study of families formed through egg and sperm donation, so we were in an excellent position to recruit a broad sample of surrogates. We also approached COTS, the UK surrogacy agency founded by Kim Cotton, which was the only one of its kind that existed at the time. Altogether, 34 surrogates who had given birth around one year earlier took part in the study in 2002.

The team visited the surrogates in their homes to interview them about their experiences and find out whether handing over the baby they had carried for nine months made them susceptible to post-natal depression. Two-thirds had undergone traditional surrogacy, like Kim Cotton's first surrogacy pregnancy, and one-third had done gestational surrogacy, like Kim Cotton's second surrogacy pregnancy. We found that their reasons for becoming surrogates were many and varied. One woman said that she had been motivated purely by money. For the rest, the incentives were personal as well as financial: a desire to help a child-less couple achieve their dream of becoming parents, the wish to gain a sense of personal fulfilment by doing something worthwhile, and, in some cases, enjoyment of being pregnant without wanting to have any more children themselves. Not one of the surrogates said that they'd had second thoughts about handing over the baby to the intended parents, or found it difficult to do so. They were able to distance themselves from the pregnancy and did not see the baby as their own, even those who were traditional surrogates and were genetically related to the child.

When asked to remember how they felt at the time of the birth, around one-third of the surrogates said that they had felt upset in the weeks following the handover but these feelings were mild and short-lived. As Hayden explained, 'People always ask whether I miss the baby. I don't, because it never was mine. What I miss is the friendship through the nine months of pregnancy. When you're pregnant with somebody else's baby they're ringing you up every other day and you see them on a regular basis, whereas after the baby's been born, when those people go away, you're not missing the baby, but you're missing the friendship. I felt a little bit empty in that respect.' By the time we interviewed them one year later, only two surrogates were experiencing psychological problems, and none was suffering from post-natal depression. Although it was widely assumed that women who used their own eggs would find surrogacy more difficult, we found that those who were genetically related to the baby were no more likely to experience psychological problems than gestational surrogates.

The intended parents didn't reject the surrogate once they received the baby, as had often been claimed. The surrogates had formed close relationships with the intended parents during the pregnancy, and most remained in contact with the family they had helped create one year on. Hayden said, 'The most rewarding aspect of being a surrogate is the look on the mum and dad's faces the day the baby's born. She still gives me hugs and says "thank you" to this day.'

Opponents of surrogacy had highlighted the potentially harmful long-term consequences for surrogates. Would they feel regret in later years? Would they experience psychological problems in the future? And what would the impact of surrogacy be on the surrogate's family, including her own children? A report by the British Medical Association in 1990 suggested that the disappearance of the baby after the birth may cause distress to the surrogates' own children. *The Times*, summarising the conclusions, reported, 'Among the potential problems arising from surrogacy are that the surrogate might decide to keep the child; the commissioning parents might refuse to take it, for example, if it was born with a handicap; the surrogate could suffer a severe reaction similar to bereavement after giving away the child; and her other children might suffer severe disturbances when a newly arrived sibling was given away.'

In order to shed light on these issues, Vasanti Jadva, joined by Susan Imrie, re-visited the surrogates in our study ten years after they had relinquished the baby. They managed to track down many of the women who had taken part in the initial phase of the research, and recruited some additional women who had been surrogates around the same time. In addition to interviewing the surrogates themselves, they interviewed the surrogates' own children, if they were 13 or older, to find out what they thought about their mother's involvement in surrogacy.

Vasanti and Susan found that most of the surrogates had stayed in touch with the families they had helped create, seeing them once or twice a year, and were happy with this. Very few felt that they did not have sufficient contact with the child. The surrogates talked positively about their relationship with the intended parents and the child, and said that they enjoyed the time they spent together. Almost all described their relationship with the intended parents as a genuine, close friendship that felt natural, easy, trusting, and supportive. Although there were no differences between traditional and gestational surrogates' feelings about the child, more traditional than gestational surrogates — although by no means all — felt a special bond with the child. As Lucy put it, 'I think the world of her, there's nothing maternal there but I love her to bits. She'll always be a special little girl to me,' and Kay said, 'I just think she'll always be really special, and a big part of what I did in my life.'

Almost half of the surrogates' own children were in contact with the families too, often describing the child born through surrogacy as a sibling or half-sibling, irrespective of whether or not they were genetically related. In the absence of terms to describe this new form of relationship, some of the surrogates' children had made up their own words, referring to the surrogacy child as their 'surrosister' or 'tummy-sister'. As Lily, whose mother had been both a traditional and a gestational surrogate, put it, 'They're really close, but it's a weird bond that you have. They're not my brothers and sisters, but it's like your cousins that you get quite excited to see.'

This was the first study to examine the experience of surrogacy from the perspective of surrogates' own children. Despite fears to the contrary, the children Vasanti and Susan spoke to said they were not upset by their mothers' involvement in surrogacy. Instead, most were supportive and felt proud of their mother for helping a woman who was unable to have children herself. As Marie, the 16-year-old daughter of a gestational surrogate, said: 'I think it's a really nice thing to do for someone. Obviously, if they can't have children and they really want a child that's a bad thing, so if someone else is able to do that for you and help you through it then it's something that's compassionate really.' Chloe, the 16-year-old daughter of a gestational surrogate, felt the same way, 'I think it's a brilliant thing. For someone to go through what my mum went through to make someone else happy, I think it's just amazing how someone would do that for someone else.'

***

Some surrogacy arrangements have gone badly wrong. Surrogates have changed their minds about handing over the baby, like in the case of Baby M, a situation that is extremely painful for everybody involved. Disagreements have also arisen between intended parents and surrogates about whether or not to terminate a pregnancy if there is a risk of a baby being born with a disorder, and whether or not to reduce the number of embryos in cases of multiple births. But disputes between surrogates and intended parents have been surprisingly few and far between, and have been much more likely to occur when surrogates and intended parents have taken matters into their own hands. When carried out under the protection of strict regulatory guidelines through reputable surrogacy organisations and agencies, many surrogates have found having a baby for an infertile couple to be a highly satisfying experience.

Sarah Jones was 25, a single mother to six-year-old Charlotte, living in a small village in the north of England surrounded by family and friends, and working in a children's care home when she became pregnant with Rose, her first surrogacy child, in 2003. When Sarah saw a newspaper advertisement for egg donors, she looked up 'egg donation' on the Internet to find out more, and quickly discovered the possibility of becoming a surrogate, which she found much more appealing. Had she donated her eggs at that time, the law in the United Kingdom would have prohibited her from knowing the identity of the family she had helped create. As a surrogate, she could have an ongoing relationship with the family if they agreed. The more that Sarah thought about it, the more she realised that this was exactly what she wanted to do. She gave up the idea of egg donation and decided to become a traditional surrogate: 'I thought, it's just like egg donation really but you hang on to it for a bit longer! Knowing the outcome and maintaining contact with the family afterwards was more of a selling point for me.'

Sarah met Lisa and Tony, the couple whose lives she would transform, at a pub lunch hosted by Surrogacy UK, an organisation founded in 2002 to connect surrogates and prospective parents based on the ethos of lasting friendship. 'I sat down next to Lisa and stayed sitting there for the next four hours!' Sarah told me. 'As soon as we started talking we just never stopped, and we never once talked about surrogacy. It was just about families and life experiences. I can be quite shy, so for me to sit and natter to a complete stranger for hours was a good indication that I felt very comfortable around her. I got on really well with her husband Tony too.' After the meeting, Sarah thought that she would really like to help this couple, so she informed Surrogacy UK, who contacted Lisa and Tony with the offer, and it turned out that they felt the same way about Sarah.

Over the next few months, they saw each other fortnightly to get to know each other better before deciding whether or not to proceed, with Sarah's daughter Charlotte included in the visits. 'We really clicked. We talked as if we'd known each other for ever. It was like meeting a best friend,' recollected Sarah. After deciding to go ahead, Sarah was inseminated with Tony's sperm, and when she discovered she was pregnant, they were all hugely excited. Throughout the pregnancy, they continued to meet up every two weeks, and Lisa and Tony were present at their daughter Rose's birth. 'It was easy because it was like watching someone else give birth,' said Sarah. 'I was so pleased my friends were having a baby. I didn't feel like she was mine. I didn't have any qualms about it.' Sarah had no regrets. Instead, she felt a huge sense of achievement.

Fifteen years on, the two families are still close: 'Charlotte and I have always been included as part of their family, all through the pregnancy, and that didn't stop afterwards,' said Sarah. 'We knew from the start that we were going to be in each other's lives pretty much for ever. They're my best friends still'. Despite the age difference, Charlotte and Rose have always been close, and have understood the relationship between them from a young age. Now they stay in touch independently of their parents.

Surrogacy was such an uplifting experience for Sarah that even before she had given birth to Rose, she knew she wanted to do it again. She had discovered her passion — helping women who could not carry their own children to become mothers. It wasn't just about the money; Sarah felt a sense of purpose. She wanted to bring joy to childless couples who could not otherwise have the children they so desired. Three months after Rose was born, Sarah offered to be a traditional surrogate for another couple who she had known for 2 years and had befriended through Surrogacy UK. Their daughter, Jessica, was born in 2005. As with her first experience of surrogacy, the families are still in touch.

Sarah's life took a surprise turn one month after she gave birth to Jessica. At a party, she met the man who was to become her future husband. The couple had two children together, a daughter and then a son. But a husband and three children of her own were not enough to dampen Sarah's enthusiasm for surrogacy, and in 2013, with the support of her family, Sarah had a son, Jude, and, three years later, a daughter, Jennifer, for Charlie and Matt, a gay couple who she had met through Surrogacy UK: 'I enjoyed it so much the first two times. It's not who I am but it's certainly a big part of my life, so it seemed a natural progression after I'd decided I wasn't having any more for me.'

Sarah was one of the surrogates who took part in our research. By the time I re-connected with her in the summer of 2018, she had three children of her own and five surrogacy children for three separate couples, all conceived using her eggs. I almost didn't ask her about future pregnancies as I assumed that, at the age of 40, she would say that her surrogacy days were over, but I was mistaken. 'I thought Jennifer was my last surrogacy child. I was really happy with where I was,' Sarah told me, 'until some friends who'd had twin boys from another surrogate said that they were thinking about doing it again. We'd been friends for years. They wrote their profile and went back on the Surrogacy UK list in January this year. I thought, "I'll wait until June and if they've been picked then that's lovely, but if they haven't,

I will think about it seriously." And that's what happened. We start treatment next month. This is definitely the last!'

Sarah is not alone in having several surrogacy children. More than two-thirds of the surrogates who took part in Vasanti and Susan's research had been surrogates more than once, and almost one-third had more than three surrogacy children. Surrogacy creates new kinds of bonds and friendships, as it has for Sarah: 'The majority of my friends are either intended parents or surrogates,' she reflected. 'I have personal friends that I've known from school, and work friends too, but the group of friends that is the largest is definitely the surrogacy people.'

Surrogacy in the United Kingdom is tightly regulated and close relationships between surrogates and intended parents are strongly encouraged, which may account for Sarah's positive experiences. However, in recent years, a growing number of people have travelled abroad in search of surrogacy, often because of lower costs and minimal regulation in low-income countries such as India, Thailand, Cambodia, and Nepal in south-east Asia, and Eastern European counties including Poland, Ukraine, and Georgia, re-igniting concerns about the exploitation of poor and emotionally vulnerable surrogates.

***

At 10.30 am on 1 April 2014, one month earlier than expected and following a difficult pregnancy, Laxmi Patel gave birth to a baby girl by caesarean section at a hospital in a suburb of Mumbai. She heard the newborn's cry from beyond the green curtain that blocked her view, but she was not allowed to see the baby she had nurtured for the past nine months. The child was immediately taken from her and handed to the Australian couple who, unable to have a child themselves, had travelled to India to fulfil their dream of becoming parents through surrogacy. All that Laxmi wanted was to see the baby's face and hold her just once. She had no wish to keep her. She already had two children of her own:

'I knew that it was their child and that after the birth they would be the parents of the child. I did not have a problem with that because I already had two kids. I just wanted a picture of her. I would have been happy if I had a photo of that girl.' On the day they were leaving for home, the couple visited Laxmi without the baby. Although they could not communicate directly because of the language barrier, Laxmi felt reassured that they were nice people. But she didn't get to keep a photo of the baby. 'They only showed me a photo,' Laxmi said. 'If they had given me the photo, I would have got it framed and kept it at home.' Laxmi thinks often about the baby girl she gave birth to in 2014 and lives in hope that she will meet her one day.

Laxmi was born in Mumbai and lived with her parents, her two sisters and her brother in the over-crowded slum district of Goregaon. Their tenement home was made of brick, a step up from the mud and plastic dwellings that were typical of the area. The family made boxes of sweets for a living and the children attended school, unlike many of their peers. But then disaster struck. First their mother passed away, and then they lost their father. There was no one to look after them. Laxmi's maternal grandmother took her to her village in Karnataka to find a husband. At the time of her marriage, Laxmi was 12 years old. By 18, she was divorced with two young sons, abandoned by her husband who had married someone else.

Laxmi first heard about surrogacy when she was 23. She was introduced to a woman acting on behalf of a surrogacy agency by an aunt. At the time, she was struggling financially, working 12 hours a day in a shopping mall in Goregaon, and taking on additional catering work at weddings when it was available. The money Laxmi received for being a surrogate enabled her to pay for her children's schooling and her brother's college fees for a course in air-conditioning and refrigerator repair, and helped her to rent a better house. Five months after giving birth, when she was back at the shopping mall for nine hours a day selling flour, Laxmi had mixed feelings about her experience of surrogacy.

The payment she had received for being a surrogate had helped her family hugely and she was happy about that, but she felt that she had not been treated with respect. She didn't like the surrogates' house where she had been required to live for some of the pregnancy, and the promise that she would receive a picture of the baby had not been honoured. 'Surrogacy has affected me in a good way but also in a bad way,' she said. 'I could not work for one year and the amount of money that they gave me to live on each month during the pregnancy was not enough for my two children and my rent. They deducted some of the money they had promised me because I had to leave the surrogate house to look after my kids. I ask them to let me talk to the madam but they did not let me talk to the madam. They said the madam does not have time.'

Laxmi was one of the women who took part in the first study of the psychological wellbeing of Indian surrogates, conducted by Nishtha Lamba at the Corion Clinic in Mumbai between 2015 and 2017. Nishtha grew up in Delhi, trained as a psychologist in Delhi and New York, and joined our team as a PhD student in 2014, supervised by Vasanti Jadva and myself. At the time, there was growing controversy around foreign couples travelling to India to have children through surrogacy. In the previous decade, following global media coverage of the birth of twins in Anand, Gujurat, in 2004, to a woman who was a gestational surrogate for her daughter and son-in-law who lived in the United Kingdom, India quickly became the go-to destination for international surrogacy. It was highly attractive to couples whose only possibility of having a genetic child was through gestational surrogacy, the only type of surrogacy permitted in India, but who could not access this in their own country because the cost was prohibitive or legislation did not permit it. Even in the United Kingdom, where commercial surrogacy is illegal, gestational surrogacy can soon add up when the IVF, legal fees, and the surrogate's permitted expenses are all taken into account. In India, at this time, surrogacy was less expensive, regulation was minimal, the intended parents' names could be on the birth certificate, and there was a plethora of surrogates living in abject poverty who were motivated by payments that were equivalent to ten years' earnings. The operators of the multi-billion-dollar surrogacy industry paid scant attention to the potential harm to the surrogates' wellbeing or the ethical issues raised by the enormous gaps in income, and discrepancies in race, social class, and culture, between the surrogates and the intended parents.

Acutely aware of the concerns that had been voiced about wealthy foreigners exploiting poor, and often illiterate, Indian women, Nishtha and Vasanti wanted to find out how the surrogates themselves felt about their situation and whether surrogacy caused them psychological harm. Nishtha interviewed 50 pregnant surrogates from a clinic in Mumbai that arranged surrogacy for foreign couples. She also recruited a group of 69 expectant mothers, pregnant with their own child, from a similar socio-economic background, from public hospitals. Comparing these two groups of pregnant women would help explain whether any mental-health problems they experienced were directly related to being a surrogate or resulted from social and economic disadvantages more generally.

When Nishtha first spoke to the surrogates and expectant mothers they were in their second or third trimester of pregnancy. She assessed the women's anxiety, depression, and stress levels, as well as the extent to which they had bonded with the baby. She also interviewed the surrogates about their reasons for becoming a surrogate, their feelings about it, and their experiences. Between four and six months after the birth, Nishtha saw them again, this time focusing on their reflections on their experiences as well as their mental health. She found that the surrogates were more depressed than the expectant mothers during the pregnancy, and continued to be more depressed after the birth. But unexpectedly, the surrogates did not show a greater increase in depression following the birth than the expectant mothers, which suggested that the surrogates' depression was connected to their life circumstances rather than to giving up the baby. As Neeta, one of the surrogates in the study, pointed out: 'All come here because they have problems, no one comes happily. Each woman has her problems and they come because of that. If they have a good home, why would they do this?' These women became surrogates because the payment they received enabled them to achieve their ambition of buying a house for their families or educating their children.

Much attention has been paid by the media to the surrogacy hostels that Indian surrogates are often required to live in during their pregnancies. As an article in *The Guardian* newspaper in April 2016 described it, 'The women sleep in cramped conditions and are controlled to the point of being told when to eat, drink, and sleep.' But many of the surrogates in our study said that they liked staying in the hostel with other surrogates because they were well looked after, they could have their own children to stay with them, and they developed strong friendships there. Another advantage was that the surrogates could hide their pregnancy and avoid the inevitable disapproval and stigmatisation that they would face from their families, neighbours, and wider communities. All of the surrogates had kept the surrogacy secret to some extent. Some explained their absence from their home by saying they had moved to a nearby town to work as a domestic helper. As one woman, Parveen, said: 'My mother keeps making excuses that I am at work or I have been to my in-laws' place or something else. We are telling them 100 lies in order to hide a single truth.'

Like the surrogates who had participated in our UK study, the Indian surrogates did not form an emotional bond with the unborn baby and did not find giving them up difficult. But not one of the Indian surrogates had been allowed to see the baby at the time of delivery, and most had had no contact with the baby afterwards. This is in stark contrast to the experiences of surrogates in more affluent countries, where such a practice would be considered inhumane. Like

Laxmi, many surrogates wished to have a photograph of the baby to keep, but only one-quarter actually received one. This caused deep disappointment and distress. 'I met the parents only once and they did not even show me a picture of the baby,' said Parveen. 'They did not do at least that much for me. I have given them a baby after 18 years. They must have thought that I would run away with the baby. If I had run, I would have run when the baby was in my tummy. It is okay if they do not want to show me the baby but at least they can give me the photo.'

The small number of surrogates who had been allowed to meet the intended parents and the baby were much happier, which suggests that the intended parents' fears that they would want to keep the baby were unfounded. Seeing the baby seemed to have the opposite effect, instilling a sense of contentment with the surrogacy arrangement and the handover experience. As surrogate Sarita, who gave birth to twins, said, 'I could deal with the situation after seeing them. Otherwise, I would always have wondered how they look and what they are like. I am peaceful now. After all, I kept the babies in my womb for nine months. I deserved to see their faces at least.'

In the summer of 2015, Vasanti and I travelled to Mumbai with Nishtha to find out how her research was going, and meet the director and staff of the surrogacy clinic. Following a hot and bumpy ride across the city, we arrived at an anonymous, slightly decrepit, three-storey modern building with a nondescript entrance on a quiet side-street off a noisy and vibrant main road. We took the lift to the second floor — the surrogates' entrance was on the next floor up — inserted our feet into a machine that covered our shoes in plastic bags, and entered. Compared to the hustle and bustle of Mumbai, it was an oasis of calm and efficiency. Intended parents, mainly foreigners and non-resident Indians, waited patiently for their appointments, and surrogates wandered in and out. It looked like any other fertility clinic the world over. Apart from the surrogates' brightly coloured saris, a large statue of

Ganesh, the Indian god of good luck, in the corner, and a poster stating that sex selection is banned in India, it was a surprisingly unremarkable environment for such an extraordinary endeavour.

**

International surrogacy does not always involve the gross inequalities between surrogates and intended parents that are apparent when wealthy westerners travel to low-income countries such as India. As cross-border surrogacy is becoming more commonplace, a growing number of couples are seeking surrogacy abroad because of restrictive legislation in their own countries, rather than a desire for cut-price treatment, and these couples often enter into arrangements with women for whom surrogacy is more of a choice than a financial necessity.

In the spring of 2016, after the birth of her third child, 30-year-old Laura was thinking about going back to her job as editor of a community magazine when she saw an advert for surrogates in a local newspaper. Laura lived in a small town in rural Maryland in the United States with her husband, Marshall, an installer of audio-visual equipment, their baby boy, Laura's 12-year-old daughter and nine-year-old son from her first marriage, and her mother and father. She had always lived in a multi-generational home, growing up with her maternal grandparents. Her family was very close. Laura joked with Marshall about becoming a surrogate so that she could stay at home to look after their baby, but didn't think much more about it. Yet the advert kept attracting her attention: 'Every time I turned around I kept seeing this advertisement,' she told me in 2018, when I was put in touch with her by a counsellor from the fertility clinic where she became a surrogate. 'I'm one of these people who thinks that if something continues to show up in your life, you need to pay attention to it. I kept seeing advertisements for this surrogacy agency and I thought "maybe I should call".'

The preliminary interview with the agency took place over the phone, and Laura gave permission for the clinic that would eventually carry out the surrogacy to request her medical records. Once the clinic gave the all-clear, the agency posted a profile of Laura with photos, detailed information about her and her family, and what she was looking for in a surrogacy arrangement. The agency's procedure was that intended parents selected potential surrogates from all of the surrogates' profiles, and then the surrogates received the profiles of intended parents who were interested in them. 'They got to pick first! They chose me and then I got to choose them,' she recounted. Laura and Marshall selected the very first couple whose profile was sent to them. The couple were the same age as them, they were close to their family, ran their own export business, liked to travel, had tried unsuccessfully to have a baby through IVF nine times, wanted to transfer two embryos, and were from mainland China.

The initial meeting between the couples took place by Skype with a translator, as Lili and Luning, the intended parents, did not speak English well. Despite the language barrier, Laura felt very comfortable with them and warmed to Shining Li, the Chinese psychologist from Shenzhen in mainland China who would support them and translate for them throughout the process. Next, they all met up at the clinic in New Jersey for an intensive day of physical and psychological tests. They learned about each other's families, shared photos, and discussed how they each wanted the pregnancy to proceed. Unlike many intended parents, Lili and Luning were not prescriptive about what Laura should and shouldn't do while she was pregnant. 'I felt good when I met them,' Laura told me. 'They saw pictures of my kids and they felt reassured that I'd had three healthy children and they didn't have to tell me what I needed to eat, how I should exercise, and how to take care of myself when I was pregnant. I felt good knowing that they had that kind of trust in me.' Following the day together, the clinic organised background checks of Laura and Marshall, including a criminal records search and a home study by a social worker. Once Laura was approved as a surrogate, legal contacts were drawn up by separate lawyers for each couple, the contracts were signed, and they were ready to go.

Lili couldn't carry a pregnancy but she did have healthy eggs so the couple opted for gestational surrogacy. They had four embryos left from their previous IVF attempts, three female and one male, and they decided to transfer one female embryo and their last male embryo. When Laura found out that she was pregnant with twins she was thrilled but nervous — she had been desperately hoping that one embryo would develop but hadn't bargained for two, although she had known that this was a possibility. The pregnancy went smoothly, and in April 2017 she gave birth to twins: a girl and a boy. Marshall was in the delivery room with Laura while Lili and Luning waited anxiously outside: 'I got to see the babies. They showed them to me right after they took them out,' said Laura. 'They lifted them over the curtain so I knew they were okay. They were so pretty! They had so much hair and I was amazed at how big they were. And they were crying loudly. I was happy. It felt so good.' When Laura was back in her room, Lili and Luning brought the babies to her so that she could hold them. Laura's parents and her two older children were there too. They took pictures of them all together. Everyone was excited.

After all they had been through together, saying goodbye to Lili and Luning was bittersweet. Laura was the first to leave the hospital: 'I didn't really get emotional until the day we were leaving. I was very aware that when we left I would never see them again. I had become very close to Lili. Although she could not speak English well, she could write in English, so we communicated by text. She and I had gotten so used to texting each other every day and talking and getting to know one another that I kind of felt like I was losing a friend.'

Laura felt more concerned about losing contact with Lili than she did with the babies. Although the couples had agreed that there would be no contact after they left the hospital, Lili and Luning asked if they could send pictures from time to time. Laura loves seeing photos of the babies. And she loves knowing that they're healthy and doing well. But to her, it feels like a distant friend sending photos of their children. She doesn't feel an emotional connection. She explained, 'I think it's because you don't do all the things when you're pregnant that help you bond, like buying baby clothes or thinking of names. I wasn't even imagining what these babies would look like, because I didn't have a clue. We weren't putting the crib together. We talked to the babies but it was always "baby girl" and "baby boy", because we had no idea what their names were going to be. You don't do all of those bonding things.'

***

In the years since the controversial births of Baby Cotton and Baby M, surrogacy has become a more accepted route to parenthood in some parts of the world. In 1998, the committee set up to review the UK's law on surrogacy, of which I was a member, published a report recommending greater regulation of surrogacy, and that payments to surrogates should be restricted to actual expenses arising from the pregnancy. The aim was to protect all concerned. Twenty years later, in 2018, by which time there was much less concern about the risks of surrogacy as it is practised in the United Kingdom, and the government had recognised surrogacy as an acceptable way of forming a family, another review of the law was initiated by the Law Commission of England and Wales, and the Scottish Law Commission, with the aim of making surrogacy more accessible and straightforward, and discouraging people from seeking surrogacy arrangements abroad. A key proposal, based on the wishes of surrogates and intended parents alike, is that the intended parents become the child's legal parents from birth, unless the surrogate applies to a court of law within a fixed period of time to withdraw her consent. This seems to be a more sensible approach than the current situation whereby the intended parents have to apply to a court after the baby is born. As the Law Commissions' consultation document points out, surrogates don't see themselves as the child's mother, and the intended parents would like the child to be part of their family from birth. In 2003, in her book, *Nature and Mortality*, Baroness Warnock, who had chaired the government Committee of Inquiry into Human Fertilisation and Embryology that reported in 1984, acknowledged that she had been too hostile towards surrogacy, partly due to the commercial nature of surrogacy as practised in the United States.

Today, in America, surrogacy is permitted in some states, but not in others, and some states allow gestational, but not traditional surrogacy, while others have no legislation whatsoever. In 2016, the Ethics Committee of the American Society for Reproductive Medicine recognised the benefits of gestational surrogacy while making recommendations on how it should be practised. In mainland Europe, some countries that have been strongly opposed to surrogacy have begun to reconsider the issue, although an alliance between feminists and conservatives resulted in the Swedish government rejecting a proposal to permit surrogacy in 2016, and a report of the Bioethics Committee of the French Parliament in 2019 concluded that surrogacy remained unacceptable in France. In Australia, like the United States, the law varies from state to state. In New South Wales, it is a criminal offence to travel abroad for commercial surrogacy, whereas this is not the case in the neighbouring state of Victoria. In India, a Surrogacy Bill was brought before parliament in 2016 to restrict surrogacy to childless, married Indian couples, and Thailand and other south-east Asian countries have banned foreigners from entering into surrogacy arrangements. Cambodia took a particularly prohibitive approach, imprisoning 43 surrogates in 2018 and 2019, releasing them on the condition that they would raise the children themselves, a disproportionately harsh treatment of women who were victims of agents operating outside the law.

Surrogacy continues to divide feminist opinion. For some, it is inherently exploitative of women and should be outlawed, as exemplified in Margaret Atwood's dystopian novel, *The Handmaid's Tale,* in which women are forced into surrogacy. For others, banning surrogacy removes a woman's autonomy over her own body. The findings of Vasanti and Susan's research on the experiences of surrogates and their families shows that surrogacy can be a rewarding experience for surrogates, and can result in close, respectful, and enduring relationships between surrogates and the families they help create. Even in India, where there are huge inequalities in wealth and social status between intended parents and surrogates, some surrogates told the social scientist Lopamudra Goswami that they did not feel exploited and were against the 2016 ban as surrogacy had enhanced their lives.

One issue that unites almost everyone is that the birth of children without identifiable legal or genetic parents should be avoided at all costs. In 2000, headlines such as, 'Nightmare of limbo twins', 'Nobody's children', and 'The scandal of "Babies to go"', highlighted the plight of twin girls conceived in Greece using sperm from an anonymous American donor, the eggs of an anonymous British donor, and a British surrogate, for an Italian man and his Portuguese wife, who then changed their minds; eventually, the twins were adopted by a lesbian couple living in California. Situations like this are shocking and clearly go against all that we know about the best interests of children. At present, there is little that can be done to curb bad actors in the field of assisted reproduction who operate across international borders, taking advantage of disparities between the laws of different countries or, as is often the case, an absence of legislation whatsoever. International regulation in the field of reproduction is notoriously difficult to achieve, but the ambition of bodies such as the United Nations, and the Hague Conference on Private International Law, offer some hope.

***

When I caught up with Kim Cotton in 2018, 1,050 babies had been born through COTS, and after a break of several years, she was back in the saddle running the organisation. She was just as passionate about surrogacy as she had ever been, and thrilled to be advising the United Kingdom Law Commission on its proposed new legislation. Kim was still in touch with the 27-year-old twins she had given birth to in 1991: 'They live in New Zealand now but they come to the United Kingdom quite frequently, so we catch up quite a lot. We're all on Facebook and when it's their birthday I'll say, "Happy birthday from tum-my-mummy," and it was my birthday last week and they said, "Happy birthday to our tummy-mummy." We talk, we laugh, they're lovely kids. I'm thrilled with them and how it has all turned out. They're part of our family. They're really special to us.' Looking back at the birth of Baby Cotton, Kim feels that it would all have been so different had she been able to meet the intended parents. Her second experience as a surrogate brought home to her how bad the first had been. Anonymous surrogacy is abhorrent to her now. Although genealogy internet sites that do DNA matching such as AncestryDNA mean that it may now be possible for her to find Baby Cotton, Kim feels it would be wrong to do that. But if Baby Cotton ever looked for her, she told me, that would be just fine.

Chapter 5

Surrogacy Families: 'No Accident'

'The surrogate baby is doomed to second best.'

DR JOHN DAWSON, BRITISH MEDICAL ASSOCIATION, (1987).

'I think it's cool. I quite like talking about it because it's an interesting fact about me.'

CHRIS, AGE 14, BORN THROUGH TRADITIONAL SURROGACY, (2015).

In 1996, in Liverpool, England, when Lynne and Peter's surrogate, Suzanne, was five months pregnant with their son, Alex, they felt it was time to tell their families. Surrogacy was still highly controversial in the 1990s, in the wake of the Baby M and Baby Cotton scandals, but the couple wanted to be completely open with their families. So they carefully planned the announcement: '"We have good news." Pause. "We are having a baby." Pause. Wait for the congratulations to die down. "And we're not pregnant!"'

To their amazement, Lynne's 72-year-old father, who was known for his old-fashioned views and inclination to inadvertently cause offence, simply said, 'Oh! Surrogacy? Is it Mandy [Lynne's sister]?' Lynne was stunned. She had expected that her father wouldn't even know what surrogacy was. It turned out that he had watched a programme about it on breakfast television and was completely accept-ing. 'That Saturday afternoon, he asked to speak to Suzanne,' Lynne told me. 'They had a wonderful conversation. My dad was in tears, and thanked her for making his daughter so happy.' It proved to be a more significant phone call than they realised at the time. The following Monday, while out driving, he had a heart attack and died. Lynne was devastated but is forever thankful that her father knew that she was to be a mother at last and that he had spoken to the woman who was making it possible.

Alex was conceived using Suzanne's egg, and is the genetic child of Suzanne and Peter. Following Alex's birth, Lynne felt under scrutiny from unthinking people who said things to her like, 'Gosh, you're just like a real mother', and 'What will you tell your son if you have a baby of your own?' Despite there being only a slim chance that she could conceive naturally, she started using contraception to prevent an acci-dental pregnancy. She didn't want her beloved and long-awaited son to be seen as second best.

Lynne grew up in a coal mining town in the northeast of England, the second eldest of five children. She loved her parents and her three brothers, but she was especially delighted when her sister was born. The two have always been close. After school, she trained as a nurse, and met her future husband, Peter, in 1979, when she was 25: 'I was thinking about learning to fly, and took my dad for a trial flight for Father's Day. I thought, "I rather like that instructor!" I started flying lessons with him and ultimately we got married.' By then, Lynne was working as a brand manager in a pharmaceutical company and Peter was training to be a commercial pilot.

Lynne put off starting a family until she was in her mid-thirties. Because she came from a large family herself, and always expected to have children, she assumed it would be fine. But it wasn't. It was only after eight trying years of fertility treatment, and six failed attempts at IVF, that Lynne and Peter turned to surrogacy as their final chance.

They met Suzanne through COTS, and Lynne was 42 when Alex, their 'perfect, angelic child', was born.

Lynne remembers her fear that Suzanne might change her mind and keep baby Alex. Back then, maternity hospitals were often hostile towards surrogacy. 'We were there, both of us, at the hospital, sitting outside like expectant fathers,' Lynne said. 'We were not allowed to be present at the birth.' Suzanne was made to stay in the delivery suite all night with Alex — now considered to be bad practice in surrogacy births — while hospital staff kept asking, 'Do you really want to do this?' The following morning, Lynne and Peter waited on tenterhooks for the phone to ring, not knowing what would be in store. 'It was awful,' Lynne told me, 'but then Suzanne rang and said, "Lynne, come and get him, come and get him now."' When Lynne and Peter arrived, the nurses wouldn't let them onto the ward because they weren't relatives, but Lynne mustered all her strength and proclaimed, 'I am the intended mother. Your patient has asked us to come. This is not a prison. I am going in.' As Lynne described it, 'We walked past the nurses, and Suzanne just said, "Lynne, put him in the car seat, take him. Go now!" And that's what we did, with a flurry of nurses running behind us, wittering. It was horrendous.'

Alex is now a young adult with a rewarding career in the merchant navy, and a girlfriend who Lynne adores. Growing up, his parents were always open with him about being born through surrogacy, and prepared him for the flack he might experience at school. Lynne used to say to him, 'You may get teased at school if you talk about surrogacy, but just turn around and say, "So what? I've got two mothers."' They also had discussions about the meaning of the word 'real', and Lynne would say, 'You've only got one real mother, and by the way, that's me.' She has a close relationship with Alex. 'I feel so lucky,' she told me. 'He sneaked up on me a few months ago and said, "I'm so glad you are my real mother!"'

The family has always kept in touch with Suzanne and her wider family, including Gee, another child born through surrogacy two years after Alex. They contact each other at birthdays and Christmas, and they all meet up at least once a year. Lynne can't put into words how grateful she feels to Suzanne, 'She's given us this amazing thing, a family, that you cannot properly thank anybody for. It's utterly fantastic.'

Unlike Lynne and Peter, who didn't ever discover the cause of their infertility, Mary had always known that she couldn't give birth to children herself — she was born with a medical condition that made it impossible — but she had always wanted to be a mother. Mary was 39, and her partner Jake 29, when they had their first child. After some research, they had decided that surrogacy would be the best way forward, and had found their surrogate, Jane, through Surrogacy UK. Mary's eggs were fertilised with Jake's sperm using IVF and the embryos transferred to Jane's uterus, just like Laura's gestational surrogacy arrangement with Lili and Luning. Nine months later, Jane gave birth to Valerie, the genetic daughter of Mary and Jake. Three years after that, Jane was the surrogate for Valerie's little sister, Coral.

Mary loves that Jane is involved in her family. The two women are very close. It was through Mary that Jane met her current husband, with whom she has two children. 'Jane is the person that I would speak to if I had a problem,' said Mary. 'She's my best friend. She's like the sister I never had.' Valerie and Coral are also close to Jane. 'Valerie calls her Auntie Jane, she loves her, and she knows that Auntie Jane was her "tummy-mummy",' Mary told us when Valerie was seven. 'The girls are fond of Jane's own children too and they all play together once a month.' As teenagers, the girls continued to be close to Jane. 'She's a really nice person,' Coral said. 'She's similar to my mum. She's funny and calm and relaxed. A bit more than mum, actually! She's a very caring person. I call her Auntie Jane and she's like family to me.'

Mary and Jake are pleased that there is no mystery for their daughters about where they came from. Their policy has always been to be open and honest so that the girls don't think it's anything to be ashamed of. 'As soon as Valerie could talk, we told her that mummy's tummy was broken and that Auntie Jane let us borrow her tummy, and she came straight to mummy as soon as she was born,' said Mary. Jane has also spoken to the girls about why she gave birth to them. All of their close family know about the surrogacy, but Mary feels that it's up to the children to decide who else to tell.

Although it might seem worrying from a mother's point of view for the surrogate to be close to the children, Mary doesn't find Jane's involvement in her family threatening. 'She's such a wonderful person. I think it's a privilege to know this person, to have this person in our life. I don't feel threatened in any way.' Mary's only fear is that one of her girls might say that she's not their real mother. 'I think that would cut very deep but it hasn't happened so far, and we have a very close relationship so I don't think it would enter their minds,' said Mary, 'but it's in *my* mind, rightly or wrongly.' Sometimes Mary feels that having children through surrogacy is a lot to live up to: 'If I'm having a bad day, I think "I'm such a bad parent. I don't deserve this wonderful outcome."' But most of the time, she just feels grateful. 'I'm still amazed by it all,' she told us when Valerie was 14. 'I do sometimes pinch myself and say, "My goodness, they're mine!"'

✳✳✳

Lynne and Peter's family, formed through traditional surrogacy, and Mary and Jake's family, created by gestational surrogacy, are nothing like the media's image of surrogacy, in which an impoverished and vulnerable woman is exploited by a wealthy couple and quickly discarded once she has relinquished the commodity they have purchased — the baby. And yet, to this day, surrogacy remains the most controversial form of assisted reproduction. Of the many criticisms of surrogacy, the issue that most interested me was the impact on families formed in this way. Would children be psychologically harmed by the knowledge that they had been created for the sole purpose of being given away to other parents? Would they feel abandoned by the woman who gave birth to them? Would they see her as their 'real' mother? What if the surrogate was also the child's genetic mother? If the surrogate had been paid, would this make matters worse for the child? And if the surrogate remained in contact with the family following the birth, would it undermine the relationship between the mother and the child? It is commonly assumed that because the mother does not experience the pregnancy, she may find it difficult to bond with her baby, a situation that is unlikely to be helped by her anxiety that the surrogate may change her mind. She may also face disapproval of her unconventional route to parenthood from relatives, friends, and her wider social circle. Because the mother does not become pregnant, it is impossible to hide surrogacy in the same way as egg, sperm, or embryo donation — openness about the pregnancy is usually the only option.

In the late nineties, we had no idea of the answers to any of these questions. Parallels were often drawn with adoption. As an article in *The Independent* newspaper in 1997 put it, 'Does surrogacy damage the psychological health of women and children? After all, the history of adoption is of women left riven with guilt in later years and children bereft at abandonment by birth parents. Why should those involved in surrogacy feel any different?'

My experience on the UK government's Surrogacy Review Committee brought home to me how important it is to have reliable evidence in discussions on this highly emotive and controversial area of family life. Listening to the testimony, it was clear that many experts believed that surrogacy would be detrimental to children, but at that time, there was no research to prove or disprove this. We didn't know whether children born through surrogacy would suffer emotionally, or whether their mothers would lack confidence in their parenting abilities, or feel or behave less positively towards their children because they did not give birth to them. Based on what was actually known at the time, our committee concluded that there should be a Code of Practice to ensure that the welfare of the child is the paramount concern of all those involved in any surrogacy arrangement, but this recommendation was never adopted, most probably because it wasn't seen as a priority for the government at the time.

Although too late for the government review, we decided to include a group of surrogacy families in our new study of children born through egg or sperm donation, to find out more. My research on lesbian mother families, and on families formed through IVF and donor conception, had shown that the widely held assumption that these families would experience problems was wrong. Perhaps that would also be true of families formed through surrogacy. On the other hand, surrogacy involved children being separated from the women who gave birth to them, some of whom were their genetic mothers. In this respect, it could be seen as similar to adoption, which can be problematic for children. I went into the study with an open mind; I had absolutely no idea what we would find.

We were fortunate in being able to enlist the help of the Office of National Statistics, the government body responsible for the registration of intended parents as legal parents in surrogacy arrangements, to help us recruit families to the study. All parents with a one-year-old child born through surrogacy were invited to take part, and COTS helped us identify other parents who had not yet been granted legal parenthood. We recruited 42 surrogacy families altogether, who we are following up with to this day.

When the children were one, mothers and fathers who had become parents through surrogacy showed greater warmth and enjoyment in their babies than the parents who had conceived naturally. They were also more emotionally involved with their babies, but not to the extent that they were over-protective. At age two, the surrogacy mothers' bonds with their children remained strong. Compared to the natural conception mothers, they saw themselves as more competent at parenting, took greater pleasure in their toddlers, and felt less anger, guilt, and disappointment in them. The surrogacy fathers found parenting less stressful than the natural conception fathers. When the children were three, the surrogacy mothers were more affectionate, and interacted more with their toddlers than the mothers with naturally conceived children. Like the families formed though egg, sperm, and embryo donation, the surrogacy families appeared to be doing better because the parents were so pleased to have children after all they had been through to make it happen.

Our next visit to the families was when the children were seven. By that time, most of the surrogacy children knew how they had been born. Although the parents still had good relationships with their children — they were warm, sensitive, and involved, and showed little criticism, hostility, or conflict with their seven-year-olds — they were no longer doing better than the natural conception parents. Some of the surrogacy children showed an increase in emotional and behavioural problems at this age. However, these psychological problems had disappeared by the time we re-visited the families when the children were ten. Interestingly, the same pattern has been found among internationally adopted children by researchers in the Netherlands. The most likely explanation for this phenomenon in both surrogacy and adoptive families, as first suggested by the Dutch researchers Femmie Juffer and Marinus van IJzendoorn, is that these children have to cope with issues relating to their identity at a younger age than most other children.

By the time they had become teenagers, at age 14, we found the children born through surrogacy to be flourishing. This was based not only on what the mothers and teachers told us, but also on what the teenagers said themselves through questionnaires about their self-esteem, mental health, and psychological wellbeing, including their feelings of happiness, connectedness, and optimism, and their relationships with their parents. We also asked how they felt about being born through surrogacy. Only one teenager expressed some unhappiness, the majority were largely uninterested, and a few saw it as an advantage.

As Simon put it, 'I was talking to someone at school and they said they were an accident. I know I was no accident. I was really wanted, and it makes me feel special.' Others, like Helen, explained that being born by traditional surrogacy does not affect her relationship with her parents, 'It doesn't bother me. My mum is still my mum. Dad is still my dad.' Most of those who were in touch with their surrogate spoke positively about her, but explained that they don't see her as their mother. 'Our relationship is a good one,' said Angela, 'but I don't talk to her like she's my mum and she doesn't talk to me like I'm her daughter.'

Some of the 14-year-olds who were not in touch with their surrogate were interested in finding out about or even meeting her. Echoing some of the children conceived through sperm donation, Ellen, born through gestational surrogacy, would like to know more about the woman who gave birth to her: 'I really want to know who she is and meet her maybe.' Others, like Sally, born through gestational surrogacy, wish to thank her: 'Sometimes I think about it ... wanting to meet my birth mum. To say thanks for being my birth mum.' They would like to ask her why she decided to be a surrogate, whether she was happy about it, and how many other surrogacy children she has had. But not all of the teenagers were interested in their surrogate. Whether that will change as they grow older remains to be seen.

Although children born through surrogacy are usually told about their origins from an early age, those conceived using the surrogate's egg don't always know the full story. Like mothers of children conceived through egg donation, the mothers in these cases were worried that it might affect their children's feelings towards them. We found that when the children in our study were seven, only one-quarter of those born through traditional surrogacy had been told that the surrogate was their genetic mother, an even smaller proportion than in egg donation families. All intended to tell their children in the future, but by age ten, almost half of the children conceived using their surrogate's egg were still unaware that the surrogate was their genetic mother. It seems that the absence of a genetic connection to the mother is a more sensitive issue than surrogacy, and also easier to hide.

An enduring question about surrogacy families is whether the relationship between the parents and the surrogate breaks down once the baby is born. This is something that we were able to look at through our repeated visits to the families as the children grew up. The pregnancy was an anxious time for some of the intended parents. They worried that something would go wrong, or that the surrogate might change her mind and decide to keep the baby. Janice, a therapist who was unable to carry a pregnancy herself because of a hysterectomy when she was 27, was nervous that her surrogate, Pat, would lose the baby, especially as their first attempt at pregnancy was unsuccessful. But the bond between mother and surrogate usually strengthened as the pregnancy progressed. The intended mother often accompanied the surrogate to antenatal appointments and ultrasound scans, where they could share the pleasure of seeing the baby grow. These visits may have helped the intended mother bond with her unborn child. As Miriam, a doctor, and mother of one-year-old Beth, described it, 'COTS found me a friend, and not just a surrogate. I went to every check-up with her, and every scan. I saw her every week or two. The bigger she became, the more we were there. We were on the phone every day. She wanted me to be at the birth. When Beth was born, we cried tears of joy.'

In the year following the birth, more than 90 per cent of the parents remained in touch with the surrogate, and two-thirds had met up at least four times. Not surprisingly, when the surrogates were relatives or friends, they saw each other more. Mostly, the parents and surrogates got on well; less than 10 per cent of mothers had reservations about their relationship with the surrogate or about the surrogate's relationship with the child, and none had experienced serious conflict. Rather than feeling undermined, the mothers felt close to the surrogate and wanted their children to stay in touch with her. 'Since Beth was born, we have visited once a month. Our relationship is even stronger now,' said Miriam. In the few cases where there was no contact, this was either by mutual consent or because the surrogate didn't want it, and not because the parents had rejected the surrogate.

Although the frequency of contact declined over time, especially with traditional surrogates who did not previously know the intended parents, a surprising 60 per cent of the surrogacy families in our study were still in touch with their surrogate when their child was ten. Whether or not the surrogate was previously known to the parents, and whether the child was born by gestational or traditional surrogacy, seemed to make no difference to how well they got along.

Our study is the only investigation worldwide to have followed surrogacy families as the children grow up, and the first to interview adolescents about how they themselves feel about being born in this way. Although we need more research to confirm our findings, the evidence so far shows that surrogacy families are doing well. The children did not see their surrogates as their 'real' mothers, even if there was a genetic connection between them. They were quite clear about that. Nevertheless, they were able to accept their surrogates, and most were happy to have them in their lives.

***

Gee Roberts was born through traditional surrogacy in 1998. Her parents had gone through IVF five times, failing to become pregnant on three occasions, and having their hopes dashed by early miscarriage on the other two. By then, they were in their mid-forties and knew that an IVF baby was no longer an option for them. If they were going to achieve their dream of having a family, then surrogacy was the only way. As they had used donated eggs in their final two IVF attempts, their jump to surrogacy seemed less enormous than going straight from IVF to surrogacy using the surrogate's egg.

Gee has always known her surrogate, Suzanne. 'She's always going to have a key role in my life,' said Gee, 'not as my mother, but as something completely different. I wouldn't be here without her which makes her important to me. But I would never, ever compare her to my mum. Suzanne and I get on really well. We're very similar in some ways, and we really enjoy seeing each other and catching up, but I see her as more of an auntie than a mother.' Suzanne has two children of her own, and has been a surrogate for other couples, giving Gee several half-siblings, one of whom is Lynne and Peter's son, Alex. All three families meet up several times a year. Gee explained, 'It's important to me to always see them and make sure that we're there for each other in whatever ways we can be. As I don't have any other siblings, my half-siblings are very special to me.'

Because she has always known about her background, something that Gee believes is important, she didn't realise when she was young that her family was unusual. 'At school, when I was about four or five, we were asked to draw a picture of our parents,' she recalled, 'and I drew a picture of two mums and a dad. My dad was called in to the school to explain!' It turned out that Gee's head teacher had been adopted as a child. This led to a special friendship between them and they are still in touch to this day. All through school, her friends were supportive. Gee feels very lucky: 'I've never met anyone who's been unsupportive or disrespectful, ever. When I say I was born through surrogacy, they always want to know more. I'm very open about it. As soon as I meet someone and they start asking, "Do you have brothers or sisters?", I tell them at that point.'

Gee has always been very close to her dad, but has had a more difficult relationship with her mum, which she puts down to her mother never quite coming to terms with having a non-genetic child. 'I look very similar to my dad, and I think that that helps,' said Gee, 'and I'm so different to my mum in every imaginable way: I'm tall, I'm brunette, I'm brown-eyed, and she's very short with red hair and blue eyes. I think she finds it difficult that we're so different.' Gee's parents also had a troubled marriage that ended in divorce when Gee was 15, which complicated the situation. 'I don't think it helped that I was so similar to my dad, because my mum and dad were having a really tough time, and I'm a mini version of my dad. I think my mum found that quite difficult.'

But Gee sees it differently, 'Even if she feels that I'm not hers in the way that she had imagined her child would be, from my point of view, she has always been my mum, and always will be my mum. Surrogacy leads to all kinds of opportunities for hurting each other and saying, "You're not mine", but that's never something I would ever say to my mum, or would even think of, because I am hers and that's always been the way it's been from day one.' Today, Gee feels that she and her mum have come out the other end of a difficult few years, and they are much closer than they've ever been before. She also feels positive about surrogacy: 'I feel very lucky to have been part of something so special and so unique. For me, surrogacy has been fantastic, and my parents are thrilled that they've gone through surrogacy and they've got me. I love the fact that I have so much family. I have a really nice relationship with my surrogate's side of my family, and if I didn't have three parents, in a sense, I wouldn't have so many people around me. So I love it. I wouldn't change it for the world.'

When I spoke to Gee in 2018, she was a third-year medical student, planning a career in paediatrics or fertility treatment. I asked whether her choice of specialty had anything to do with her own experiences. 'Absolutely!' she replied. 'It's important. If it wasn't for medicine I wouldn't be here, so it's important to give back.'

***

The first surrogacy agency in the world, the Center for Surrogate Parenting, opened its doors in 1980 in California. It all started when

Bill Handel, who had recently completed a law degree, was asked by a fertility doctor for legal advice. The doctor had been approached by a married couple whose friend had offered to have a baby for them because the woman was unable to carry a pregnancy herself, and he needed to discover whether the couple could become the legal parents of the child. The assignment the doctor offered Bill was to find out how to practise surrogacy legally. It was 1979, and only traditional surrogacy was possible, so the plan was to conceive the baby using the friend's egg and the intended father's sperm. At that time, Bill had no idea what surrogacy was, but he agreed to look into it.

Bill went back to his law school, and spoke to all of his professors, including his ethics professor, one by one, to ask how they thought he should approach the problem and what the obstacles might be. The consensus was that step-parent adoption — with the intended mother adopting the baby — was the way to go. First, they had to prove that the friend and the intended father were the genetic parents of the child through genetic testing, something they couldn't do until the baby was born. Armed with the results, they went to court to request that the intended father's name be added to the birth certificate, which already named the friend as the baby's mother. That done, they returned to court for a second time where the friend asked for her parental rights to be relinquished to the intended father. The judge agreed, opening the way for the intended mother to request a step-parent adoption of her husband's child. Following this ruling, California became the most popular destination for surrogacy in the United States.

One year later, in Cape Town, South Africa, Karen Synesiou, then an 18-year-old high school graduate, was watching television with her parents one evening when an episode of the influential US news magazine programme *60 Minutes* was aired. The topic was surrogacy, and it featured Bill Handel and the story of the beginning of surrogacy in the United States. Karen's parents were appalled, she told me. The idea of taking parental rights away from a woman who gives birth to a child, and giving the child to a woman who is not the child's mother, was abhorrent to them. Karen saw it differently. She said, 'I found it fascinating that we, as women, could decide to help someone else. I thought it was amazing that we could be empowered to do that.'

Ten years later, following an undergraduate degree in Cape Town, and a law degree in England, Karen moved to the United States. The week she arrived in California, she saw an advert in the LA Times for the position of Office Manager at the Center for Surrogate Parenting, Bill Handel's surrogacy agency. Still fascinated by surrogacy, Karen applied, and was offered the job. Two and a half years later, in 1993, she and Bill became business partners. Today, the agency has been responsible for the birth of almost 2,500 babies, and an article in US *Vogue* magazine in 2019 reported that there are more surrogacy agencies in California than in any other state.

Fay Johnson and her late husband Bob were among the first couples to have children through the Center for Surrogate Parenting. Fay was unable to carry a pregnancy because she had been exposed to the drug Diethylstilbestrol, commonly known as DES, when her mother was pregnant with her, which caused her womb to develop abnormally. DES was prescribed in the 1940s to prevent miscarriage and pregnancy complications, but was later withdrawn because of its serious side effects.

Fay had no idea that she was a DES baby when she met her future husband in 1979. Fay worked in Hollywood for First Artist Productions, a film company owned by some of the leading actors of the day. Bob worked in film distribution for Warner Brothers in the building next door. It was Fay's job to take the box office returns to Warner Brothers. One day, there was a new person there — it was Bob, the man who would become her husband and, eventually, the father of her children.

But the journey to parenthood was long and hard. It was only after two failed attempts at IVF that Fay discovered she had been a DES baby and that her womb had been damaged by the medication. Having children seemed out of the question, and may never have come about had it not been for two coincidences. The first was that Fay happened to see the same episode of *60 Minutes* that Karen had watched in her home in Cape Town, and through this learned about surrogacy, something she had not heard of before. The second was that one day in 1987, Bob called the wrong number. As Fay remembered it, 'Bob came home and said he'd made a really crazy wrong number phone call that day and ended up with this guy named Bill Handel who ran a surrogacy agency. One week later we were there for a consultation.' The couple's daughter, Lily, was born in 1990, and their son, Chase, followed in 1994. The children were born to different surrogates through traditional surrogacy.

Fay has always been open with her children about how they arrived in the world. 'I started telling them their stories as infants. I mean at six weeks old. I would tell them the same story every night. I figured children love stories about the day they were born, and they love stories where they're the main characters, so I just developed this little story, and that was it. I wanted Lily and Chase to appreciate all that had been done to have them, rather than my shame that I couldn't carry them. They never didn't know their own story.' Fay can see resemblances between her children and their respective surrogates. As she described it, 'They are both very much like their surrogates. Chase is very outgoing and has a big personality, and so is his surrogate. Lily and hers are very quiet.'

Lily and Chase have grown up knowing their surrogates and their half-siblings through surrogacy. In 2019, when he was 25 and studying Business Management in California, Chase spoke to me about his experiences of growing up as a child born through surrogacy. He was very clear about who he saw as his mother — it was most certainly Fay. 'My surrogate mom and I are related by blood. I look a lot like her. I have a lot of features like her, but I don't feel like she's my mom,' he told me. And Chase feels differently towards Lily than to his other genetic half-siblings. 'I've got a half-brother and a half-sister out of my surrogate's kids, and then a half-sister who's another surrogate child that she has. And there are similarities between my half-siblings and I, but I wouldn't say we're super close. We have dinner with them probably twice a year, hang out with them. I grew up with Lily, she's my sister.'

Chase appreciates his parents being open with him: 'My whole life, I was told that I was born through surrogacy. I met my surrogate mom all the time when I was young. We're friends with them. I would guess though, I could get mad if I went through my whole life with my mom saying I was from her, and then when I'm 25 she said, "Actually, it's all a sham." Then I'd be like, "Whoa, this changes things." That would upset me. But if you're told the truth your whole life, then it's nothing new.' And Chase never felt stigmatised by his peers because he was born through surrogacy. 'I was never picked on by people saying, "Oh, you were born different." It's never ever been a thing. I always thought it was cool because it was different, and then if anyone ever said, "You were a mistake", I could say, "Actually, man, I cost a lot of money." I know that I was both time-consuming and expensive, so I really was wanted.'

A distinction is often made between commercial surrogacy in the United States, where the surrogate is paid, and altruistic surrogacy in the United Kingdom, where she is not. Although surrogacy is permitted in the United Kingdom, commercial surrogacy has been outlawed since the Surrogacy Arrangements Act came into force in 1985. Nevertheless, surrogates may receive reasonable expenses in the United Kingdom to cover maternity clothes, travel to hospital appointments, domestic help, medical expenses, legal fees, and loss of earnings, which often amount to not much less than commercial rates for surrogates in the United States. Many European countries, such as France, Germany, Denmark, Italy, and Spain have banned surrogacy altogether, as have other countries around the world.

***

The increasing number of people who are travelling abroad for surrogacy has pointed the spotlight on the potential pitfalls, including babies being left in legal limbo for months on end, unable to return with their parents to their country of origin because of a mismatch in the law between the country in which the babies were born and the parents' country of residence. In 2008, a British couple who entered into a surrogacy arrangement in Ukraine, resulting in the birth of twins, became embroiled in a dispute over who were the legal parents. According to Ukrainian law, which gives legal parentage to the intended parents at the time of conception, it was the British couple, but British law states that the surrogate and her husband are the parents until parentage is transferred through a strict legal process. This meant that the parents couldn't obtain passports for the twins to bring them back to the United Kingdom. There was stalemate. When it became clear that the only option for the twins was to be raised in a Ukrainian orphanage, the British judge relented, declaring the twins to be, 'marooned, stateless, and parentless', and granted legal parentage to the British couple.

Unlike couples who have children through surrogacy in their own countries, those who go overseas are much less likely to keep in touch with their surrogate, especially if they go to countries in Eastern Europe or Asia where language barriers, and the mediating role of the clinic in contact between the parents and the surrogate, mitigate against it. This may create future problems for children who are curious about their surrogate, or who wish to meet her. We don't know how children will feel about having a surrogate from a different country, and most likely from a different cultural, religious, and socio-economic background to themselves.

A further problem with cross-border surrogacy is that surrogacy is practised in some countries in the absence of regulation or clear guidelines to protect all of those concerned. Under these circumstances, surrogacy can go badly wrong, as happened in 2014, when an Australian couple entered into a traditional surrogacy arrangement with a woman in Thailand. The surrogate conceived twins, but when one of the unborn twins was found to have Down's Syndrome and congenital heart problems, the intended parents asked the surrogate to abort the twin. The surrogate refused on religious grounds. After the birth, the couple took the unaffected twin back to Australia, abandoning 'Baby Gammy', the twin with Down's Syndrome, to be raised by his surrogate in Thailand. This case attracted international condemnation. It was only thanks to donations from around the world that the surrogate could afford to care for Baby Gammy.

***

As we have seen, children born through surrogacy often stay in touch with the woman who gave birth to them, but they don't see her as their mother, even when she is genetically related to them. But what if the surrogate is the child's grandmother? How does that affect relationships within the family? And does it cause confusion for the child?

Linda Robinson and her husband, Henry, met by chance at a friend's wedding in Melbourne, Australia, in 1975. A bridesmaid pulled out at the last minute and Linda was asked to stand in because she fitted the dress. Linda and Henry soon married, and had a daughter, Lauren, followed by a son, Ryan. They enjoyed a happy and stable family life. But their bubble burst when Lauren was diagnosed with cervical cancer at the very young age of 21. The treatment left Lauren with functioning ovaries, enabling her to produce eggs, but unable to carry a baby because her womb had been removed. When Lauren married Nicholas in her early thirties, and wanted to start a family, her sister-in-law offered to carry a baby for the couple, but the first attempt was unsuccessful and the second ended in miscarriage.

Unbeknown to Lauren, her mother, Linda, had a plan. She would carry a baby for her daughter and son-in-law. But there was an obstacle in her way — she was 57 at the time! Not only did she face all of the usual challenges of surrogacy, but she was way past the age at which it's seen as acceptable, safe, or even possible to have a baby. After consulting many doctors, having myriad tests, and attending counselling to ensure she fully understood the implications of what she intended to do, she was given the go-ahead. Linda's heartfelt desire was to help her daughter experience the joy of motherhood, but would Lauren agree?

Linda rang her daughter and said, 'We would like to help you,' but Lauren didn't answer her for quite some time. Linda kept thinking, 'She does realise I'm getting older, doesn't she?' It was when they were on holiday together one month later, that Lauren said they'd like to proceed: 'There were big cuddles all round. Lots of excitement. It was lovely.'

Linda's saving grace was that she had been taking hormone replacement therapy and hadn't gone through the menopause, because the idea of carrying a baby for her daughter had been at the back of her mind for some time. Amazingly, she was first-time lucky in becoming pregnant. It was only when she received a call from the clinic to confirm the pregnancy that the enormity of her actions hit her — she was having a baby at the age of 57 after a gap of almost 30 years. First she rang Lauren to tell her the good news, and then she rang Henry and confided, 'I don't know about this! What have I done?' But whatever her misgivings, Linda knew she was at the point of no return.

Nine months later, following a surprisingly easy pregnancy, tainted only by the disapproval of some family members and friends, Linda gave birth through caesarean section to baby William, the genetic child of her daughter and son-in-law. 'It was wonderful, just wonderful,' Linda recollected. 'It was late at night, Henry had just gone home with Nicholas, and Lauren was sitting there nursing him. She thought I was asleep, but I could see her. She was crying, just looking at him.'

Nine years later, when I met with Linda and Henry in Melbourne, they had no regrets whatsoever. 'Lauren has been through so much. It was a way we could help her,' they told me. 'She's a wonderful mother, and he's a gorgeous child.' And how is William doing, now that he's nine, I asked? 'He's a very, very well-adjusted young man,' Linda replied. On seeing photographs of his grandmother in hospital, he worked out for himself that she had given birth to him. He asked, 'Who had me? Was it Gran, or was it you, Mum?' William was five at the time. He told his school friends all about it, and they didn't bat an eyelid. How is your relationship with William, I was curious to find out? 'We know what our role is,' they replied. 'We are his grandparents.'

***

Since the early days of surrogacy in the 1980s, attitudes have become more accepting, especially in countries where surrogacy is regulated or practised according to strict legal and ethical guidelines. But surrogacy remains a contentious topic, and one in which the views of supporters of traditional family values have coalesced with those of some feminists who consider surrogacy to represent the ultimate exploitation of women. But one strongly held belief about surrogacy — that the children would suffer psychological harm by being born to one woman and raised by another — has not been borne out by the evidence. We found the opposite; the children were doing well and had good relationships with their parents. And the answer to the question of who they saw as their 'real' mother was crystal clear. It was the one who raised them. Some of the children were close to their surrogate, but they didn't see her as their mother.

In 2016, Kim Cotton interviewed Alice, one of the twins she gave birth to in 1991, for an article on surrogacy that she had been invited to write for a law journal. Alice has known that she was born through surrogacy for as long as she can remember, and is proud of who she is and where she comes from. She said, 'Surrogacy has not affected me in any negative way. I have grown up in a normal family household, having a normal childhood, and now feel as "normal" an adult as anyone else.' At school, many of the children did not understand about surrogacy and asked her questions. When Alice was born, she was front page news, so she used these articles to explain her birth. Growing up, surrogacy didn't impact upon her life on a daily basis, but when she thought about it, she felt special, wanted, and loved. Alice ended by saying, 'To the surrogates, you are truly amazing and selfless. You give a gift that can never be equalled. Without women like you, the world would not be as bright. I am thankful every day for my mum and Kim, for fighting science and the media, and to Kim for carrying my brother and I for nine months, only to give my mum the biggest gift in the world. To the families, treasure your precious babies for they are the most special of all.'

Gee Roberts, writing about her experiences as a young adult born through surrogacy for the COTS Christmas Newsletter in 2018, shared similar sentiments. She said: 'As a surrogate baby, I feel privileged to have been born in a way that makes me so different from everybody else that I know. It means that I always have that "tell me an interesting fact about yourself" question covered, and my answer of "I was the 250th surrogate baby born through COTS" takes people aback. It has shaped my life massively and will continue to do so forever, and I am very lucky to exist as part of a wonderful story of human goodness. Surrogacy is a very special thing, and to be born based on dedication and unconditional love from my parents, and selfless kindness from my surrogate, is a blessing.'

Chapter 6

Gay Father Families: 'Beyond Our Wildest Dreams'

'Please don't pretend two dads is the new normal.'

DAILY MAIL NEWSPAPER, (2018).

'Everyone looks at me and thinks: she's got gay dads, how cool. Lots of people have divorced parents but my story's special. I'm the one with the gay dads. It makes me feel special, in a good way.'

LAUREN, AGE 17, (2009).

When Anthony Brown and Gary Spino moved into their modest apartment in New York's Greenwich Village in 1990, it was some time before they met Janet McDevitt, their elderly neighbour on the second floor. Janet only ever left the apartment block to go shopping, always at night. She was fiercely independent but physically frail because of a chronic lung disease. When Janet returned from her outings, she would sit in the lobby to collect her breath before tackling the stairs. Whenever they saw her, Anthony and Gary carried Janet's bags upstairs and left them hanging on her doorknob. They gave her their phone number and encouraged her to call them if she needed anything, but despite their friendship, Janet never let them past her front door.

Anthony and Gary did not see inside Janet's home until one morning in 2002 when their phone rang at 4 am. Janet had fallen and couldn't get up. The moment they entered her apartment, they understood why she had never invited them in. Janet was a hoarder. Her small, one-bedroom apartment was packed floor to ceiling with her belongings. It was filthy, there were vermin, and there was food everywhere. Fortunately for Janet, Gary, an avid watcher of the TV show *Hoarders*, had taken a class on 'How to declutter your home' and knew exactly what to do. He asked Janet for permission to clear a space on the sofa so that he could sit her there. Janet agreed, and Gary slowly began to move a few of Janet's possessions. That was the night their friendship really began.

From then on, the couple kept a close eye on Janet. When she was first diagnosed with cancer, they visited her regularly in hospital, taking her mail and her cheque book with them so that they could attend to her affairs for her. Following a spell in rehab for the cancer, Janet was signed out to Anthony and Gary. They informed the social workers that her living conditions were not conducive to her health, and that she would end up back in hospital if nothing was done, but their warnings fell on deaf ears. Altogether, Janet went through the cycle of hospital, rehab, and discharge home three times. The last was terminal. Janet passed away six years after she had first met Anthony and Gary. She was 76.

It turned out that Janet McDevitt, in her earlier days, had been a very different person from the woman Anthony and Gary had befriended. They were amazed to discover her story. She had come from a wealthy Cincinnati family whose fortune had, against the odds, survived the Great Depression of the 1930s. As a young woman, she had lived in Positano, Italy, then a sea-side haunt of the rich and famous. Janet had fallen in love with a Berber and moved with him to Morocco, but her North African sojourn ended suddenly when she discovered she was pregnant with a child she did not want. She'd retreated to Italy for an abortion. Perhaps the experience was too unsettling, even for intrepid Janet. She returned to New York when she was in her early thirties, married an oil magnate, and lived a conventional life on Central Park West. Whether or not the abortion played a part in this we'll never know, but the couple were unable to have children. For Janet, her marriage was a loveless one that had lost its meaning without children. She did not want her husband's money, but she did want her name back and to return to her old apartment in Greenwich Village. She divorced her husband and built a new life among the up-and-coming artists of the day — Jackson Pollock, Lee Krasner, Mark Rothko, and the emerging group of abstract expressionists that were to define American art in the mid-20th century. The gift of a painting from Janet that Anthony and Gary had thought ugly, but hung in their apartment to please her, turned out to be by Theodoros Stamos, one of the original abstract expressionist painters living and working in New York in the 1940s and 50s. But the biggest surprise of all came when Janet passed away, and they discovered that she had left half of her estate to them.

'We didn't know she had money,' said Gary. 'We loved her and we took care of her. It was literally on her death bed, on the last day she could talk, that she told us.' Because of the way she'd lived, the couple had always assumed that Janet was hard up. For Anthony and Gary, the inheritance meant that they could have the family they had always wished for. In August 2013, their son Nicholas was born with the help of Shannon, their surrogate, and Holly, their egg donor.

Anthony and Gary's route to parenthood was long and complicated. Anthony had grown up in suburban Richmond, Virginia, with a brief spell in California, before returning to his home state when he was 12 years old. Moving back to Virginia and coping with a new school was traumatic for him. Although he didn't know he was gay, the children in his class teased and bullied him about it.

'One of the things that the kids did was that they carved the initials "TBIG" into every desk. It was written on every wall, in every bathroom,' he told me.

'What did that stand for?' I asked.

'Tony Brown is Gay,' he replied drily.

Anthony bottled up his feelings for three years until he broke down one day and opened up to his parents. They moved him to a different school, but it was not until he went to college and developed a passion for acting that he found his calling, eventually graduating from the renowned Juilliard School in New York. Although Anthony lived with a woman who he loved all through his time at Juilliard, they split up when he graduated. One year later, in 1989, he met Gary.

Anthony's mother was immediately supportive, but the prospect of telling his father was terrifying to him. Their relationship was more distant and, like many fathers and sons, they didn't find it easy to talk about their feelings. 'I planned a trip home to tell my dad, and my mom knew what I was doing, so she told him. My father called me and he said, "There is nothing that you could ever say to me that's going to make me stop loving you,"' Anthony recollected with tears in his eyes. From then on, their relationship became closer: 'And the first time that I took Gary home to meet my parents, they picked us up at the airport and they had a bottle of champagne in the car waiting to drive us back home, to celebrate!'

Gary's background was quite different from Anthony's. All four of his grandparents had emigrated from southern Italy to the United States, and Gary had grown up with his sister and two brothers in a traditional Roman Catholic family in the Italian neighbourhood of a small town in Pennsylvania where, as he described it, 'Everybody was related and everybody married each other and even their kids married each other.'

Coming out as gay at the age of 20 was extremely difficult for Gary and his family because of his strict Catholic upbringing. His parents took it badly, and he was treated cruelly by his classmates. But when he met Anthony, Gary's parents welcomed his new partner into their family, and when Gary's mother realised that gay men could have children, it changed everything. When she met Nicholas for the first time, she was overwhelmed with joy. The couple, who had met when they were 27, married on their 16th anniversary. When Nicholas was born, they had been together for 24 years.

Since the millennium, a small but rapidly growing number of gay couples like Anthony and Gary, mainly living in the United States, have become fathers with the help of a surrogate. Their children are conceived through IVF using one father's sperm and a donor's egg, and the resulting embryos are implanted in the surrogate who carries the pregnancy but has no genetic connection to the baby. In some cases, the surrogate's egg is used instead of a donor's to avoid the need for IVF, but that is less common as laws on surrogacy in the United States encourage the use of gestational surrogacy to give the intended parents greater security over parental rights. Children growing up in gay father families formed through surrogacy usually have two fathers — a genetic and a non-genetic father — and two biological 'mothers' — a gestational mother (the surrogate) and a genetic mother (the egg donor) — but don't have a mother who brings them up.

Although decades of research, including my own studies dating back to the 1970s, had shown that children with two mothers fare no differently to children with a mother and a father, it was widely assumed when married gay men began to be open about their sexuality in the 1980s and 90s that male same-sex parents wouldn't match up because men are less naturally suited to parenting than women. The belief that children need mothers is so ingrained that gay fathers face prejudice in their daily lives even now, not just from strangers but also from family and friends.

Until the 1970s, fathers were not believed to have a direct effect on their children's development; that was considered to be the domain of mothers. As the respected child psychiatrist, John Bowlby, put it in his landmark book, *Child care and the growth of love*, in 1953: 'Fathers have their uses even in infancy. Not only do they provide for their wives to enable them to devote themselves unrestrictedly to the care of the infant and toddler, but, by providing love and companionship, they support the mother emotionally and help her maintain that harmonious contented mood in the atmosphere of which her infant thrives.' It was only when the psychologist Michael Lamb, a leading expert on fathering, and others began to investigate fathers in their own right in the 1970s that it became clear that fathers are important too.

Today, following more than 40 years of research, not only is it accepted by psychologists that fathers do affect the development of their children, but also that the ways in which fathers and mothers influence their children are essentially the same. Just like mothers, fathers who are warm, sensitive, involved, and engage in appropriate discipline are more likely to have well-adjusted children than fathers who are distant, hostile, and over-controlling. But the research on fathering is based on families with a mother and a father. What about children with two fathers?

***

As with our previous research, we wanted to address the questions that were being asked about this new kind of family, and find out whether there were any grounds for the criticisms that were being directed at them by the Church, politicians, and the media. In 2002, the American Academy of Pediatrics published a report endorsing the adoption of children by lesbians and gay men, and the British government passed a law allowing same-sex couples to adopt children jointly. Both decisions triggered an onslaught against same-sex adoptive parents, especially if the parents happened to be men. The *Washington Times* wrote, 'How unfortunate that such a respected body as the American Academy of Pediatrics has opted to advance the militant homosexual agenda at the expense of scientific honesty and the very children it seeks to serve.' In the United Kingdom, the Children's Society, the Church of England's leading adoption agency, refused to comply with the law, although it later changed its position, against the will of many senior members of the church.

Is it really true that men are less nurturing and generally less competent at parenting than women? And do their children develop psychological problems as a result? By comparing families with two fathers to families with two mothers (so that both types of family are alike in having two same-sex parents but differ in the sex of the parents) we were able to examine whether men can parent as well as women. To me, gay father families formed through surrogacy were particularly interesting because they differed from the traditional family more than any other type of family that I had ever studied. In addition to having two fathers, the children were conceived using the egg of a donor, born to a surrogate, lacked a genetic connection to one parent, and did not have a mother. If these children did not experience psychological problems, I thought, this would tell us more clearly than any of my other studies that the structure of families mattered less for children than we had previously believed. We were interested in other questions too. Why had the fathers chosen surrogacy as a path to parenthood? What were their experiences of surrogacy? How did they get on with their surrogates and egg donors? And how did they explain to their children about their family? Unlike heterosexual couples who become parents with the help of a donor, like lesbian mothers, gay fathers don't have the choice of keeping it a secret; they will be faced with their children's inevitable questions about how they were born.

I was first inspired to embark on this research by a chance encounter with Jamie Marks, a civil rights lawyer who had represented the first same-sex couple in New York to be granted joint parental rights, at a conference on LGBTQ+ families organised by the Family Pride Coalition in Philadelphia in May 2006. Jamie, a father of two children born through surrogacy with his husband, Mark, thought that a study of the children of gay fathers similar to our previous research on the children of lesbian mothers would be helpful in informing policy-makers and legislators about gay father families, and hopefully disproving some of the prejudices his clients faced. Jamie's enthusiasm sparked my own, and following a long lunch at Le Cirque restaurant on my next visit to New York, I decided to go ahead. As few children had been born to gay fathers through surrogacy in the United Kingdom when we were planning our study, I approached my friend and colleague, Anke Ehrhardt, Director of the Division of Gender, Sexuality, and Health, and Vice-Chair of the Department of Psychiatry, at Columbia University in New York, where I had spent an inspiring and enjoyable sabbatical as a Visiting Professor in 2004–5, to ask whether she might be willing to collaborate on a study of gay father families in the United States. Anke was a trailblazer, one of the foremost scholars of human sexuality worldwide, and founder of the HIV Center for Clinical and Behavioural Studies at Columbia University, established in 1987 to help combat AIDS. I had met her at an early meeting of the International Academy of Sex Research in Haifa, Israel, in 1978, and had followed her ground-breaking work ever since. If anyone could help make my study of gay fathers happen, it would be Anke. We planned the project in New York in the spring of 2013, and got started in the autumn of that year.

Our first task was to construct the team. The study would be run from Cambridge by Lucy Blake, a psychologist at the Centre for Family Research, assisted by researchers in New York. As this study had been included in the five-year grant awarded to me in 2013 by the Wellcome Trust, for once, funding did not present a problem. We received a great deal of help from a number of LGBTQ+ organisations, who agreed to spread the word, including the gay fathers' association, Men Having Babies, the Family Equality Council, and the LGBT Center in New York. Surrogacy agencies that worked with gay men also helped us recruit families to the study. Lucy, together with Susan Imrie and Sophie Zadeh from our team in Cambridge, also collected data at Family Week in Provincetown, Cape Cod, in 2014 and 2015, an annual vacation for families with LGBTQ+ parents, and made all of us in Cambridge feel quite envious when they sent back photos of swimming pool parties and campfire nights on the beach.

We enrolled 40 gay father families to the study, and a comparison group of 55 lesbian mother families, all with a child aged between three and nine years. The lesbian mothers had used donor insemination to become pregnant, so both types of family were similar in that they had been created through assisted reproduction. Comparing gay fathers with lesbian mothers would tell us more clearly about any differences that existed between men and women as parents than a comparison between gay father families and traditional families in which there was a father in the home.

Together with our team in the United States, we interviewed the families about their experiences, using similar assessments to those in our earlier studies. Our findings clearly refuted the idea that men are less capable parents than women. Not only did the gay fathers have just as positive relationships with their children as the lesbian mothers, which demonstrated that fathers can parent as well as mothers when motivated to do so, their children showed even lower levels of emotional problems than the children of lesbian mothers. This result was unexpected. Why were the children of gay fathers particularly well adjusted? One possible explanation, put forward by a reviewer of our study when we sent an article on the findings to an academic journal for publication, is that men may be less sensitive to children's emotional problems than women because men may be less 'tuned-in' — and so failed to describe them to our researchers. Alternatively, gay fathers may make especially good parents. The teachers seemed to think so, giving these children very positive assessments.

But one finding from our study was less heartening. Like the children of lesbian mothers, some children were stigmatised by their peers because their fathers were gay. Not surprisingly, in both family types, children whose parents experienced greater stigmatisation showed higher levels of behavioural problems. In the study we carried out in the

United Kingdom with Stonewall, in which we looked at the school experiences of children with same-sex parents, the children with gay fathers were very positive about their families. Some enjoyed feeling special. But others felt unfairly singled out, just as we found with children of lesbian mothers. As William told us, 'Normally people just say "gay dad" and stuff like that, and then some people pretend they just found out and say, "Is this true and this true?" and just keep asking. I know they know so it gets annoying. Normally I try and say something back because it makes me feel better. Or I just try and ignore it. That's harder obviously. I wasn't happy to go to school because I knew it would happen.'

***

Like Anthony and Gary, the gay men in our study had grown up thinking that they would never be fathers. John came out as gay when he was 17. It was 1978, and gay people faced enormous prejudice, but he considered himself fortunate. He was at college in Cambridge, Massachusetts, and there were gay support groups, gay social groups, and, as he described it, gay dances with more than a thousand people. But he had one regret. He was extremely close to his family and was distraught that he wouldn't be able to have a family of his own: 'The hardest thing for me was not being able to have children,' John explained. 'I really, really wanted to have kids, but I pushed it into the background. I thought I could be fulfilled and do things for society and have a successful career. And so I sort of made my peace with it because at that time there was never any possibility of having kids.' But times changed, and after 20 years together, in 2012, John and his husband Alan had their first daughter, Kate, through surrogacy, soon followed by their second daughter, Anne.

Peter, another participant in our study, also thought that parenthood was not an option for him. But, like John, his closeness to his own family made him think again. It was when he moved back to the area where he grew up, around family, that he began to feel he would like to have children. Peter had been in a committed relationship with Sean for 15 years when their daughter, Jodie, was born in 2009.

When we asked the fathers why they had chosen surrogacy as a path to parenthood, we found that some had initially thought about adopting children but discovered that adoption by gay men was either prohibited or not encouraged in their state at the time, and international adoption by gay men was usually illegal. Adoption also raised complications that some prospective gay fathers found daunting, such as the possibility of being required to stay in touch with an adopted child's birth parents. A particular advantage of surrogacy, important to some, was that it enabled one or both partners to have a genetic connection to their children. But surrogacy is not available to everyone: at a cost of $100,000 and upwards in the United States, it is an option for only a tiny minority of gay men, and elsewhere, with the exception of a handful of countries including Canada, Denmark, the Netherlands, the United Kingdom, and some Australian states, it is illegal, although, like heterosexual couples, some gay couples travel to countries in Eastern Europe or Asia where laws are more lenient. Gay couples usually opt for gestational rather than traditional surrogacy, with some saying that they had decided upon a separate surrogate and egg donor to help cement their own family as their child's primary family unit.

One decision gay couples who opt for surrogacy have to make is who will be the genetic father of their children. Although some couples say that it is not important to them, having a biological link to their child may matter more to one partner than the other, or both partners may wish to have a biological child. Sometimes the couple will decide to mix their sperm together and leave biological paternity to chance. John and Alan intended to have two children from the start, and took it in turns to be the biological father. The first time, the clinic mixed sperm from both men with the donor's eggs. It turned out that John was the biological father of their first daughter. The next time, only

Alan's sperm was used, and he became the biological father of their second daughter. As their girls were born from eggs from the same donor, they are half-siblings and look similar to each other. For couples who mix their sperm, genetic testing can establish biological paternity, but gay fathers usually do not need to take a test. Children look like their parents and, as they grow older, it becomes hard to ignore these resemblances. John said that within two years, it was apparent who was the biological parent of each of their daughters. But the couple made a point of not discussing it outside the family as they didn't want people to focus on that.

Surrogacy also offers the possibility of having twins, with one twin genetically related to one father and one twin genetically related to the other. For this to happen, each partner creates embryos using his sperm and the donor's eggs. Twins are by no means guaranteed. Sometimes only one embryo, and sometimes neither, will develop. But if only one baby is born, each father has had an equal chance of being the genetic parent. Gay fathers who mix their sperm may end up with more than they bargained for. In 2016, a gay couple in South Africa became the fathers of triplets after they each contributed an embryo and one divided into twins.

The announcement that John and Alan were having a baby was greeted with delight by John's parents. They hadn't expected him to have children, and they were overjoyed. Alan's mother was not so thrilled by the news. She had refused to meet John for the first five years of the couple's relationship. When the couple told her they were expecting a baby, she said that they were going to ruin a child's life. But when the children were born, everything changed. Now she is an adoring grandmother of two little girls.

When gay couples tell their gay friends that they are going to be parents, the reaction is sometimes less than enthusiastic, and they often lose touch with their gay friends who don't have children. John and Alan's friends were positive at first, but soon there was a parting of the ways. 'We straddle both worlds now,' John told us, 'but most of our world is families, kids, and school. And most of that world is straight, so we've become the straightest gay people on the planet.'

Derek and Jeremy, who live in California with their five-year-old twins, Callum and Hannah, had a similar experience. 'Our friends were very excited and supportive, with the exception of our gay friends,' explained Derek. 'We do have gay friends who we have become a lot closer to who are also parents. But we don't have a lot of gay friends who are not parents, and the ones that we do have are generally those who are interested in becoming parents themselves.'

Some of the fathers in our study felt stigmatised by strangers. Occasionally, this took the form of outright hostility. More commonly, the stigmatisation was subtle. They were excluded by the mothers at their children's schools — left out of coffee mornings and other social events — and mothers proffered unsolicited advice on how to bring up their children that the fathers felt they wouldn't have given to other women.

Many gay fathers, like Anthony and Gary, involve their surrogate in their lives as their child grows up; this was true of 85 per cent of the fathers in our study. 'The agency matched us with a really fantastic woman, we couldn't have asked for a better person, she was just wonderful,' said Peter. The families meet up once or twice a year, call each other on holidays, and send each other Christmas packages.

John and Alan have had a more problematic relationship with one daughter's surrogate than with the other daughter's, which they put down to her issues with her own family. They are still in touch with both of their surrogates, and both read a poem at their wedding, but they have a closer relationship with their older daughter's surrogate. The two families have been on holiday together and all of the children get on very well. 'I wish we did have a little bit better relationship with our younger daughter's surrogate,' said John. 'I just feel bad for our younger daughter that she doesn't see her surrogate nearly as much as our older daughter does. And I feel badly for the surrogate because she's got such a lot going on.'

When distance makes visiting difficult, the families stay in contact in other ways, such as through social media. This is how Derek and Jeremy keep in contact with their surrogate. 'She did an amazing thing for us and she's a wonderful woman. Shortly after the children were born, she and her family moved to Oregon. It's quite far. We stay in touch via Facebook. So we get to see pictures of her and her family, and her kids as they've grown older, and she can do the same. We send her flowers every year on the children's birthday. It's important to us to know how she's doing, and to let her know that we think of her often and fondly, and appreciate the gift that she gave us.'

Although most fathers in our study had met, or had been in contact with, their egg donor before or during the pregnancy — something that is not always possible in countries that permit egg donation — they were less likely to keep in touch with their egg donor than with their surrogate once their baby was born, although the majority of fathers had deliberately chosen an egg donor who was open to being contacted in the future if that was their child's wish. When John and Alan met their donor, the most important question for them was whether or not she would be willing to meet their future children, and she agreed. They wanted to be able to tell their children that if they ever want to contact their donor, they could. Derek and Jeremy also met their donor, an occasion Derek described as, 'The world's most awkward first date.' He explained, 'There were so many things that we wanted to know. What we focused on was just the element of warmth, which is something that you can't get from a piece of paper, or even a video. This was somebody who we may never see again, and certainly not for many, many years. But in the back of our minds was that at some point down the road this woman might be back in our lives, and so from that perspective, I think it was very good that we met her.'

A task that gay fathers, like lesbian mothers, are faced with early on is talking to their children about how their family differs from other families. This can help children cope with the questions and comments that they will inevitably encounter. Just as adoptive parents are advised to respond to children's questions about their adoption as and when they arise, gay fathers are recommended to do the same. Often these conversations are triggered by the child and come up at unpredictable moments, as happened to Peter. 'It was funny, when Jodie was around two, I remember potty training her and she was sitting on the potty and I'm sitting in the bathroom and we're waiting for a million years for her to go and then she was like, "I don't have a Mommy", and I was like, "No you have two daddies, a Daddy and a Poppa." It was a surprise.' As well as talking about having two dads, gay fathers have to tell their children about their birth. Surrogacy and egg donation can be difficult to explain to young children so initial conversations need to be simple. 'We just say that she came from our surrogate's belly, that's really about it,' said Peter. 'We'll say "Where do you come from?" and she'll say "Jesus" which is very cute and endearing, but that's it. She hasn't really asked so we haven't pushed it further because, you know, she is only five.' Derek and Jeremy have taken a similar approach. 'We've never used the word surrogacy,' said Derek. 'They are still five. What we have told them is that there is a wonderful woman, and when Daddy and I decided that we wanted to have a baby we asked her if we could borrow her belly, and she agreed. That's where you came from. You were in the surrogate's belly, and as soon as you came out Daddy and I were there in the hospital, so we've been with you since the day you were born. Your parents are me and Daddy, and you have two dads instead of a mom and a dad, and that's all that we've really said about the way that they were born.'

Our study was the first in-depth investigation of parents and children in gay father families formed through surrogacy, and so the results must be treated with caution. Because we recruited volunteers, it's possible that those fathers who had a particularly positive experience were more likely to participate in the research. Also, given the high cost of surrogacy in the US, these fathers generally had a high income, although this did not seem to explain why the children were thriving when we explored this possibility in our statistical analyses; those on lower incomes were doing equally well. Although we must keep these issues in mind, the findings so far tell us that gay fathers with children born through surrogacy do just as good a job as other parents.

The fathers we spoke to felt extremely fortunate to have been able to have children through surrogacy. 'I feel very blessed that I was born at a time, and at a place in the world, where it was a possibility,' said Derek. 'I can't imagine my life without kids in it. And I don't know how that could have ever happened if I had been born in just about any other place in the world and, certainly, if I had been born any other time in the world. I think about that all the time.'

John feels the same way, 'It's the best thing we've ever done in our lives. I feel like saying to my gay friends who don't have kids, "You should all have kids. You don't know what you're missing!"'

***

In September 2018, when I visited Diego Diaz and Melvyn Jones, adoptive fathers of Kerry, 15, Robert, 11, and Jamie, four, in their comfortable and stylish home in a picturesque street in a city on the south coast of England, the family was still reeling from a visit from the police. Kerry's birth father had just been released from a 13-year prison sentence for violent crime, and had been housed just three streets away. This blow came on top of the discovery, a few years earlier, that Kerry's birth mother also lived nearby, and that her son, by a different father, was at the same school as Robert. Kerry's birth mother, whose sisters had all had children under the age of 16, was 13 and in foster care when Kerry was born, and couldn't look after her baby. Kerry had been taken into care and adopted by Diego and Melvyn when she was 18 months old. She occasionally bumps into her birth mother in the street. Sometimes that makes her happy, and at other times, angry and upset.

Robert, the youngest of his birth mother's 14 children, ten by one father and four by another, was also placed with Diego and Melvyn when he was 18 months old, three and a half years after they adopted Kerry. Like Kerry, Robert's birth father had committed serious crimes and was considered to present a risk to children. Robert was already an uncle to five nieces and nephews, some of whom are older than him, because his eldest sisters, aged 28 and 32, had already had children. Diego and Melvyn didn't know it at the time they adopted Robert, but he was badly affected by foetal alcohol syndrome, caused by his birth mother's alcohol dependence when she was pregnant, which has had a profound impact on his learning ability. Robert is very behind at school, performing at the level of a seven or eight-year-old although he is 11, and he is struggling to adapt to his recent move from junior school, where everyone knew him, to a senior school with 2,000 children.

Jamie, the youngest, joined the family as a baby, three and a half years after Robert. His birth mother, who had grown up in the care system, became pregnant when she was 18 with her 14-year-old boyfriend. Jamie was born with cerebral palsy and, as a result, has impaired speech, mobility issues, and behavioural difficulties, often flying into a rage out of frustration because he can't speak. The day I visited was Jamie's first day at school, and his fathers were concerned that Jamie might not receive the support that he needed for his physical and developmental problems.

Diego, a part-time customer service agent at London Airport, and Melvyn, who runs a bespoke artisan business, decided on domestic adoption as there were so many children in need of an adoptive family in the United Kingdom, and they wanted to be open about their relationship which would not have been possible had they embarked on international adoption in a country such as India or China. Diego and Melvyn love their children to bits, and are completely dedicated to them, but acknowledge that adopting children from the child welfare system can be extremely challenging. 'These children were in care for a reason,' said Diego. 'I think all the love in the world cannot, sometimes, plug the hole that these kids have got in their soul. They will push you to the limit and back, time and time again, because the worst has already happened to them. You cannot use the same parental skills that you have learned from your parents. You were given up at birth, you feel neglected, you were rejected, so saying to a child, "If you carry on speaking to me like that, you're not going to watch your favourite television programme" … it just doesn't work!'

Despite the immense challenges, Diego stressed to me the pleasures of being adoptive parents: 'It has enriched our lives. We have done amazing things, we've been on wonderful holidays, and even the little one who has cerebral palsy loves football, and he is in a special football team for children with cerebral palsy. The paces are small and tiny, but in a way I think they're more special because they're huge steps to these kids. Our middle one still wets the bed, but he's been on a school trip and we've managed that, and he came home full of pride, and a sense of belonging to the rest of them, because he was able to go on the school trip.'

Diego is the first to admit that bringing up three adopted children who were maltreated by their birth parents is not for the faint-hearted. As he put it, 'These kids come from trauma, they are traumatic to handle, and they give you trauma.' He added, 'I think it's very helpful to sometimes take time out and think, "Okay, we are doing well. Everyone's dressed, everyone's clean, no one's got nits, they've all been fed, and everyone's where they're supposed to be." That's very cathartic to me!' It's the routine of family life that Diego finds most rewarding: 'I'm delighted when they come in. They'll say, "Hi", they give you a kiss and say, "What's for dinner?" You'll polish their shoes and they'll sort out the homework and you help them where you can. And you thank your lucky stars every morning that you've got these kids and then you sometimes think, "Oh my gosh, imagine if they were still in care!'"

***

It wasn't until a new law was passed in the United Kingdom in 2002, allowing same-sex couples to adopt children jointly, that gay men began to be considered as prospective adoptive parents. The change in legislation was a long time coming. In the late 1990s, I was invited to attend a meeting with the Health Minister and, among others, a representative from Stonewall and a member of the House of Lords who had been raised by his mother and her lesbian partner. It was at that meeting that the British government began to seriously consider this issue. To my amazement, the Health Minister was so persuaded by the evidence presented by those around the table that she instructed the civil servants who were drafting the bill to be presented before parliament to alter the clause on adoption by same-sex parents to enable both partners to be the legal parents of their adopted children.

When the new legislation eventually came into force in 2005, many adoption agencies had concerns. Some social workers felt that because children who had been put up for adoption were emotionally vulnerable due to the traumas that had led to them being removed from their birth families in the first place, being adopted by same-sex parents, especially gay men, would be an additional burden for them. The arguments against adoptive gay fathers were similar to the objections to gay men having children through surrogacy; not only were they gay, but they were also male, neither of which was assumed to be conducive to caring for children. The combined effect of these two factors was thought to be detrimental to the social, emotional, identity, and gender development of already at-risk children.

In 2009, the British Association of Adoption and Fostering, the national organisation for adoption agencies, held a conference to discuss this issue, at which I was invited to give the opening lecture. It became clear from the adoption professionals present that there was a need to understand the outcomes for children adopted by gay men. Were adoptive fathers as effective as parents of vulnerable children as adoptive mothers? And did children who were adopted by gay fathers face greater difficulties than children with adoptive mothers? Because of our background in studying lesbian mother families, the Centre for Family Research seemed the obvious home for the research, so our first UK project on gay father families was initiated that day.

With the support of the British Association of Adoption and Fostering, who helped us recruit families to the study, and a grant from the Economic and Social Research Council, the government body responsible for funding social science research in the United Kingdom, we began our investigation. My colleague, Michael Lamb, a world expert on fathering, and Fiona Tasker, who had worked with me on our follow-up study of people raised by lesbian mothers, joined the project, together with Laura Mellish and Sarah Jennings who visited each of the families in their homes. The study included adoptive gay father families and comparison groups of adoptive lesbian mother families and adoptive families with heterosexual parents. All of the families had two parents who had been together for an average of 12 years. The ages of the children ranged from almost four to just over eight. The children had all been adopted from the child welfare system because their birth parents were unable to look after them, and they had lived in their adoptive families for at least one year.

The fathers in our study chose adoption as their route to parenthood for a variety of reasons. Adoption not only gave them the status of joint legal parents of their children, but also an equal, non-genetic relationship to their children. Many said that having a genetically related child was not important to them. They also felt that adoption was an ethical way to become parents because there were so many children in need of adoptive families. These fathers did not want the complications of sharing parenting with a birth mother in a different family, and on top of the prohibitive cost, some felt uncomfortable about surrogacy.

As with our previous research, we were interested in different aspects of family life; the psychological wellbeing of the parents, the quality of the relationship between the parents and their children, and the adjustment of the children. We used a similar approach to our earlier investigations — involving parents, teachers, and children — but tailored our assessments to the specific types of family in the study.

Although the parents in all three family types had low levels of psychological and relationship problems, and were highly committed to their children, gay fathers showed lower levels of depression and found parenting less stressful than the heterosexual mothers and fathers. The gay fathers also showed higher levels of warmth and responsiveness towards their children, lower levels of aggression when disciplining them, and spent a greater amount of time with their children, compared to the heterosexual parents. The lesbian mothers fell in between.

Not surprisingly, the children in all family types showed high levels of behavioural problems according to the parents and teachers. Research on adopted children generally has shown that children who are maltreated in the years before their adoption are at high risk of developing psychological problems, and the older they are before being placed in their adoptive families, the greater the risk. Although we were unable to obtain accurate details on the experiences of all of the children in the study before they were adopted, from the information that we had, we discovered that more than one-third of the children's birth mothers had mental health problems, were dependent on alcohol, or had been victims of domestic violence, and more than one-third of the children's birth fathers had been convicted of criminal behaviour, just like Kerry and Robert's birth fathers. Many of the children had experienced horrendous abuse. More than two-thirds had been neglected, almost half had endured emotional abuse, almost one-fifth had been victims of physical abuse, and just under 5 per cent had suffered sexual abuse. A similar proportion of children in each family type had experienced these traumas.

A child psychiatrist, who was unaware of the children's family backgrounds, examined the section of parents' interview transcripts on the children's emotions and behaviour. One quarter of the children were classified by the child psychiatrist as having a psychological disorder, a learning difficulty, or both. A higher proportion of these children were from the heterosexual parent families. To answer questions raised by social workers, we also looked at the gender identity and gender role behaviour of the children, and found no differences between family types for either boys or girls.

We can't be sure why the gay father families were found to be doing better than the heterosexual parent families. Perhaps it was because the gay fathers had not experienced the stress of infertility and failed fertility treatments that all of the heterosexual parents, and half of the lesbian mothers, had gone through. The gay fathers also appeared to have less challenging children — possibly because the most troubled children were less likely to be placed with them due to the uncertainty about gay men as suitable adoptive parents — which may explain their more positive relationships with their children. On the other hand, these gay fathers were some of the first to adopt children in the United Kingdom, and may have been subjected to a particularly stringent screening process owing to the concerns about their parenting abilities, and may have been especially motivated and dedicated to parenting adopted children.

Adolescence can be a difficult time for adoptive families. This is when young people focus on their identity, asking themselves who they are, and who they want to be. Adopted adolescents are faced with the additional question of who they are as an adopted person. As described by Hal Grotevant and David Brodzinsky, the leading American experts on the psychology of adoption, adolescents need to integrate the experience of being adopted into their life story in order to develop a secure sense of identity. As part of this process, some adolescents become curious about their birth family, searching for information about them, and trying to find them, if they are not already in contact. But not all do. The challenge for parents is to communicate openly and supportively about their children's birth families, and the reasons for their adoption, in order to promote a positive identity in their adopted children.

Because of the special significance of adolescence for adopted children, Anja McConnachie and Nadia Ayed from the Centre for Family Research began to follow up with the families in our study in 2015, approximately six years after we had first met them, when the children were aged between ten and 14. As expected, parents in all three family types reported greater difficulties now that their children were adolescents; half were now considered to have a learning difficulty, an emotional or behavioural disorder, or a mixture of psychological problems. Many of the parents were struggling to cope, and had to fight hard for the support their children needed. We interviewed the children to explore their attachment to their adoptive parents, using a method developed by psychologists Howard and Miriam Steele from the New School for Social Research in New York, both highly respected scholars in the field of children's attachment relationships. In line with the findings of the first phase of the study, we found that the children in gay father families were more likely to be securely attached to their parents than the children in heterosexual parent families.

Diego and Melvyn's daughter, Kerry, is one of the teenagers who took part in our study when she was 13. Kerry likes exploring the woods and having adventures near her grandparents' farm, climbing trees, riding horses, and going out for family dinners. When asked to describe herself she said, 'I am not a serious, sensible person. I like being funny and joking around.' She thinks the best thing about herself is that she has a good family and nice friends: 'Papi is really, really kind.

I think he loves me very much. We get on brilliantly.' When they argue, it's about tidying her bedroom; Kerry thinks that Papi cleans too much. 'Daddy loves me too. He goes out a lot and I like to go with him. We go cycling together and walk the dog. It's really nice.' Kerry adores her adoptive brothers. She likes to play with Robert, read to him, and watch *Harry Potter* films with him, and she finds her younger brother very cute: 'When I'm doing my homework, I get distracted and give him hugs. I let him ride on my shoulders. He loves it. He's adorable.' At school, Kerry likes sport best and is not so keen on geography. When she grows up, she thinks she might like to be an author or a vet. Kerry says that her friends like her dads because 'They're both nice, kind, and caring,' and recently one of her friends said, "Lucky you!"'

In a similar study to ours, the psychologist Rachel Farr and colleagues in the United States compared gay father, lesbian mother, and heterosexual parent families, all with adopted pre-school children, and followed up the families when the children were school age. In contrast to our UK study, the researchers found no differences in parenting quality between the family types, and the children showed few behavioural problems. The reason for the discrepancy between the findings of the two studies most probably lies in the different backgrounds of the children. All of the children in the US study had been adopted at birth or in the first few weeks of life, whereas many of the UK children had been neglected or abused by their birth family, and all had been in foster care, sometimes for several years. Children who are adopted at an older age are more likely to experience psychological problems than children adopted in infancy because of the adversities they experienced before being adopted.

***

While families with lesbian mothers can help us answer the perennial question, 'Do children need fathers?', gay father families can enlighten us about the much less common and more unexpected question, 'Do children need mothers?' This question is rarely asked simply because the answer is assumed to be an unequivocal 'yes'. This is partly because, even now, mothers in traditional families spend much more time caring for their children than fathers, and also because mothers are believed to be more nurturing and sensitive. Our research suggests that fathers who take responsibility for the upbringing of their children can be just as competent at parenting as mothers, and that children can flourish in the absence of a mother. Gay couples who have children through surrogacy, or who adopt children, go to great lengths to become parents, so perhaps it's not surprising that they become devoted fathers.

In striking contrast to the hostility experienced by lesbian mothers less than 40 years earlier, public reaction to gay fathers has been more subdued. In 2010, the birth of baby Zachary to the singer, Elton John, and his husband, David Furnish, through surrogacy and egg donation was greeted with congratulations rather than condemnation. With some exceptions in the right-wing media, the same was true when Olympic diver, Tom Daley, and his husband, Dustin Black, welcomed their son, Robbie, into the world in 2018. But gay fathers have not been universally accepted. In 2017, the McCain food company capitulated to public pressure by removing a television advertisement featuring a gay father family. And hostility comes from even the most unexpected quarters. In 2015, the gay fashion designers Dolce and Gabbana criticised Elton John and David Furnish for having children through surrogacy, describing their IVF children as 'synthetic'. Social attitudes have a long way to go, even in countries with relatively liberal legislation.

***

In July 2018, I caught up with Anthony Brown, who I had first met in November 2014 when I was invited to speak about our research on surrogacy at a Men Having Babies conference in New York, in his office in mid-town Manhattan. Anthony had given up acting many years earlier to become an attorney, focusing his practice on family law for lesbian and gay couples. His son Nicholas was now nine years old and flourishing, a happy child doing well at school, passionate about swimming, tennis, dancing, and reading. The family was still in touch with their surrogate, Shannon, and egg donor, Holly, mostly through postcards and social media, but meeting up whenever they could, and both women had met each other as well as Anthony and Gary's wider family. Anthony couldn't imagine being closer to Nicholas if he was biologically his son.

When I asked Anthony about his hopes and dreams for Nicholas, his answer was clear: 'More than anything, I want him to be happy. I want him to find whatever it is that makes him happy. I want him to like who he is. Because I struggled so much with not knowing who I was and then taking a long time to actually like myself. So that's my greatest dream for Nicholas.'

Anthony grew up in the generation of gay men for whom marriage and family seemed impossible. It was always a sadness in his life that he would never have children, but he accepted the reality of his situation. He is still incredulous that his dream of being a father came true. 'Having Nicholas is beyond our wildest dreams. Surrogacy is a leap of faith, and it is one that I thank God for every day. I wish it was available to more people. I'm just over the moon.'

Chapter 7

Single Mothers by Choice: 'Different Shapes'

'Some women are unfortunately forced to become single parents but to start out as a single mother from the outset on purpose is extremely selfish.'

DAME JILL KNIGHT MP, *DAILY TELEGRAPH* NEWSPAPER, (1991).

'I am very happy in my life. My mum's been two, three, four parents to me. She's been everything.'

JANE, AGE 18, DAUGHTER OF A SINGLE MOTHER BY CHOICE, (2010).

At the age of 40, two years after the break-up of a relationship, and following a series of unrewarding dates, Patricia Rhodes, who worked in publishing, decided it was now or never if she was going to have a child. 'I had held out hope that I would meet someone and everything would turn out how I wanted it, but it didn't happen,' she told me when we met in New York in the summer of 2018, over twenty years later. Knowing that she would have to take matters into her own hands, Patricia contacted the organisation Single Mothers by Choice: 'I went to a few meetings, which were pretty supportive because there were mothers who had already had children on their own. You could actually talk to living representatives and ask them about their experiences. It gave me the courage to try it,' Patricia explained. 'I didn't feel like a pioneer. It felt more to me like, "Damn it, if this is what I have to do, I'm going to do it!" I didn't think it was necessarily the best thing for a kid and sometimes I wondered if I was being selfish.'

At first, Patricia was unsure whether to ask someone she knew to be the biological father or whether to use a sperm donor. In the end, she decided on a sperm donor because she was fearful somebody she knew might demand involvement with her family in the future; a donor would have clearer boundaries. She looked for characteristics in her donor that were complimentary to her own; Patricia was good at art so she chose a donor who was good at maths, and who also seemed to be a nice person. Patricia's daughter, Cassie, was born in New York City in 1996.

Patricia moved to a neighbourhood in the New York borough of Queens where her brother, his wife, and their two-year-old son were living. 'I imagined Cassie and I would enjoy a loving, close-knit extended family and, in particular, I would get the support and experience of another mother,' said Patricia, whose own mother had passed away when she was 18 years old. 'Well, that turned out to be a big disappointment. On the other hand, I learned so much from my Italian and Greek neighbours about generosity, kids, and family relationships,' she remembered fondly, with tears in her eyes. Also, when Cassie was first born, Patricia's father and stepmother came to Queens often, 'My parents were great. It was very helpful to me just to have them there.'

Single mothers were viewed with suspicion in Patricia's conservative neighbourhood, no matter how the child was conceived, but as Patricia settled in, she found a wonderful child-minder for Cassie, and things got better. 'Cassie spent hours each day with a woman who could barely speak English and watched TV. It was against all the rules of what you're supposed to do with your child. But she was loved in that home. She was family.'

When Cassie was eight, they moved to New Jersey: 'We moved to a town that had been recommended because a lot of people from Manhattan and Brooklyn and Queens had moved there. It has a cosmopolitan, liberal vibe. There's a lot of single families and gay families and I felt it would be a really great place. It was a good choice. Cassie was very happy there. She loved her high school and she had great friends.'

Patricia began to talk to Cassie about her donor when she was four years old, and Cassie has always been open about her origins with friends and at school, speaking out in class when the topic was discussed to correct teachers who didn't get it right. 'I felt really cool,' said 16-year-old Cassie when she took part in a study of teenagers who had met their donor siblings that we carried out in 2013 in collaboration with colleagues from the New School in New York. 'I thought it was awesome. I guess everyone wants to have that one quirky story, and this was mine. It was a fun thing that made me unique, so I liked it.' When Cassie was 13, Patricia contacted the Donor Sibling Registry to try to discover whether any other children had been born from the same donor. Two weeks later, an email arrived; Cassie had a half-sister, Holly, who was exactly the same age.

With a mixture of apprehension and excitement, Patricia and Cassie set off to meet Holly and her mother at a Mexican restaurant in New York City. Cassie recalled, 'I was really excited, because it's so cool to find out you have a sister, but I was really nervous. I thought, "What if I don't like her, what if she's really obnoxious, or prissy, or really weird, and that we won't get along. Or what if I'd be the weirder sister." At dinner, after awkward hellos, we were both really quiet, just fiddling with napkins, and smiling and nodding. We were shocked and speechless.' Afterwards, they all went for a walk and the girls went ahead and had a chance to talk by themselves. 'When we walked together, we went through a list of questions to see if she and I had similarities. I was really excited. It was fun comparing her to myself.

We kept turning round to our moms and asking if we walked the same way, and things like that,' Cassie recollected. 'We really like to have the "Do you like that? I like that. Do you look like this? Oh, I look like this", conversation. If you were to meet a new friend, you'd have to go through a year of chit-chatting, getting to know them slowly. I feel that we skipped all that and went straight to being really close friends. I can talk to her about absolutely everything, just as much as I can my best friends. I feel that we just clicked, really, really quickly.' Now the girls meet up several times a year. 'We give each other the low-down on how our lives have been since the last time we met — friends, how things have changed, guy stuff. It's been a really positive experience.'

Cassie hopes to meet her donor one day. She doesn't want to have a close relationship with him, but she'd like to be on good terms and be able to ask him questions so that she can fill in the gaps in her knowledge of him and his family background, 'to see where the other half of me is from'. From the profile her mother received from the sperm bank, Cassie knows that if he could go anywhere on vacation it would be Aruba, he likes chicken, his favourite colour is blue, he's tall with wavy hair and brown eyes, he's really good at maths and science, he's athletic and musically talented, and his family are originally from Eastern Europe. As Cassie described it, 'It's like match.com but for your donor.' Cassie calls him her donor, never her dad: 'It's always been donor. It makes me uncomfortable when people say father. Father seems too literal. He's not my father. So there's just no point in calling him that.' But he does have a place in her life, 'It's like having a mystery as a father. He's omniscient in a sense. He's special to me because without him I wouldn't be here.'

***

In the United States, the terms 'choice moms' and 'single mothers by choice' are used interchangeably to refer to mothers like Patricia who choose to go it alone from the start and use sperm donation to conceive their babies. This became possible through the growth of sperm banks in the United States in the 1980s and 90s, which meant that single women could have children without the risk of the donor claiming parental rights. In 2000, Australia was one of the first countries to enact legislation allowing single women to have children using assisted reproduction procedures such as sperm donation and IVF. When a group of Catholic Bishops challenged the decision on the grounds that pregnancy should involve a man and a woman, and that a child has a right to be raised by a mother and a father, the High Court of Australia, the highest court in the land, ruled that it would be discriminatory not to give single women the same access to assisted reproduction as partnered women. But public opinion in Australia remained against it. A survey conducted at the time found that only 38 per cent of the population were in favour of single women having children through sperm donation; despite the High Court's decision, the traditional family continued to be seen as the optimal environment for raising children.

Four years later, in the United Kingdom, Suzy Leather, the Chairperson of the Human Fertilisation and Embryology Authority, announced that the law should be changed to give single women the same rights to fertility treatment as heterosexual couples. Although it was not, strictly speaking, illegal to do so, most clinics didn't offer sperm donation to single women, as the existing legislation required fertility clinics to consider a child's 'need for a father', which was widely interpreted to mean that single women should be excluded from treatment. In response to Suzy Leather's statement, *The Independent* ran a front-page story on the issue with the inflammatory headline, 'Fathers no longer required.' When the new legislation was passed in 2008, in which the clause on the need for a father was replaced with the 'need for supportive parenting', Iain Duncan Smith, a prominent member of the British parliament and former Leader of the Conservative Party, described it as 'the last nail in the coffin for traditional family life'.

In 2005, in Scotland, almost ten years after Patricia gave birth to Cassie in New York, Alice Ferguson, a 39-year-old graphic designer, decided to have a baby as a single mother. She had been in a three-year relationship with a man she loved, and wanted to have children with him, but he didn't want to be a father. 'I definitely wanted a child, and I thought it would be with him,' said Alice when she took part in our research in 2011. 'He was so bright and funny, and we got on so well. It seemed perfect, at first. But he just didn't want to have kids, and so that was that.' Alice then met someone else who was keen to have children, but she was not in love with him. As she was almost 40, her only option, she concluded, was to have a baby on her own even though it was not ideal. 'I'm not a single mother by choice. I wanted to have a husband,' she said, 'I don't know what we should call ourselves, but "by choice" sounds really militant, "by desperation" maybe!'

Alice conceived her daughter, Maria, by donor insemination at the London Women's Clinic, the first fertility clinic in the country to open its doors to single women. She chose the donor online from the catalogue of an American sperm bank so that she could find a donor who was willing to be identified in the future. This was important to Alice as she wanted her child to be able to contact the donor, should they wish to. The law had just changed in the United Kingdom to remove donor anonymity, and there was a shortage of donors who were willing to be identified. Her friend helped her choose and then she bought vials of his sperm. Alice had already made her decision but she paid extra for a 14-page profile of the donor, which she described as 'unbelievable'. 'There's so much detail. You know what hair colour everybody in the family's got and what any of the grandparents may have died of. I found out that the donor's grandfather had run as a Democratic candidate and lost by four votes.' Alice was surprised by how many similarities there seemed to be between this donor's family and her own. 'The thing that was heartening, but it spooked me as well, was that lots of the people in his family sound like our family. They're all sort of lefty, and there are music-y people, one of them is an anthropologist, and the donor's dad is a designer, like me.'

The donor's physical appearance was also a deciding factor for Alice as she thought it would be best to choose a donor who looked like her and the rest of her family. If her child looked different, she felt that it would automatically raise more questions in people's minds about who the father was, and maybe more questions in the child's own mind every time they looked in the mirror. 'I'm half Finnish and he's half Norwegian,' said Alice. 'I've got all these Finnish cousins that are quite tall and blonde, and it seemed like people in his family were tall and blonde as well. I really wanted someone who looks like me.'

It has always been important to Alice to be open about her daughter's conception. But it has not always been easy answering Maria's questions about her dad. When Maria was four she asked, 'Can we get a daddy?', and suggested they find one at the train station. When she was ten, she still wanted a dad, and wished that Alice would get married so that she would have one. Maria knew about her donor, and that one day she might be able to meet him and her donor siblings. She would ask questions about him. Why didn't Alice know him? What did she know about him? Did he know she had been born? These were conversations Alice hadn't anticipated having until Maria was much older. 'The other night, Maria said to me, "My friends think it's weird that you've never met my dad." I'm really aware that there's a sad tinge to it for her. When she was born I was very excited about it but I think now it's not quite as straightforward for the child. It's their life and they're having to figure it all out.'

In 2019, I caught up with Alice and Maria at their family home in Corstorphine in Edinburgh. They both welcomed me warmly and it was clear that the two were close. At 13, Maria's favourite subjects at school are science, art, and Spanish. As well as seeing her friends, she loves gymnastics and dancing. But her passion is cheerleading. Her team takes part in national competitions and has won medals. Maria still thinks it would be good if her mum married one day. She wishes she had a dad and would like Alice to 'go online dating'. Maria is happy to tell her friends about her family as long as she doesn't have to spend too long explaining, but sometimes her friends say they feel sorry for her which she finds annoying. When she's older she would like to meet her donor siblings; her 'squad', as she calls them. She thinks she might like to meet her donor too if she could do that together with her squad.

*****

On 11 March 1991, the revelation that a heterosexual woman who had never had a sexual relationship with a man had conceived a child using donor insemination in the United Kingdom was greeted with outrage. Articles with headlines such as, 'Storm over virgin births', 'Woman on course to claim science's first virgin birth', and 'Why one virgin birth was enough for us all', decried the practice. The *Daily Mail* claimed that it 'strikes at the very heart of family life', and that science is being misused to produce 'supermarket laboratories whose best-selling line is one-parent babies'. Members of the British Parliament called for it to be banned, insisting that the children would suffer. Dame Jill Knight MP said, 'To bring a child into the world deliberately with only one parent is highly irresponsible with no thought for the child', and Anne Winterton MP declared, 'The practice is wrong because it does not consider the best interests of the child. It is immoral and unnatural.' Doctors saw it as a medical problem, and labelled it the 'Virgin Birth Syndrome'. The Church was particularly opposed. A member of the Conservative Family Campaign, a Christian pressure group, described the phenomenon as 'repellent and selfish', and the Pope appointed a special commission to investigate it.

Antagonism against single mothers is nothing new. It is often claimed that single mother families are at the root of society's most chronic problems. Teenage delinquency, school drop-out, drug and alcohol abuse, antisocial behaviour, unemployment, and dependence on the welfare state have all been placed squarely at the feet of single mothers. But so-called 'virgin births' were something different. The announcement that single heterosexual women were actively choosing to become mothers — and didn't need to have a sexual relationship with a man to do so — caused consternation about the imminent demise of fathers and death of the traditional family.

Who are single mothers by choice? Why do they do it? And are they all virgins, as implied by the press? These were some of the questions that were being asked when the story broke. Our research on families formed through donor insemination had focused on two-parent families, so we were curious to know what happened if the mother was single. To find out, we began our first study of single mothers by choice in the early 2000s. By working closely with fertility clinics, we recruited 27 heterosexual single mothers by choice with babies born through donor insemination. In stark contrast to the picture that had been painted of them — as women who were deliberately setting out to undermine the traditional family — the large majority told us that they would have preferred to start their family with a partner. But by their late thirties, the time during which they would remain fertile was running out, and so they decided to have a biological child by themselves while it was still possible. Many felt that they did not have a choice. What's more, not one of the women was a virgin, and most hoped to have a partner in the future; they wanted companionship for themselves and a father for their child.

In 2008, I was visited by Mikki Morrissette, the founder of the Choice Moms website in the United States. She asked us to carry out a survey to find out more about who 'choice moms' are and what they are like. The survey, which was posted on the Choice Moms and Single Mothers by Choice websites, the two largest websites aimed at single mothers by choice, enabled us to access a larger group of 291 single mothers. We found that they were educated, financially secure, professional women. The majority had been in long-term relationships in the past but decided to go it alone, either because they didn't want to have a child with the wrong partner, or their partner didn't want to start a family. Single women do not take this decision lightly; they think long and hard about raising a child by themselves, and make sure that they are financially secure and have good support networks in place before they embark on motherhood, sometimes changing their career or moving to a child-friendly neighbourhood in advance. But this is not how they are portrayed. Single mothers by choice are often chastised for being selfish. A journalist writing in *The New York Times* in 2005 reported, 'Many single women still find the choice to get pregnant met with incomprehension or even hostility from friends, family, and some strangers. The most common accusation is that they are selfish, because of the widely held belief that two-parent homes are best for children.'

Making an active decision to become a single mother is not easy. Our survey found that three-quarters of the mothers had concerns about their child not having a father, especially if they had sons. Jane, mother of a four-year-old, was anxious that her son might 'not learn to do masculine things like house repair or manly sports, and not learn how to be a loving father', and Poppy, mother of a one-year-old, worried that 'my son will miss out on father-type activities and seeing male behaviours'. Mothers of girls were more likely to have misgivings about their daughters not being able to form healthy relationships with men. Georgie, a mother of two daughters, aged five and two, was concerned that, 'they will seek the attention of males at a young age to make up for the loss of attention they may have received from a dad', and Tessa, mother of an eight-year-old, said, 'I hope she doesn't think men are useless or bad. I try to let her know that marriages can be great.' Almost all of the mothers in our survey thought that it was important for children to have men in their lives to make up for not having a father, and most had enlisted male relatives and friends to play an active role. But not all of the mothers were concerned about their child not having a father. As Jackie, the mother of three sons, a seven-year-old and two-year-old twins, put it, 'I think if I prepare my kids properly, it'll be a confirmation that families take different shapes and it's not always a bad thing.'

Although some women have sex with a man who will not play a role in the child's life to get pregnant, and others go through the adoption process, the most common route to motherhood for single women is through sperm donation. Many single women prefer anonymous donors to avoid the unwanted complication of the biological father making a claim on the child in the future. Dee said, 'My concern was that a known donor would at some point decide he wanted to co-parent my child.' Another reason for choosing an anonymous donor is to protect the child from rejection. As Tanya explained, 'I worried about my child feeling rejected by a man that knows she is in the world, but doesn't want to be her "Daddy"'. Others, like Jan, opt for identifiable donors so that their children have the opportunity to contact him should they wish to do so: 'I used an "identity-release" donor, so my child can contact him when he turns 18. I was not comfortable with forever anonymous donors, because I want my son to decide whether to know his donor or not.' Kitty also chose a donor who is willing to release his identity when her child grows up: 'For me, this was the best choice — a donor who would have no part in our lives, so that I could anonymously raise my children, yet one who wouldn't always be some unknown background "spectre" in my sons' lives, but could be made tangible and real to them.' A small number chose a known donor. Janet said, 'I felt it was best for my child to have the option of knowing her biological father throughout her life, and if I could give this to her, I should.'

Single mothers worry about how their children will feel about being donor-conceived, and are faced with the complex decision of whether and what to say about the donor. Our survey of members of the Donor Sibling Registry found that single mothers are more likely than heterosexual couples to search for donor relatives; around 45 per cent of parents searching for donor relations were single mothers whereas only 20 per cent came from heterosexual couples. The main reason single mothers search is to give their children a clearer sense of identity by knowing about, and possibly meeting, their donor and donor siblings; 60 per cent of the single mothers gave this as a reason for joining the Donor Sibling Registry compared to 9 per cent of the heterosexual couples, and three times as many single mothers as heterosexual parents had met donor siblings. Single mothers are also more likely than heterosexual parents to tell their children about their donor conception, and to tell them when they are young, but this is not surprising as they have to explain to their children why they don't have a father.

Just as single mothers are more likely than heterosexual couples to search for donor siblings, so are their children. And children of single mothers by choice are more likely to search for their donor than children of lesbian couples, which suggests that knowing about their biological father is more important to children with one mother than it is to those with two mothers. Although most children use the term 'donor' to refer to their genetic father, children of single mothers by choice are more likely to call him 'father' or 'dad' than the children of heterosexual couples. Jim, aged 17, said, 'I dislike the word donor. He is my father. I have no other man as father.' Others referred to their donor as their father or dad, but didn't see him as a prominent figure in their lives: 'I'd like to know my dad,' said 16-year-old Keith, 'but since I've grown up without him, it's really no biggie.'

***

Is it the case that children in single mother families do less well than children in traditional families, as is claimed by the press? Two types of studies have set out to answer that question; studies of children who are being raised in single mother families because of their parents' divorce, and studies of children of unmarried single mothers, many of whom had unplanned pregnancies. The research on children with divorced single mothers was initiated in the 1980s, most notably by the psychologist Mavis Hetherington and her colleagues at the University of Virginia, in response to the increasing divorce rates in the United States, and in the 1990s by the psychologist Judy Dunn and colleagues in the United Kingdom. The research shows that these children are, on average, more likely to experience emotional and behavioural difficulties, and less likely to do well at school, than children who grow up with both parents at home. But many children whose parents divorce show no negative effects, and many of those who do, improve over time, especially if the divorce results in a more amicable relationship between their parents.

The studies of families headed by unmarried single mothers were prompted by the sharp rise in the number of children born to unmarried mothers from the 1960s, when the rate was under five per cent, to the early 2000s, when it rose to 20 per cent in the United States and 15 per cent in the United Kingdom. Two of the most highly regarded investigations are the Fragile Families Study in the United States, which looks at children born between 1998 and 2000, and the Millennium Cohort Study in the United Kingdom, which focuses on children born around 2000. Like the children with divorced single mothers, the children of unmarried single mothers had more educational, emotional, and behavioural problems than those with married parents.

But just because children in single mother families show poorer outcomes than children with two parents does not necessarily mean that the absence of a father is to blame. Researchers have found that growing up with a divorced single mother does not, in itself, appear to be harmful. Instead, it is the experiences that often accompany single motherhood that are responsible for children's problems. One important factor is the drop in income that many single mothers experience following divorce, often necessitating a move to a different neighbourhood where the family has no roots or support networks, and the children have to

189

start over with new friends and a new school. Another cause of children's difficulties is witnessing arguments and bitterness between their parents, sometimes for years before the parents separate. And children often have to cope with their mother's vulnerable emotional state after the divorce takes place. Depression is high among recently divorced mothers, which can impair the ability to be an effective parent. Similar factors are at play among children of unmarried single mothers. As with the children of divorced mothers, the poorer outcomes for the children of unmarried single mothers, compared to children with two parents, are largely explained by greater socio-economic disadvantage and the mothers' poorer mental health, rather than single parenthood, in itself.

Much of the concern about single mothers by choice stems from the assumption that if children of divorced or unmarried single mothers whose pregnancies were not planned do less well than children with two parents, then the children of single mothers by choice will experience difficulties too. But that's not necessarily true. Single mothers by choice are different from divorced or unmarried single mothers. Like Patricia and Alice, they have made an active decision to parent alone rather than finding themselves in this situation unintentionally, and the financial hardship, parental conflict, and maternal depression associated with negative outcomes for children in single mother families don't usually apply to children of single mothers by choice. Also, unlike children whose parents divorce, the children of single mothers by choice have not been separated from a father with whom they may have a strong bond. But they do face a situation that children from other kinds of single mother families do not — unless they have a known donor, they don't know who their biological father is and may never be able to find out.

In 2011, Sophie Zadeh, a social psychologist and expert on how different types of families are represented in society, and Tabitha Freeman, began a new study to examine the impact on children of this new kind of single mother family. They compared 51 families with single mothers by choice with 52 families with a mum and dad. All of the families had a child between the ages of four and nine conceived by donor insemination. The research focused on children's relationships with their mothers and their psychological wellbeing, and on how children feel about not knowing the identity of their biological father. The children of single mothers by choice were found to be just as close to their mothers, and just as well adjusted, as the children in two-parent families. The greater the stress and financial hardship that the mothers faced, the greater the likelihood of the children experiencing emotional and behavioural problems, but this was just as true for children with two parents as it was for those with single mothers.

From the low level of psychological problems shown by the children of single mothers by choice, it seems that not knowing the identity of their biological father does not impair their wellbeing when they are young. But single mothers by choice do have to confront their children's questions about their fathers from as early as two or three years old. Louise Hendey, a children's nanny, was 32 when her son Alex was born through donor insemination. Louise has always been open with everyone, including Alex, about his conception. When she took part in our study, Louise told us, 'I get a real bee in my bonnet, I never ever want someone to think that Alex was a mistake, or a result of a fling, or that he wasn't wanted, so I would much rather people knew how I became pregnant and my reasons, so that they know he was completely wanted. I would hate for someone to think that I just messed up my life by having him, because this was the whole plan, and this is what I wanted.'

Louise began to talk to Alex about his donor conception when he was very young. But Alex will never be able to meet his donor because he is anonymous. Alex finds this hard to understand. Louise recollected: 'I quite distinctly remember coming home from work when he was about two and a half, and he said to me, "Ian's got a daddy, Sally's got a daddy, and Pat's got a daddy, and I haven't." And I just said, "That's right", and he said, "Why?"' Louise was shocked that this came up at such a young age. 'I just said, "Mummy couldn't find a man to be a daddy, and there's a special way to have babies where a doctor can help you, and that's what Mummy did."' Alex seemed to take this in stride. But by the time he was seven, he had begun to ask more probing questions about his donor. 'The conversation was along the lines of why can't he know the sperm donor that was used to conceive him,' Louise told us. 'I had to explain that he was anonymous, which is quite hard to explain to a seven-year-old. I told him that we know that the sperm donor is a very kind man, and Alex's comeback was, "How do you know? You've never met him," which I thought was very sensible. And he also said, "If he was so kind and nice, why can't you just marry him?"'

Even at ten, Alex didn't understand what an anonymous donor was. On a drive home from a visit to see his uncles, he commented that being with them made him wish he had a dad. He still didn't grasp why his donor was anonymous. Louise told him that anonymous donation was like taking clothes to a charity shop: 'We take a bag of clothes to the charity shop and leave them there, nobody ever knows about that bag of clothes apart from that someone gave them with love. Somebody else comes and buys our coat and they love it, they got a great thing but they never know that it was us that donated but it was done with love on both sides. That's what anonymous is.' But Alex remained confused.

Like Alex, most of the children in our study began to ask why they didn't have a dad from a young age, often at the most unexpected times. Sonia, mother of five-year-old Ruth, said, 'She really took me by surprise when she said it. We were driving in the car and completely out of the blue she said, "Why do I have to only have a mummy?" Sometimes comments from others trigger children's interest in this issue. The mother of seven-year-old Jimmy said, 'The first time it came up in conversation he was three, and a friend of his who was nine months older, asked him, "Where is your dad? Have you got a dad?" And I could see him thinking, "Hold on a second, I don't know."' Spending time with other children's fathers also sparks some children's curiosity. Lisa, who has five-year-old twin girls, told us, 'When they see the daddies of their friends they keep on mentioning that they would like a daddy.' Just as we found with children of lesbian mothers, schools that are not sensitive to diverse family forms can upset children of single mothers. Father's Day activities, in particular, can make the children of single mothers feel bad. As Naseem, mother of six-year-old Jamila explained, 'She only gets bothered when it's coming up to Father's Day, when they're doing stuff at school. Sometimes she will say, "I'm not special because I haven't got a dad."'

Although the children wanted to know why they didn't have a dad, most of those who were aware of their conception using sperm donation, showed little interest in their donor. As Katrina, mother of seven-year-old twins, explained, 'They don't talk about the donor. They talk about a father figure and say, "You need to go out and find somebody to be a dad to us." They don't talk about the biological father. They haven't made that connection.'

As the oldest children in our study had just turned nine, and some were as young as four, they were too young to fully understand the meaning of sperm donation, so Sophie, with the help of Kitty Jones and Jo Lysons, revisited the solo mother families three to four years later, when the children were between seven and 13 years old, to ask them about their thoughts and feelings about their family. Almost all of the children had been told about their conception by age four, and most had some understanding of what this meant. Eleven-year-old Freddie explained, 'There's a special part in the hospital where you can go if you don't have a boyfriend. So you can just go and ask if people volunteer to help make a baby,' and Belinda, aged nine, said, 'To make a baby you need sperm from a man and an egg from a woman and some very kind men helped my mum make me and they donated their sperms.' Some children, like Sam, felt confused when their mother tried to explain how they were born. He told us, 'I really didn't know what my mum was talking about. I thought she was talking gibberish.'

Most of the children talked about their donor in either neutral or positive terms. Jackson, aged eight, said, 'I think he would be kind. He would be caring. He would be nice.' And 11-year-old Maggie said, 'He's probably quite a kind person, the sort of person who wants to help people.' Some children, like 13-year-old Martha, had mixed feelings, 'I felt fine when I was told about him because I was used to not having a dad, but I wish I could just meet him because he's my dad after all,' and Alistair, 11, said, 'It's normal for me because I'm used to not having a dad. I don't really want to meet him because if I do I'll probably just miss him, because I guess he is kind of my dad.' But a few, like nine-year-old Katie, viewed him in a more negative light, 'I really don't think he'd be the best dad because if he doesn't even want to see his own child then I don't think he'd be the best.'

The children differed in how they saw their connection to the donor. To some, like 11-year-old Joy, he was a complete stranger, 'He's got no role in my life. He's not part of my family or anything. He just feels like another person in the world.' Others thought about the characteristics they may have inherited from him. As Jon, aged ten, described it, 'I think he's quite a lively and musical person who enjoys going outside and running around and being all crazy because that's a bit like me.' And yet others viewed him as more of a father-figure who they might like to meet one day. Louise's son, Alex, said, 'I wouldn't describe him as part of my family. I'd describe him as a half dad. He's half not my dad but he half is my dad,' and nine-year-old Lizzie mused, 'I really want to meet him some day but I also don't because I'm not sure what he'll be like, and I'm not sure if he will want to see me.' When asked what questions they would ask their donor, some children wanted to know what he looks like, what he's like as a person, and whether he has a family of his own. Others were interested in why he became a donor: 'Why did he feel like that was a good thing to do?', and whether he would like to form a relationship with them: 'Would you ever like to be my actual dad?'

One question that particularly interested Sophie and Kitty was why some children of single mothers by choice are accepting of their donor conception whereas others express mixed or negative feelings. The answer seems to lie partly in the quality of their relationship with their mothers. They found that children who feel secure in their relationship with their mother — who see her as sensitive to their feelings, supportive, and there when they need them — view their donor more favourably than those who have a more insecure relationship with her. Our US study of older children born by sperm donation to single mothers that Cassie took part in came up with a similar result. Most of the teenagers were securely attached to their mothers, and those who were securely attached were more likely to be curious about their donor — they thought about donor conception and the characteristics they might share with their donor, and saw being donor-conceived as part of who they are. In contrast, those whose relationship with their mother was characterised by greater insecurity were more likely to avoid the topic — they were more likely to keep their donor conception secret, be ashamed of it, and feel embarrassed if others found out they were donor-conceived.

The mothers in our study admitted that parenting as a solo mum can be hard. 'It's full on the whole time,' said Rose, 42, who juggles her job as a teacher with bringing up her four-year-old son. 'When issues come up, I can talk to my friends, but at the end of the day, it's my responsibility, and that can be quite difficult sometimes. But I don't regret a single instant. It's been without doubt the best thing I've ever done.' For Louise, it's when she has to make important decisions, that she most misses having a partner, 'I found that choosing a school for Alex was really difficult. You become aware that you're boring people because, at the end of the day, no one cares as much as I do about Alex's school. If he had a dad, it would be great to talk to him about that. And it would be lovely to have somebody who just comes in and takes him off my hands, so that you don't feel you're asking a favour, and you don't feel guilty that you're not with him. But I think that there are lots of positives about parenting on your own, it's definitely not all bad.' Louise worries about the impact on her child of being a single mother by choice. The media coverage of boys without fathers underachieving at school and becoming delinquent is a source of concern to her. When Alex was 12, she said, 'I think he's actually very well adjusted, but there's always that nagging doubt in the back of your head: did I do the right thing?' When I last spoke to Louise, Alex was 14, and behaving like many teenagers — he was obsessed with screens and quite uncommunicative, although Louise wasn't worried about him getting into trouble. She trusted him completely. 'I've found the last year the most challenging since Alex was born,' she said. 'This teenage stage — it's hard doing this part alone. I've got no one to bounce it off, so I worry a lot. But I think I'm doing all right.'

***

Studies of families created by single mothers by choice tell us something different from studies of families of divorced or unmarried single mothers — they tell us not just whether children need fathers but whether children need to know who their father is. Our findings that these children are just as likely to have good relationships with their mothers, and are just as likely to be well adjusted as children with a mother and a father, show once again that fathers are not essential for children's wellbeing. But these children's interest in their fathers from as early as two years old, together with our discovery that, when they are older, they are more likely to search for their sperm donors over the Internet than the children of heterosexual couples, suggest that, for many children of single mothers by choice, knowing the identity of their biological father is important. And for some of these children, the distinction between donor and dad seems to be more blurred than it is for children in other new family forms.

For Alice Ferguson, being a single mother has been rewarding, but not always easy. Reflecting on the first ten years of Maria's life, she said, 'I do think that having a kid was unmissable for me. I'm so grateful to be in this world of "kiddom". But the disadvantage is that I am doing everything. If I had somebody to share it with, that would be fantastic. People say, "Hats off to you, it's amazing what you're doing," so I have a lot of support. But it's definitely not as easy as being with somebody you're in love with and having a baby together.'

Looking back, 21 years on, Patricia Rhodes has no regrets. 'I didn't realise how hard it would be to be a single parent, but Cassie and I have a fantastic relationship and I'm so lucky. We talk about everything and sometimes I get more information than I really want to know! But that part is great and she's a wonderful human being. I hear such nice things from other people which to me, as a parent, is the bellwether of whether or not you did a good job. I guess, despite everything, she turned out all right.'

Chapter 8

Trans Parent Families: 'Same Person, Just Happier'

'I fear this child is going to grow up confused. It is confusing for me.'

THE UNCLE OF THE UK'S FIRST TRANS MAN TO GIVE BIRTH, (2017)

'He's still my mum.'

ETHAN, AGE 12, (2017).

In 2008, Katie Cornhill's relationship with her two daughters, Tayla, six, and Mandy, two, to whom she was known as Dad, was severed by the courts when she began to identify openly as a woman. Despite the girls stating that they wished to spend an equal amount of time with each of their parents following their mutual separation, and a glowing court report highlighting how much Katie and her children loved each other, the judge ruled that Katie should only be allowed to see her daughters every other weekend and for one night each week. Over the next seven years, following repeated visits to the family court, the children were removed almost completely from Katie's life.

Katie grew up in London in an energetic and hard-working family. She has an older sister and a twin brother. Like many twins, the two were very close and remain so to this day. But from the age of four, Katie, who was assigned male at birth and brought up as a boy, knew that she was different. 'I just knew that I didn't fit in properly,' she told me over afternoon tea in her seaside apartment on the south coast of England. 'I used to observe my sister doing things that you would associate, stereotypically, with someone who identified as a girl. And that appealed to me. I didn't understand why. I just thought, "Actually I should be doing that. That's where I fit."' At first, her family was supportive, and let Katie play with her sister's toys and wear a nightdress in bed. But when Katie started junior school, her parents told her that she was just going through a phase, and that she was a boy and had to grow up as a boy. They did it out of love, to protect her from the rejection and ridicule that she would undoubtedly experience from her classmates. But Katie didn't understand. She wondered why she was not allowed to wear her nightdress in bed. Each night, she cried herself to sleep.

At junior school, Katie found it hard to make friends. 'I would go into school, play with the boys, and think, "Oh, I don't want to play with you," and go and play with the girls, and they would say, "Why are you playing with us? Go away! You're a boy!" So I'd play with the boys, and they would shout, "You queer boy, you faggot. Go and play with the girls!" and I'd think, "Oh! Where do I go?"' By the age of ten, Katie knew that she wanted to live as a girl, but she also knew that she was not allowed to do that. The early years of senior school were especially hard because she was going through puberty. 'I didn't like it,' she told me, 'but I had to deal with it, and kept thinking, "I've got to fit in, I've got to fit in, I've got to fit in."'

Salvation came in the form of the Sea Cadets, an organisation that gives young people a taste of navy life. As Katie was a naturally sporty teenager, she flourished there, and could escape her struggles at school. It was at the Sea Cadets that Katie met her future wife. The couple started dating when they were 17, fell in love, and married five years later in April 1995. Meanwhile, Katie had joined the armed forces. Six years later, she followed her grandfather's footsteps into the Fire and Rescue Service, where she now holds a senior position in charge of traffic accidents, fighting fires, and saving lives. The couple's first child, Tayla, was born in 1999, followed by Mandy in 2003. 'I loved my children completely. I was besotted by them like many loving parents,' said Katie. 'When they were in my life, I was extremely close to my daughters.'

From the outset, Katie's ex-wife was aware of Katie's gender identity and was supportive of her cross-dressing, but the couple grew apart and separated in 2005. In 2007, Katie found the courage she needed and began to live as a woman. 'I no longer wanted to struggle with who I was. I wanted to be myself. I wasn't happy with my body. It didn't align with my mind and my soul and my heart,' she said. 'I knew for me it wasn't just a social challenge. It was going to be medical and it was going to be surgical. I had my surgery in 2015.' But the court saw her as a threat to her children. 'I was going through what is often mis-defined as a transition, but what I knew was an affirmation, knowing I was going to end up living in my true identity. I told them, "I'm a good parent. I'm not a weirdo. I'm not someone you have to worry about. I'm not a risk to my children." I tried to take the court with me, but they didn't understand.' Katie's ex-wife turned against her, as did her ex-wife's entire family. 'My mother-in-law phoned me and said that this wasn't right, that I shouldn't be doing what I was doing, and that it would ruin the kids for life. "You're not their mother, you're their father!" she exclaimed.'

Katie first spoke to Tayla and Mandy about identifying as a woman while they were watching a television programme featuring a man dressed as a woman as part of a game show. Mandy, then nine, was not particularly interested, but Tayla, 13, was supportive. She asked lots of questions and wanted to see Katie's wig, make-up box, and clothing. Katie explained to her daughters that she was becoming a happier person because she was finally living as the person she truly felt she was. She assured them that being a woman wouldn't affect her love for them. The revelation didn't seem to have much of an impact on the girls at the time. It was only when Katie grew her hair long that Tayla became upset. She was concerned about the reaction of her friends at school. But she need not have worried. 'Her school was great, it was very inclusive. They already had a young person who identified as a trans boy.' Katie told us, 'Tayla's friends engaged with me. They were really interested to know all about it.' But Mandy was not so fortunate. 'My younger child's school was the complete reverse. They were very clear that I was not to be me in front of everybody. They didn't want me to go anywhere near the school, and they were supported by the Education Department in that decision through their omission to act. I was ostracised from my daughter's life.'

***

When we are born, we are welcomed into the world with cries of, 'It's a boy!' or 'It's a girl!' depending on our physical appearance, and most children develop a gender identity — a sense of being male or female — that is in line with the sex they are assigned at birth. But that is not always the case. A transgender (or trans) woman is assigned male but identifies as female, and a transgender (or trans) man is assigned female but identifies as male. Terms such as gender non-conforming are also used by some trans people to describe their gender identity, and some people describe themselves as non-binary, defined by Stonewall as an umbrella term for people whose gender identity doesn't sit comfortably with 'man' or 'woman' (or 'boy' or 'girl'). There are many different gender identities and many different terms to describe them. For the sake of simplicity, I shall use the term trans.

When people transition, this usually happens in stages, and not everyone goes through every stage. Initially, the transition may involve a change in outward appearance, pronouns, behaviour, and lifestyle. This can include wearing dresses, wigs, and make-up for trans women, and a wardrobe of shirts and trousers for trans men. Many trans people take hormones to feminise or masculinise their bodies. Trans women take feminising hormones to develop breasts and a more female body shape. The masculinising hormones taken by trans men cause deepening of the voice, increased muscle volume, and facial and body hair. Some trans people have gender reassignment surgery, which may involve genital reconstruction surgery to create a penis for trans men or vagina for trans women, or other types of surgery such as breast removal. In addition to a change in gender identity, gender transition may involve a shift in sexual orientation, so that a heterosexual man may identify as lesbian woman following transition, or a lesbian woman may identify as heterosexual man.

Trans parents have become increasingly visible in recent years, reflecting growing public awareness of trans people more generally in the western world, accompanied by rising levels of hate crime. *Time* magazine named 2014 as 'The transgender tipping point', and *Prospect* magazine listed the rights of transgender people as one of the big new issues of 2015. Just two years later, in January 2017, *National Geographic* published a special edition on the 'Gender Revolution' examining why beliefs about gender are shifting so rapidly and radically. The cover featured a photograph of a nine-year-old trans girl dressed top-to-toe in pink, including her hair, with the caption, 'The best thing about being a girl is, now I don't have to pretend to be a boy.'

Just three months later, Olympic gold medallist and prominent member of the Kardashian family in the reality TV series, *Keeping up with the Kardashians*, Caitlyn Jenner (formerly known as Bruce Jenner) announced that she identified as female and was in the process of transitioning to be a woman. She changed her name to Caitlyn in July 2015, and underwent gender reassignment surgery in 2017. When she appeared on the cover of *Vanity Fair* magazine in 2015, her tweet, 'I'm so happy after such a long struggle to be living my true self. Welcome to the world Caitlyn. Can't wait for you to get to know her/

me', reached more than 1 million followers in just four hours. With six children, Caitlyn Jenner is the most high-profile transgender parent in the world.

In 2016, a report from the Williams Institute at the UCLA School of Law showed that 1.4 million adults identify as trans in the United States, representing 0.6 per cent of the adult population. This figure had doubled in ten years. Amnesty International published a report in 2014, estimating that there are 1.5 million trans people in Europe. In 2015, in the United Kingdom, the largest gender identity clinic for children revealed that the number of children under age ten presenting for treatment had quadrupled over the previous five years, and a later report from that clinic showed that the number of referrals per year for children up to age 18 had risen from 97 in 2009–10 to over 2000 in 2018–19. The number of trans parents is not known, however estimates produced in 2014 by the Williams Institute suggest that between one-quarter and one-half of trans people are parents. Media attention has focused on the small number of trans men who have given birth to children, so-called 'pregnant men', but currently most trans people with children undergo their gender transition once they are already parents.

**

A parent's desire to transition is often — although not always — a source of conflict between couples, resulting in the breakdown of their relationship and a tug-of-war over custody of their children. Echoing the custody battles of lesbian mothers in the 1970s, it is commonly assumed by lawyers and judges that children will suffer psychological harm, and will become confused about their own gender identity, if they remain in contact with their trans parent.

In 1982, in *Cisek v. Cisek*, one of the first custody cases involving a trans parent, the Ohio Court of Appeals removed a trans woman's right to see her two daughters, citing an expert witness's claim that, 'the transsexualism of the [parent] would have a sociopathic affect [*sic*] on the child.' The expert believed that the girls would find it difficult to adjust to their father as a woman, and recommended that contact between them should be stopped. The court's ruling asserted, 'The duty of all courts is to protect these two girls from whatever physical, mental, or social impact might occur. There is evidence that there might be mental harm. Common sense dictates that there can be social harm.'

In 1986, in *Daly v. Daly*, a trans woman, Suzanne Daly, lost custody of her daughter, Mary, following her gender transition because of 'the substantial risk of emotional or mental injury were [Mary] forced to visit with her father'. The Supreme Court of Nevada described Suzanne as 'selfish' and laid the blame at her feet, 'It can be said that Suzanne, in a very real sense, terminated her own parental rights as a father. It was strictly Tim Daly's choice to discard his fatherhood and assume the role of a female who could never be either mother or sister to his daughter.'

And in 1997, in the Missouri case of *J.L.S. v. D.K.S.*, the Court of Appeals cut off contact between a trans woman and her children, in spite of describing her as 'a loving and caring father', based on an expert witness's belief that it would be 'emotionally confusing' for the children to see their father as a woman. The children were not allowed to see their trans parent until they were, 'emotionally and mentally suited for physical contact with their father'.

The first custody case involving a trans parent in the United Kingdom took place in 1981. It centred on whether a four-year-old girl should be allowed to have contact with her father who now identified as a woman. It was argued in court that the child should have no further contact with her father, and that she should be told that he had died or moved far away. The psychiatrist, Richard Green, an expert witness in the case, disagreed with this proposal. He maintained that the child would feel angry and deceived when she later found out the truth, and that she should continue to see her father during her transition. The judge ruled that the father could see her daughter once every three weeks, and only when dressed as a man with no make-up, jewellery, or female clothing. The Court of Appeal later overturned this condition. Mirroring the summing up in one of the first UK cases in which a lesbian mother won custody, the judge, Lord Justice Ormrod, concluded, 'It is very finely balanced whether it is in the interests of the child to keep contact with the father in these confusing circumstances.'

Trans parents continue to lose custody of their children to this day. In one of the most extreme cases, Jessica Lynn, a trans woman living in California, lost all parental rights to her 12-year-old son, and her name was removed from her son's birth certificate by a Texan Court in 2013, following her gender transition. It was claimed by her ex-wife's lawyers that her chosen lifestyle endangered her son's emotional wellbeing, and she was not allowed to see her son again. She was devastated. When Jessica visited the Centre for Family Research in 2017 to speak about the challenges she had faced in fighting to keep her child, she said, 'Court-ordered psychiatric evaluations speak to my merits as a loving parent, but the judge ruled not only to remove my parental rights in full, but to smear my name off my son's birth certificate, like a blemish.' Although a private investigation found Jessica to be clearly discriminated against, her case will never be reopened. I was struck by how similar her experiences were to those of the lesbian mothers I met in the 1970s.

What these cases have in common is that decisions to deny parents the custody of their children, or the right to have contact with them, are based on the assumption that children will experience psychological harm from maintaining a relationship with their trans parent. Prejudice, rather than evidence, drives these rulings. At the time the early cases went to court, the only research that existed was a study conducted in the 1970s by the psychiatrist Richard Green of a small group of 16 families with a trans parent in the United States. This study looked at the gender development of the children only, finding that it was typical. It did not examine the psychological wellbeing of the children, or the quality of their relationships with their trans parents. Since that time, no further investigations have been conducted on young children with trans parents. In the absence of research on what the consequences for children really are, decisions about trans parents' custody and visitation rights are being made purely on the assumption that their gender transition will have a damaging effect.

What exactly is it about trans parents that worries the courts? There has been much speculation about the potential risks for children. The early fear that children of trans parents would be confused about their own gender identity, and would behave in ways that are atypical for their sex, hasn't gone away, despite the lack of evidence to support it. Today, there is greater diversity in the ways in which young people express their gender identity, and our increased understanding of children's development shows that parents have little influence on the gender identity and gender-role behaviour of their children, but the idea that children may follow in their trans parents' footsteps remains a concern of the courts, showing how little has changed since the 1980s.

There is also the worry that children will find it hard to accept a parent's transition and will have difficulty in relating to them as a result. When the person they have always known as Dad becomes a woman, or the person they have grown up knowing as Mum becomes a man, it is thought that this will be profoundly upsetting and confusing for children. On top of that, children may witness their parents' distress as they confront the difficulties and challenges that come with the decision to transition, difficulties that may be compounded if the trans parent is rejected by their family, especially by their own parents. Courts also worry about the negative effects of prejudice against trans parents on children. All of this may be intensified by the animosity between parents that led them to the divorce courts in the first place. Parental Alienation Syndrome, where the child is turned against one parent by the other parent, in this case against the trans parent, is a common feature of these disputes.

But divorce is not always the way. Unlike Katie, who was denied contact with her children, Hannah, a trans woman and a writer, lives in Newcastle, England, with her wife, Leia, a teacher, and their son, Ben, who is 15. When Hannah was five, she used to wish she could wake up the next day as a girl. She also used to imagine that she was a princess who had been magically changed into a boy to save her from something bad. 'I wanted to be a girl, but I knew I was a boy because I *was* a boy,' she said. 'It was the mid-70s and not much was known then about gender identity.' Hannah started cross-dressing when she was 11. She kept it hidden at first, but when she was in her late teens she started telling people about it: 'My mum was absolutely fine. My dad didn't understand it, but he was supportive. It's the same now that I'm their daughter.' Hannah and Leia met when they were at university, and Leia was accepting of Hannah's cross-dressing. Almost 30 years later, the couple are still together.

Before Hannah began to transition, she told Ben when he was nine that sometimes she dressed as a woman, using David Walliams' book *The Boy in the Dress* to explain. Ben accepted this, and when the transitioning process was underway, Hannah and Leia described in detail what this would involve. They told him about the problems they might face and assured him that the transition would not change their relationship. Hannah told Ben that she would still be his dad. Ben's response was: 'You've got to do whatever you have to do to be happy.' 'And then I cried!' said Hannah. She was overcome with happiness.

Ben is close to his parents and enjoys spending time with them. 'My mum likes everything to be tidy and in its place, and she likes cooking and gardening, but she does procrastinate sometimes, so she doesn't always get those things done,' said Ben. 'My dad loves to read, and she also goes on Facebook quite a lot. Me and my dad go to a comic book shop. It's fun. I like it. We also play quite a lot of board games, and we watch TV and Netflix together after dinner every night.' As well as board games, video games, and reading, Ben loves roller-skating with his friends, soldering and gluing things, and computer programming. He goes to code club every week. When asked to describe Ben, Hannah said, 'He's great. He's fun. He has a great sense of humour. He's somebody I really enjoy talking to. He's intelligent, he's loving and caring, and he's a complete geek, which I'm really proud of! We get on really well.'

Hannah and Leia's main worry is that other people won't understand Hannah's transition. They have told Ben's school, and unlike the experiences of many trans parents, the school has been understanding and helpful. 'They were brilliant. They were really supportive and took it on board entirely. They understood that there might be repercussions with Ben, the whole aspect of bullying, and that he might have problems in coming to terms with it. There was also the changing of all my details on the system to Ms. They even get the pronouns right and all that sort of thing, and they're friendly and happy to see me, which is always nice as well.' But his loving family and supportive school can't always protect Ben from the hostility of strangers. When they were out together as a family last year, Hannah was accused of child abuse by a passenger on the train. 'We talked about it. I think Ben was actually more upset for me than for himself. He said if it happened again he would come and stand up for me. We talked it through and he understands that some people are just unpleasant.'

Alma, a trans woman, and her wife, Joanna, parents of three, also stayed together following Alma's transition, but it wasn't easy. 'The main challenge was to avoid the breakdown of my relationship with my wife. I thought that would have more impact on the children than anything else,' said Alma. 'We were planning our wedding, but there was a huge elephant in the room which was my gender identity.' When Alma revealed to Joanna that she needed to transition, they decided to call the wedding off. They wrote an email to the wedding venue to cancel their booking, but when neither could bring themselves to press the 'send' button, they realised that they wanted to stay together and agreed to overcome the challenges that lay ahead. They were happy together, they didn't want to break up their family, and they decided to make it work.

Looking back several years later, Alma admitted that it had been traumatic at times, but they got through it. They had argued a lot. Joanna was not a lesbian and was losing her husband. That was difficult for both of them. Alma knew that if she wanted the family to stay together, she had to make sure that Joanna was with her every step of the way. 'There was lots of crying, lots of screaming, lots of cold shoulders. It wasn't a pleasant time.' But they always made a point of ensuring the children knew they still loved each other, they still loved the children, and they were still a family unit.

Sheila, Alma and Joanna's youngest daughter, was seven when her father began to transition. When she was 12, she told us, 'I was quite sad at first because I felt like they were a different person, but then I thought, "Actually no, they're the same person, just happier and stuff. I kind of like it because it makes our family unique."' Sheila continues to call Alma 'Dad' because that's what she's always done. She explained, 'I just kept calling her Dad, but if we're in the toilets — she goes to the ladies' toilets — I don't call her Dad then because people would think it's really weird. I just say her name.'

On Sheila's last day at junior school, her teacher took Alma aside and showed her one of Sheila's essays. 'The title was "My Hero",' Alma recalled with tears in her eyes. 'Sheila had written about her dad. She said she was really proud of her dad because he'd transitioned, using male pronouns so that the reader would understand. Having a trans parent was something she was actually proud of, and that was quite a revelation.'

✳✳✳

In 2015, when I was invited to join a discussion hosted by the UK Government Equalities Office on how to improve public services for LGBTQ+ families, it became clear that practically nothing was known about children's experiences of a parent's transition. In order to fill this gap, Susan Imrie and Sophie Zadeh from the Centre for Family Research initiated the first in-depth study of what it means for children when their father or mother changes gender. They began the study in 2017. Thanks to the involvement of organisations that promote under-standing of trans issues, such as Gendered Intelligence and Stonewall in the UK and the Family Equality Council in the US, 35 families agreed to take part.

Most of the children were accepting of their parent's transition and discussed it in a matter-of-fact way. To them, having a trans parent felt normal. Susanna, 14, was a toddler when her father transitioned, 'I don't remember when it actually happened, so it's basically been for as long as I remember. Chloe's always been Chloe.' Vicky, 12, who also experienced her father's transition when she was very young, said 'He's been wearing skirts for as long as I can remember. To me, it's not strange. To someone else, maybe, having a dad who wears skirts and likes pink would be weird, but to me it's perfectly normal.'

Mike, nine, clearly remembers the moment when his parents told him, and his brother and sister, about his father being trans. The family were on holiday, sitting in front of a roaring fire one cold, dark evening. 'They explained what gender means, even though we already knew, and then they explained about being transgender,' Mike said. Mike's response was, 'I bet I'm going to be a proud son.' When asked how he felt about it one year later, he replied, 'Now I feel as proud as I thought I was going to be.'

Justin, now 15, was eight when his mother transitioned. 'It didn't make any massive difference to us,' he said. 'He was the same person, just with different body parts and sounded a bit different. He's a man, that's all there really is to it.' Brad, 12, explained, 'It's fine, they're still

211

your parent, they haven't changed, it doesn't change who they are.'

But experiencing their parent's transition can be difficult for some children. As Susie, whose father transitioned when she was seven, said, 'Thinking that my dad was becoming a mum was very hard, and I couldn't stop thinking about it.' Sometimes children hear arguments between their parents, which adds to their distress. Aaron, 13, whose father transitioned when Aaron was 11 and his sister, Mia, was seven, said, 'Sometimes they'll be arguing for loads of time, and me and Mia would sit in our rooms crying. A few days ago they were arguing about why my dad couldn't go to different events dressed like that.' For some children, not understanding what's happening to their parent is a greater source of distress than the actual transition. 'It would have helped if he had explained things a bit better. It wasn't so much him wearing dresses, but more him being a bit manic and doing strange things,' said 18-year-old Henry. Chris, also 18, offered advice to other children in the same situation: 'Try to get them to communicate with you as much as possible because it's worse if things are happening and you don't know why.'

As time goes by and families adjust to their new situation, the parent's transition often becomes easier for children to understand and accept. When Susie was nine, two years after her father transitioned, she said, 'We're a good family. I'm very proud of my family and I love them.'

Jade, who was six when her father transitioned, was upset about losing her dad: 'When she transitioned, I felt like there was a hole in my heart because I missed my dad, and every time somebody talked about their dad, I got really upset. My parents convinced me that I still do have a dad, but sometimes I don't actually remember what he looked — she looked — like.' Over time, Jade became more accepting. Looking back, when she was nine, she said, 'When she transitioned, it made her a lot happier 'cos when she was a boy, she was really unhappy. Ever since she's transitioned, she's come home from work, hugged us, and been really happy. It's changed a lot since she transitioned.' Jade's sister, Grace, five, who was three when her father transitioned, told us, 'She really wanted to be a girl 'cos she wasn't happy when she was a boy. She's being much more kinder.'

One challenge for children is to change the names and pronouns they use to refer to their trans parent, something that is often hard to do when their mum, whom they have always known as 'she', becomes 'he', or their dad becomes 'she', and sometimes their parent wishes to be referred to as 'they'. As Justin, 15, described it, 'Most of the time, when I first found out, I'd say "he" instead of "she", and then I'd go, whoops, sorry, "she".' Children also need to get used to their parent's new name following the transition, and some children help decide what their name should be. Freddie, eight, helped choose his father's new name, Lily: 'I thought of names, all the girls' names I could think of. Mostly flower names. It was my idea.'

It usually falls on children with trans parents to explain about their family to their peers, and just as we heard from children with same-sex parents, this can be an unwelcome burden. Susanna said, 'My problem has been having to explain it to other people constantly because no one really understands,' and Josh, Freddie's 15-year-old older brother, told us, 'Sometimes random people ask me questions and I have to explain it to them. That gets tiring for me.' Susanna has to remind herself that others don't understand what she's telling them: 'When I'm explaining to someone, I don't have as much patience as I probably should because I'm used to it. I've thought, how do you not understand this, and then I've realised that because I've grown up with it, it's a lot more normal for me than it is for other people.'

Many of the children in our study told us about positive reactions from their friends. For some, it wasn't a big issue. Mike said, 'I did tell my friends. But I think they've probably forgotten by now because they didn't find it as important as we did because it's not their parent.' Other children's friends thought it was cool. Callum, 15, said, 'I like when I tell people. They say, "Oh, that's really cool"', and Susanna told us, 'They've always said it's cool, and that I should write an auto-biography.' Some children, such as Isobel, who was 13 when her father transitioned, were able to turn to their friends for support: 'They were very understanding and comforting if I ever wanted to talk about it during the transition.' Vicky's friends were so accepting that she didn't worry about her trans parent attending school events, 'He wore a skirt to our music evening at school and nobody questioned that. In fact, there was a boy in my year who came up the day afterwards and said, "Your dad looks amazing, I really like him."'

But outside their friendship group, some of the children experienced teasing and bullying. Callum said, 'They take the mick out of it, but I'm not friends with these people because they're stupid', and Sonny explained, 'Unfortunately, I have to go to school surrounded by a lot of transphobes and homophobes.' Just as schools can play an important part in making children with same-sex parents feel accepted — or not — the same is true for children with trans parents. Wendy's school is a good example of an inclusive school. She told us, 'I put my hand up and said, "I don't have a dad because my dad's transgender," and I got an award for it 'cos that was actually really brave of me to say.'

Being out in public with their trans parent can present problems for children. As Jenni, 14, explained, 'Out in public, I'm worried about people seeing me with him and then being mean to me. I always think about what other people are thinking.' Joe felt the same way, 'The bit I found hard was going out in public when he was in full make-up and dress, mainly because I was worried about running into people who weren't very nice, or just getting stares.' Sam, nine, also worried about being stared at, 'People might stop and stare because it's like a woman speaking with a man's voice.'

Some children whose fathers transitioned pointed out that having two mothers can attract more attention than having a trans parent. 'I've had more issues with having two mums because people don't realise that the transition has happened, but having two mums can be quite a standout thing,' said Theresa who is 17. 'I get questions like, "How were you born? How are you here? Which one's your real mum?" That's a classic!' Charlie, 12, has had a similar experience, 'Sandra being trans isn't a big deal to me, it's never really affected me much. It's having two mums that's affected me. I've had people saying things about that, but not so much about Sandra being trans.'

Sometimes trans parents are rejected by their wider family, either by their own family or, more commonly, by their partner's family, which may mean that children lose contact with their grandparents, aunts, uncles, and cousins. This happened to Theresa, whose father transitioned when she was six, 'People on my mum's side of the family really struggle with it. Her parents and brothers, and basically everyone over there, cut us off. It made me sad and kind of angry because it's really no reason to be horrible.' But grandparents may keep in touch with their grandchildren, as happened to Eva when her father transitioned, 'When Ma told my grandad, he didn't take it very well and he doesn't talk to Ma, only us.'

Occasionally, children with trans parents risk being rejected by their whole community, as happened in 2017 in Manchester, England. A trans woman, known in court as J, who left the ultra-Orthodox Jewish community that she had belonged to all her life, was refused contact with her five children aged from 12 to two years old on the grounds that the children would be ostracised by the community if contact was allowed; this could include not being allowed to play with their friends, not being invited to social occasions and religious festivals, and not being accepted into the community's schools. The judge, Lord Justice Peter Jackson, who took the 12-year-old's wishes into account, said, 'I have reached the unwelcome conclusion that the likelihood of the children and their mother being marginalised or excluded by the ultra-Orthodox community is so real, and the consequences so great, that this one factor, despite its many disadvantages, must prevail over the many advantages of contact.' The Court of Appeal reversed the judgment later that year on the grounds that courts should not bow to intolerant communities, referring the case back to the Family Court for reconsideration. In January 2020, it was reported in *The Guardian* that the woman had withdrawn her case to protect her children from emotional harm.

In society at large, there appears to be a gradual acceptance of families with trans parents. Luke, 43, a therapist in Manchester, England, who specialises in adult mental health problems, has had a more positive experience than some of the trans parents in our study. Luke was fortunate to grow up in the 1970s with liberal parents, and at a time when unisex fashion was all the rage. He never felt under pressure to wear girls' clothes or take part in girlish activities that made him feel uncomfortable. Although he always felt he should have been a boy, he came out as lesbian as a teenager, and had his first serious relationship when he was at college. In his twenties, he met his long-term partner, Amanda, later to become his wife, and they adopted two children, Matthew, 15, and Jess, 13, when they were four and two.

When Luke embarked on his transition at the age of 35, when the children were eight and six, he thought about what people might feel awkward and embarrassed about, and wrote a letter to everyone he knew, explaining what was going to happen, what he had said to the children, and what he was going to be called. Amanda decided that they should celebrate. 'A few days before my first surgery, we threw a party to say goodbye to the person I was and hello to Luke,' he told me when we spoke on the phone two years after he had taken part in our study. 'We thought that a party would make it easier for people to know how to deal with it. The kids were at the party, and their friends from school, and the parents who we knew, and all of our family and friends. We had cake — it's not a proper party without cake! — and a band. It let people say goodbye to the old me. After Christmas, I went back to work as Luke.'

Luke had delayed his transition to protect his children, 'My absolute fear was that it would ruin their lives, that they would be bullied, that they would be humiliated by it, that it would be awful. If anything, at the moment, there's a bit of kudos in it. Many of their friends have come out as LGBTQ+ and they've told people when they didn't have to tell them. My daughter goes to a school that's quite far away, and she could easily not have told people, but she has chosen to say. My son has also told people he didn't have to tell.'

Luke's children have been on-board from the start. 'The kids were the ones that checked people on their pronouns and seemed very embracing of the idea of me as Dad,' said Luke. 'I think what was weird for them was thinking that I was going to go to hospital and then this strange bloke was going to turn up at the door and say, "Hi, I'm your dad." Once they realised it was just me but without boobs, which is in effect what they saw, they kind of relaxed. Now it's just normal. It's what we do. It's part of our family life.' Luke feels that his transition has improved his relationship with his children, 'I think it's better, I think I'm more real, I think I'm more there for them. I don't know how much that's to do with my transition, but I think everything has improved because I think I'm more me.'

As well as finding out about children's experiences of their parent's transition, our study examined whether there is any evidence for the common assumption that growing up with a trans parent is psychologically harmful for children and damaging to their relationship with their parents. The families all volunteered for the research which means that trans parent families who were experiencing serious problems might have been less inclined to take part, but we did include parents who had stayed together, parents who had split up, and parents with new partners, which means that many of the children had experienced family breakdown.

In contrast to the fears raised in child custody cases, the children were no more likely than other children to show emotional or behavioural problems. Just as we found in our previous research, the make-up of the family didn't make a difference to children's psychological wellbeing. Instead, the children who were experiencing problems were those whose parents were depressed, or were under high levels of stress, and who lacked social support. It wasn't their parent's change of gender identity, but the difficulties that sometimes accompanied it, that seemed to upset the children. As expected from what we know about trans people more generally, the trans parents in our study were more depressed than other adults, and they were more likely to be separated or divorced. Nonetheless, most of the children had not experienced serious animosity between their parents which may well account for their positive psychological wellbeing.

***

In April 2008, Thomas Beatie, a trans man who was married to a woman, became a public sensation when he appeared on the *Oprah Winfrey Show* as the world's first pregnant man. He had his first child, a daughter, in June that year, becoming the first ever legally recognised man to have a baby. He has since given birth to two more children, both sons. This was possible because he had retained his internal reproductive organs when he began to publicly identify as a man, and had conceived his children using donor sperm.

A small but growing number of trans people are turning to assisted reproduction to have children *following* their transition. In addition to becoming pregnant themselves, trans men can freeze their eggs before or during their transition for later use. Depending on their sexual orientation as heterosexual or gay, and whether or not they have a partner, the eggs can be fertilised using sperm from a male partner or a sperm donor, and the embryos implanted in a female partner or a surrogate. Trans women can freeze their sperm and have children with a female partner. If their partner is male, they can use donated eggs to conceive and enlist the help of a surrogate.

The use of assisted reproduction by trans people is highly

controversial, and has attracted opposition from both within and outside the medical profession. Although later resolved, the UK Equality and Human Rights Commission announced in 2018 that it was planning to sue the National Health Service for failing to provide egg and sperm freezing to enable trans people to have biologically related children following their transition. Just as those who transition after becoming parents are often seen as a threat to their children's development and wellbeing, so too are trans people who transition first and have their children at a later date, even though their children don't witness the transition or need to adjust to their parent's changed gender identity. Once again, there is no research to shed light on what happens to these children. But professional bodies including the World Professional Association of Transgender Health, the Endocrine Society, the American Society for Reproductive Medicine, the European Society for Human Reproduction and Embryology, and the American Congress of Obstetrics and Gynecology have all come out in favour of allowing trans people to access services to preserve their fertility before they transition.

In England, in 2019, Freddy McConnell, a trans man who had given birth to a son conceived through sperm donation — whose journey to parenthood is featured in the documentary *Seahorse* — had his request to be named on his child's birth certificate as either 'father' or 'parent', instead of 'mother', turned down by Sir Andrew McFarlane, President of the Family Division of the High Court, on the grounds that a 'mother' is the person who carries the pregnancy and gives birth. In his written judgment, Sir Andrew acknowledged that legal definitions of motherhood and fatherhood do not match new family structures, stating that there was a 'pressing need for Government and Parliament to address square-on the question of the status of a trans male who has become pregnant and given birth to a child', and that, 'the social and psychological reality of McConnell's relationship with his child was as a father and this was in tension with the law as it stands'.

Freddy McConnell said to *The Guardian*, that the ruling, 'has serious implications for non-traditional family structures. It upholds the view that only the most traditional forms of family are properly recognised or treated equally.'

Although unusual because of the widespread antipathy towards it, adoption is another way in which trans people can become parents. One Friday morning in September 2011, Biff Chaplow received a phone call at his home in Los Angeles that would change his life. It was from a social worker who was calling to tell him that his sister Rachel's children would be taken into foster care on Monday unless Biff could persuade her to let him look after them. Rachel had mental health problems and was a drug user. She had become a danger to her son Cody, three, and daughter Bea, who was only one. Her boyfriend was a meth addict and drug dealer who had been violent to Rachel and the children. Biff, himself a social worker, had been worried about his niece and nephew for some time. He wanted to do whatever it would take to protect the children, but what about his partner, Trystan? Would Trystan agree to have Cody and Bea live with them? The couple had been together for only one year and had just begun to share a home. They were in their mid-twenties and their life was centred on the beach, clubbing, weekends in Las Vegas, and having fun. How would Trystan feel about giving up their hedonistic lifestyle for the daily responsibilities of family life?

During the two-hour drive from Los Angeles to his sister's house in Bakersfield, Biff told Trystan that he didn't know whether they were having the children for a weekend, for a month, or forever, and that by agreeing to look after them, Trystan might be agreeing to staying with him for 18 years because Biff didn't want to take the children from one unstable situation and put them in another. Trystan's immediate response was an emphatic 'yes!' The couple were aware that problems lay ahead. Because of the neglect and abuse that they had suffered in their birth family, Cody and Bea were troubled children who were likely to be difficult to manage. On top of that, Biff and Trystan knew that being accepted as the children's parents would be a struggle. Not only were they a gay couple, but Trystan was also a trans man.

Biff and Trystan offered to take the children for the weekend and Rachel agreed. When they took Cody and Bea back to their home in Los Angeles, the children were in a poor state. 'It was terrible,' recalled Trystan. 'Bea had a terrible infection that made diaper changes painful. When we changed her, she would just scream and scream and scream and scream and scream. Cody had been abused pretty horribly. He couldn't speak. He was terrified. He would hide under the table. He would cling to our legs.'

It soon became clear that Rachel was not capable of caring for her children, and that Biff and Trystan needed to apply for emergency guardianship. They knew they wouldn't succeed in Bakersfield. A lawyer there told them that a judge in Bakersfield would rather the children lived in a meth home with straight parents who are abusive than live in a happy, stable home with gay parents. So Biff and Trystan turned to the court system in Los Angeles. As Trystan described in the podcast, *The Longest Shortest Time*, they lived in terror every single day. For three months, they didn't have any legal rights to the children. At any time, Biff's sister and her partner could have asked for them back, and they would have lost them. They were caring for two deeply traumatised children and, at the same time, defending their right to parent them. Trystan said, 'If you have no legal rights to a kid, you can't put them in school. You can't take them to a doctor. You can't put them in pre-school. You can't do almost anything with them.' They described the court process as 'incredibly difficult'. They had to be assessed to ensure that they would provide a good home for the children, a procedure that was especially anxiety-provoking for Biff and Trystan because of the prejudice they feared. It took months for the couple to be granted emergency guardianship by the courts. It was only then that Bea could be enrolled in day-care and Cody could go to pre-school, and only then that Biff and Trystan could begin the arduous process of becoming Cody and Bea's permanent guardians, and eventually, their adoptive parents. It was hard on Rachel too. Sometimes she wanted her children back, and at other times she wanted them to remain with Biff and Trystan. In the end, she agreed to let Biff and Trystan adopt them. The whole process was gruelling. In July 2015, almost four years after the children had first gone to live with them, Biff and Trystan became the legal parents of Cody, who by then was seven, and Bea, who was almost five.

Thanks to the love, stability, and commitment that Biff and Trystan have given them, Cody and Bea have progressed by leaps and bounds. But it has not been easy, especially for Cody, who was badly treated in his birth family until he was three. 'The change was very slow,' said Trystan. 'When I tried to read a book to Cody that was appropriate for his age, he would just squirm and run off to play. He'd never been read to. We had to revert to baby books. We home schooled him for a year to help him catch up. His behaviour was overwhelming to deal with all day. He would have meltdowns. Sometimes he would cry for hours. Every single day, we were trying, trying, trying. It was very, very slow.' At ten, Cody, like other children who were neglected and abused when they were young, still has difficulties. Trystan said, 'He feels really insecure if somebody gets picked for something and he doesn't. If he gets into trouble he goes into a shame spiral. He's quite depressive. It's like living with Eeyore.' But Trystan and Cody are very close and enjoy each other's company. They love doing outdoor activities together; backpacking, hiking, baseball, football, and walking the dog. Bea, who was only one when she left her birth family, is much easier to live with. 'Bea is my best buddy,' said Trystan. 'She is precocious, funny, and very smart. She won the Kindness Award in school last year. She's very concerned about other kids doing okay and helping and supporting them. She's very positive. She's a delight.'

For many parents, two adopted children who had been badly

treated in their early years would have been quite enough to cope with, but Trystan had a secret wish. He wanted to have a baby with Biff. At first, Biff couldn't understand it. Why would they have a biological child when there were so many children in need of a family? But he could see how much this meant to Trystan, and after a great deal of thought, he agreed.

Because Trystan had not had gender reassignment surgery, he could carry a pregnancy, but it meant having to stop the masculinising hormones he had been taking for 12 years, which made him feel irritable and moody. The couple's first pregnancy ended in miscarriage, which was deeply upsetting. But they persevered, and in July 2017, Trystan gave birth to Leo, a beautiful baby boy. Leo was greeted with open arms by his immediate family, including his grandparents. Trystan's father, a doctor, took a particular interest in the pregnancy, and was overjoyed when Leo was born. But the hostility that Trystan encountered from the wider public was shocking. The episode of *The Longest Shortest Time* in which Trystan announced his pregnancy went viral. Trystan was bombarded with hate mail. As he described it on the programme, 'I got hate messages by the hundreds, by the thousands, by the hundreds of thousands, in every language you could imagine. I was getting these messages every day. The hardest part was realising that people hate trans people. I didn't realise that before. That people hate me, and wish that I was dead.'

***

Families with trans parents challenge conventional ideas about what it means to be a mother or a father, but our research so far has shown that changing gender identity does not preclude parents from being protective of, and loving towards, their children, and neither does it cause children to develop psychological problems. In spite of the hurdles that they face, children seem to adapt to their parent's transition.

When asked if there's anything he'd like other people to know about his family — anything he'd like to shout from the rooftop — Mike said, 'What I'd like other people to know about our family is that we're a happy family — we're all really happy and joyful.' For Theresa, it's that they are close, 'We always support each other and listen to each other, and it's just easy to be around each other.' She also said, 'It's not that you're losing a parent, you're just gaining a different one.' And for Ben, 'The best thing is they're mine, they're my family and not anyone else's.'

Katie Cornhill fully reconnected with her elder daughter, Tayla, in 2017. By then, Tayla was 18, living with her boyfriend and working in a nursing home for the elderly. 'We're really good friends now. I feel that I'm more of a friend than a parent at the moment because of all the years she was removed from my life. It takes a while to rebuild the parental bond,' said Katie. 'She calls me Dad, and I'm very happy with that. That's who I am to her. I realised that I was never going to be her mum. I'm her parent at the end of the day, and I consider myself a woman, and that's it.'

The day I visited Katie, Tayla was in labour with her first child, and Katie was about to become a grandparent. Katie is still estranged from her younger daughter, but dreams of being reunited with her one day. 'I hope that she will realise that she has two parents in her life and that she'll want to re-engage and see who I am as a person. I hope that she will remember that we were really close when she was younger and that we did have a fantastic relationship back then.' Katie doesn't regret the path she took. She feels that it's important to be her true self in order to rebuild her relationships with her children. Although Katie is fully supportive of people who identify as transgender, she doesn't use the term herself because it would imply that she has changed her gender identity; Katie has always thought of herself as female through and through. She said, 'I do not feel that I went through a transition because I have never changed who I am. I went through an affirmation, not a transition. I have always been who I am today.' In spite of all that happened, Katie doesn't feel bitterness against her ex-wife, 'I don't hate her for what she's done. In fact, I had an immense amount of love and respect for her, for the support she gave me when we were together. It's partly because of her I'm the woman I am today.'

Chapter 9

Future Families: 'Pioneers'

'Egg-freezing clinics are aggressively courting a new generation. Younger millennials are heeding the call.'

THE NEW YORK TIMES, (2018).

'My sisters were put in the freezer.'

DAISY, AGE 8, (2018).

Daisy Bowman entered the world in January 2010, almost four years before her triplet sisters, Scarlett and Connie, who had been conceived at the same time. Their mother, Louise, and father, Steven, had struggled to have children, and after several years of trying, they turned to IVF. 'I produced twelve eggs,' Louise told me. 'I could hear people at the clinic saying, "I've got one egg", and "We've got two". The doctor came up to me and said that we had twelve eggs and I thought, "Oh my god! That's a lot!" The couple waited anxiously for a phone call the following morning to find out if any of the eggs had fertilised. Ten embryos had survived the night, and five made it to day three, ready to be transferred to Louise's womb. 'They put two back in, that first time,' said Louise. 'One took, and we had Daisy from that. We froze the other three.'

Louise was thrilled to discover that she was pregnant. 'I was naughty. I did an early pregnancy test,' she said. 'I felt so sick and so tired. But I wondered, "Am I imagining it again?" after all we'd been through. The test was positive. I called the clinic, but they said that it was too early to accept the test result. I did the proper one about five o'clock in the morning on the day we were supposed to, and it was positive. I took the pregnancy test to my mum and dad's house. I just handed it to them and we were all in tears.'

At first Louise was anxious that something would go wrong. But once her pregnancy reached 20 weeks, she relaxed: 'That's when I began to love every moment of being pregnant. I thought, 'This might be the one and only time I experience it.' I didn't find out whether it was a boy or a girl. We were so excited we didn't care.' The pregnancy went smoothly and Louise opted for a water birth. She recalled, 'I got into the water about three o'clock and Daisy was born sixteen minutes later. They left us to cuddle her. I don't know how long it was, but I just remember Steven and I looking at her in awe. She was tiny; she was six pounds. We had a few possible names, but we just looked at her and said, "She's definitely Daisy!" We named her then, and they wrote it on her little band, and then Steven cut the cord and it was lovely.'

Each year a letter arrived from the clinic asking what they wanted to do with their frozen embryos. At first Louise and Steven were fully occupied looking after Daisy and moving house. But when Daisy was three, they decided to have another go. On the designated day, Louise and Steven again waited anxiously at home for a phone call, this time to find out if their embryos had thawed successfully. When the call came, the news was good; two of the three embryos had survived. But they were faced with a big decision — the doctor recommended that they should use both embryos because Louise was in her mid-thirties by then. This would increase the couple's chances of having at least one child. Louise was unsure because she hadn't imagined having twins, but they decided to follow the doctor's advice. That day, they travelled to London and had both embryos transferred.

Once again, Louise became pregnant, but after what seemed to be a miscarriage six weeks later, she was referred for an ultrasound scan. Expecting to have lost the pregnancy, she was shocked and amazed to hear the nurse say there were two heartbeats — they were having twins! 'We thought, "What have we done?"' said Louise, 'We were expecting them to say, "There's nothing there."'

When I spoke to Louise five years later, Scarlett and Connie had just started school, and Louise was beginning to emerge from the unrelenting demands of caring for twins. It had been a struggle, both financially and emotionally, but the support of her family and friends got her through. 'When I found out I was having twins, I thought, "I can't do this." The first few years were very hard, but it was amazing at the same time. It's been a rollercoaster,' said Louise. 'When they turned five and started school, we said to ourselves, "We've managed, we've survived five years!" It's good now. We can have family days out. We both feel that the hardship is forgotten when you experience the nice moments.'

Louise and Steven worried that Daisy might feel left out because they had to lavish so much attention on the younger ones, so they initiated 'Daisy days', when they take Daisy somewhere special on her own. Daisy loves family outings. Her favourites were a trip to the theatre in London with her mum and dad to see *Matilda*, and a visit to the zoo with her dad and her sisters. Although she occasionally feels left out, her parents' understanding makes all the difference to Daisy. She said, 'There was one time when I was upset. I think I was seven years old and it was New Year's Eve. I was really sad so I just went upstairs to my sisters' bedroom and looked outside and it was snowing. I was crying because my mum hadn't spent so much time with me playing games, she was more with Connie and Scarlett because they were young. And then my mum came and said, "Daisy, what's wrong?" And then I told her and she helped me. She said, "I'll play more games with you when they're in bed." I felt much better after that.'

Daisy enjoys playing with her sisters, even though, like many siblings, they can be annoying at times. 'I think Connie's fun to play with, when she's not moaning, because Connie does moan quite a lot,' said Daisy. 'I like being her little girl in "mums and dads". The best thing is when Scarlett's away at a sleepover and then me and Connie have our own time to play games, like Lego.' She plays different games with Scarlett. Daisy said, 'It's really fun being with Scarlett. She can be really bossy, but I still love playing with her. She likes playing games with me in the garden. What I also love, is when we do shows together. That's probably the best thing I do with Scarlett, happy shows.'

Having the girls has left Louise feeling grateful to medical science. 'I'm fascinated by the whole process. I think it's amazing what science can give you. I'm such an advocate. I'm very open about it. The twins don't understand much yet, but they love saying that they're triplets, which is really quite funny. People say, "What?" and then I explain, and they say, "Oh, that's awesome!" It's astounding what science can do. We're so lucky that it worked for us both times.'

Families like Daisy's are becoming increasingly common. In 2016, the International Committee Monitoring Assisted Reproductive Technologies reported that the number of IVF babies born throughout the world had grown exponentially from 5 million in 2013 to 6.5 million in 2016. The most significant change in the practice of IVF over these years was a shift from the use of fresh embryos to frozen embryos. Today, the majority of IVF births result from frozen embryos. This has come about for a number of reasons. Firstly, the cost of a frozen embryo cycle is less than that of a fresh cycle, while the chance of having a baby with frozen embryos is more or less the same. Also, the use of frozen embryos reduces the risk of over-stimulating the woman's ovaries, a potentially life-threatening condition caused by the use of fertility medication to galvanise the growth of eggs. This is because freezing the embryos means pregnancy won't occur in the same cycle, which allows the ovaries to recover before being exposed to the ovarian stimulating hormones produced by pregnancy.

A further reason for using frozen embryos is the potential for reducing chromosome anomalies, the largest single cause of pregnancy failure and miscarriage. An increasing number of fertility clinics are now carrying out pre-implantation genetic screening to check that embryos have the correct number of chromosomes. This is performed by removing cells from the embryo when it is around five days old, and only using embryos without chromosomal abnormalities to try to create a pregnancy. Any embryos that are not being transferred straight away are frozen for use at a later date. Pre-implantation genetic screening is a controversial procedure, especially when used with younger women, as there is no clear evidence that it increases a woman's chances of having a baby. Pre-implantation genetic screening is different from pre-implantation genetic diagnosis, which tests for genetic disorders in embryos that are likely to be at risk.

***

It is not just embryo freezing, but also egg freezing, that is changing how babies are made. In 2010, in a debate hosted by the University of Cambridge's Centre for Gender Studies and *The Guardian* newspaper, Carl Djerassi, an inventor of the contraceptive pill, predicted that egg freezing would have as great an impact on society as oral contraception. Whether his prediction will come true remains to be seen. But it is certainly the case that a small but growing number of women are taking advantage of technological advances in egg freezing to store their eggs until they are ready to have children. Egg freezing first became possible in 1986. But it was not until the introduction of the fast-freezing process of vitrification in 2005 that a sufficient number of eggs remained viable once they had thawed. Egg banks have since sprung up in the United

States and other countries around the world. In 2018, an article in *The New York Times* claimed that more than 20,000 American women had frozen their eggs. The largest egg bank in the United Kingdom, which opened in 2013, saw three times as many women freezing their eggs in 2017 as in 2014. Women who freeze their eggs go through the same procedure of egg retrieval as women who donate their eggs, but as soon as the eggs are collected they are frozen for future use. While some women freeze their eggs to avoid the damaging effects of medical treatments such as chemotherapy or radiotherapy, others do it for social reasons — to postpone starting a family until a later date.

Hannah, who works in advertising, took part in a study of egg freezing that Zeynep Gurtin carried out at the London Women's Clinic. Hannah first heard about egg freezing through a friend. She has a demanding job, a busy social life, and had recently split up with her boyfriend. She hadn't been thinking about having children when she first learned about egg freezing but was immediately intrigued. She started looking into it, but it was not until her thirty-sixth birthday that she became serious about it. 'I went online and I found the London Egg Bank and I saw that they were doing an open day. So I went along to learn a bit more about it and signed up straight away for my first consultation.' Leading up to her appointment, Hannah had moments during which she felt sad. But once the process was over, she felt empowered, and proud of herself for doing it. 'I felt amazing. I felt elated. I remember, after my eggs were collected, crying in happiness. I've got eight eggs in the freezer. I felt the pressure had been taken off. I'd spent a lot of time being really concerned and worried about my situation, being single, and this meant I could take back control.'

To Hannah, these eight eggs feel like a safety net. She can focus on other parts of her life and on finding a partner who is right for her. But she knows that a baby is not for certain. 'When I first started looking into egg freezing, I knew that it wasn't going to be a guarantee. That's something to consider when you are thinking about doing it because it's expensive. It might be a big waste of money. But for me, there were more positives than negatives about it, and it's kind of an insurance policy.' For Hannah, the best outcome would be never to need to use these eggs: 'We'd all prefer to have a baby naturally, and with someone we love. We all want the fairy tale. But there's also the possibility that it might not happen, so you have to be prepared for another option, and it certainly is that.'

Hannah's concerns are justified. Figures published by the UK Human Fertilisation and Embryology Authority in 2018 show that few women who try to have a baby using their frozen eggs are currently successful; only one in five IVF treatment cycles using a woman's own frozen eggs were found to result in a pregnancy. That's partly because the likelihood of success depends on the woman's age when she freezes her eggs; the younger she is, the greater her chances. The ideal time is in her twenties or early thirties. For women who freeze their eggs in their late thirties or forties, it's often too late. The age of the eggs matters more for achieving a pregnancy than the age of the woman when she uses the eggs. The number of eggs that are frozen also makes a difference; the more eggs there are, the greater the chance of having a baby.

Media reports on women who freeze their eggs imply it's about women putting their careers ahead of motherhood. *Bloomberg Businessweek* ran a cover story in 2014 with the headline, 'Freeze your eggs, free your career: A new fertility choice gives women more choice in the quest to have it all.' This idea is partly fuelled by tech companies such as Facebook, Apple, and Google paying for their female staff to put their eggs on ice. An article in *Time* magazine in 2014 described company-paid egg freezing as the great equaliser because women can choose when to have children and climb the career ladder just like men. But the women we have spoken to in our research on egg freezing tell a different story. For them, it's about finding the right partner, as it was for Hannah, 'People have this assumption that women are doing it to further their careers, but for me, I was just not in the place where

I'd met somebody and was ready to have a baby with them, and so I wanted to steal a little more time for myself. I don't know any women who are just focusing on their careers and thinking about egg freezing for those reasons. It's just not something that women are talking about. It's a lot more about eligible men and finding the right person to have a baby with rather than someone that you're not sure about.'

We have found from our interviews that lack of commitment from men is a common reason heterosexual women are freezing their eggs. Some men are not ready to start a family before women's fertility begins to decline in their mid-thirties. Other men end the relationship when the issue of having a baby comes up. A 2013 report by the American Society for Reproductive Medicine found that 80 per cent of women who froze their eggs did so because they didn't have a partner. Would-be grandparents may also be behind the increase in the use of this technology. *The New York Times* revealed in 2012 that some parents are so eager for grandchildren that they are paying their daughters' egg-freezing bills.

When Claire Blaise read about egg freezing in a woman's magazine, she was still hoping to meet Mr Right and have a family in the traditional way. But she was in her late thirties, and worried about leaving it too late. 'I always wanted children, but I wanted them with the right person, and I think that's what scuppered the plan, really,' she told me. 'I've been looking for, not Mr Perfect, but someone who's right for me, and he's never really come along.'

Claire had had several boyfriends when she was in her twenties, but she didn't want to settle down. 'There was the big wide world out there and I didn't want to do the thing that a lot of my friends were doing. You know, getting engaged and buying a house and getting married and having a baby.' Claire travelled to Australia, and lived in France for a while, eventually becoming the global recruitment manager for an international organisation based in London. By the time she returned to England, she was in her mid-thirties. 'I was ready to have children. It was just when internet dating was starting, but you didn't tell anybody that you were doing it! I had boyfriends, but I went through a period of having relationships that just didn't get off the ground.' Claire worried that she would miss the chance to have children. She said, 'I thought if I freeze my eggs then at least I'm buying myself a little bit of extra time to try and meet somebody and have a better chance of having kids.' In 2008, Claire froze 21 eggs. She was 39.

But her plan didn't work out. Many of the men Claire met were divorced and already had children, and they didn't want more: 'There was one guy I met through work when I was about 40, and that lasted a couple of years, but he was going through a divorce. He knew I wanted to have kids, and he wasn't really into it. He already had children, and he didn't want to do all of that again.' Claire felt that waiting for the right relationship was holding her back. In October, 2016, she called the clinic where her eggs were stored and asked to have them thawed. The doctor recommended that they thaw ten. All ten were fertilised with donor sperm, but only one developed into an embryo. On the day the embryo was transferred to Claire's womb, she found out that the company she worked for had gone into liquidation. Two weeks later, Claire took a pregnancy test and it was positive. Claire recalled, 'I went back to the clinic and had a scan and they said, "Yes, there it is." And I thought "Oh my god, what have I done!"'

Claire was 47 when her son Frankie was born. When she was pregnant, she worried about him not having a dad. She was also concerned that people would gossip about her. 'But when he arrived, I didn't care what anybody thought,' she said. 'I was just so happy with him. And actually people have been really positive about it. They say that I'm brave. But I think when people say, "Oh, you're brave", it means, "I wouldn't do that!" But my sister says I'm a pioneer, doing it this way.'

When I spoke with Claire, Frankie was almost one, and she was thinking about whether to have another child. 'It's not because I want a big family,' she told me. 'It would be a lot easier if it was just one, but

I've got a brother and sister and I'm close to them both and I know how good it is. So I'd like Frankie to have that too. I also think to the future and how I'm going to cope with a teenager. I'll have a 12-year-old when I'm 60! But I've got all those eggs left and if I don't even try, then I might regret it.'

Although the opportunity to freeze their eggs can be liberating for women who wish to break free of their biological clock and embrace motherhood when the time feels right for them, there is a darker side to the story. Egg freezing 'parties' are being hosted by fertility clinics to encourage young, professional women to sign up. In 2018, the Ethics Committee of the American Society for Reproductive Medicine expressed concern about the aggressive marketing of egg freezing, claiming that it may generate disproportionate fear and give women false confidence in the effectiveness of the procedure. A further concern of the Committee is that the promotion of egg freezing by companies such as Facebook will put women under pressure to comply. To date, so few women have thawed their eggs to try to have a baby that we don't yet know the personal or social implications of this new way of making families, or what the verdict of those who don't succeed will be. Neither do we know whether we are on the cusp of a sea-change in childbearing that will lead to increasingly older parents, or whether egg freezing for social reasons will wither on the vine.

Fertility specialists have begun to call on schools to teach children about age-related fertility decline, which has now been shown to occur in men as well as women, in an attempt to reduce the increasing numbers of people having to resort to fertility treatment to start a family. For women, the chance of getting pregnant goes down from around the age of 37, and a recent article in the medical journal *Human Reproduction* showed that women who wish to have a good chance of having three children, should start their family by the age of 23.

***

Co-parenting — another new way of forming families — lacks an element of parenting that is usually taken for granted: a romantic relationship between the mother and father. This kind of family raises interesting and important questions. How does the partnership between co-parents evolve over time? Does it last or does it break down? What is the nature and quality of each co-parent's relationship with the child? And, crucially, what are the effects on children?

Little is known about families created by heterosexual parents who are not in a romantic relationship. But gay men and lesbian women have been co-parenting for some time. Daniel and Richard and Lorraine and Jemma became the proud parents of baby Jamie in 1997. Daniel and Lorraine had been good friends for six years and had set up a business partnership together. When Lorraine mentioned that she wanted to have a baby, Daniel offered to be the biological father as he had always wanted children but, like many gay men, had not thought that this would be an option for him. Lorraine had a home birth with all four parents present. 'The plan was that we would have Jamie for one night per week and one weekend per month,' Daniel told me when I visited him in his London home 20 years later. 'In actual fact, when Jamie was very little and Lorraine was breast feeding, she used to stay over at our house a lot or we'd stay at hers. We spent a lot of time together. Jamie didn't stay over with us alone until he was nearly one because Lorraine was breastfeeding and also because she didn't want to be apart from him.' Before Jamie started school, Daniel took one day off work each week to look after him with his partner, Richard, who worked from home. Lorraine worked part-time so she had him for two days per week. Jamie also had six very involved grandparents who were delighted to fill the gaps.

As time went on, Jamie would stay with Daniel and Richard one or two nights each week. When he was four, the two couples bought a house in the country together. Sometimes Jamie would go there with his two mothers, and at other times he would go with his two fathers. Often, all four parents and Jamie would spend Christmas, Easter, and summer holidays at the house together. It has been a very special place for Jamie. As he grew older, Jamie would spend part of the weekend with each set of parents and see his dads twice during the week. When he turned 13, he wanted to have more ordinary time with his dads, doing homework and hanging out. So for one week in three he would stay with Daniel and Richard for the entire week. Towards the end of his school days, the arrangement became much more fluid. Jamie would spend two-thirds of his time with his mums and the rest with his dads.

For Daniel and Richard, raising Jamie has been the most wonderful experience. 'I can't imagine what life would be like not having had a child. It has been the most astonishing thing. We are very lucky,' says Daniel. 'All four of us come from happy families where the parents haven't divorced. Jamie has basically been another grandchild. For my parents, he's simply my boy. My parents love all their grandchildren and Jamie is as much their grandchild as their other grandchildren. Jamie is Lorraine's mum's only grandchild and she is extremely fond of him. Richard's dad lives next door and is very much involved. They are all part of Jamie's family life. It has just felt normal. Not an experiment. Everyone has been on board. He's just another kid. Another grandchild. Another cousin. There's no sense that he's any different. He has that sense of belonging.' What struck me speaking to Daniel was how well it had turned out. The parents had not fallen out as many would have feared — they remained extremely close. And Jamie is a happy, stable, and accomplished young man now doing well at university, and still the apple of the eye of his four devoted parents and six doting grandparents.

An increasing number of co-parenting families are being formed by men and women who use connection websites such as Pride Angel, Pollen Tree, Modamily and Just a Baby to meet each other and create families. These parents are very different from Jamie's parents who were close friends long before they decided to embark on parenthood together. It's too early to tell whether co-parenting by former strangers

— whether heterosexual or gay — will turn out so well. Sarah Foley, a developmental psychologist at the Centre for Family Research, and Vasanti Jadva, have begun a study of co-parents and their children in arrangements like this to find out. From what we have learned so far, good communication between parents is essential, and a warm and cooperative relationship between the parents is likely to be key to children's wellbeing. But we don't yet know how children will feel about their family situation, and how it will play out over time.

✳✳✳

While heterosexual single mothers by choice are becoming increasingly visible and accepted, it is perhaps more surprising that heterosexual men are becoming single fathers by choice. In May 2019, in Los Angeles, a few months after I spoke with Kelley Hageman about her experiences as an egg donor, I met Adam, the father of the second set of twins, Lea and Mike, conceived using her eggs. I noticed many similarities between Adam's experiences and the stories I heard from single mothers by choice. Adam had always wanted to be a father, but after a ten-year relationship and then a seven-year marriage ended because neither of his partners wanted to have children, Adam felt that his only option was to go it alone. By that time, it was too late for women of his own age to have children, or they had already had children and didn't want any more. Like many single mothers by choice, Adam hopes that he will meet a new partner one day who will be a mother to Lea and Mike.

Bringing up the twins as a single father has not been easy for Adam. For the first two years, he tried to juggle his demanding job as a computer scientist in a large banking corporation with childcare, but it didn't work out. At first he hired nannies, but when one nanny, who the children were fond of, left without warning, he decided to enrol the twins in pre-school instead. That brought different problems, as his demanding working hours were incompatible with the pre-school day. After being late for work once too often, he was demoted, and eventually laid off. 'I decided to become a stay-at-home dad,' Adam told me. 'I started to take care of the twins myself and I am pleased I did that because I can spend time with my children and they are much happier. It really helped them a lot. They don't have nightmares anymore, they don't cry at night, and they sleep well. I think that's the best thing I've done. Financially, it's not as good as working, but we're good.'

When I visited, it was just after Mother's Day which can be a difficult time for children with single dads. Adam said, 'For a week or two beforehand, my children are exposed to all these songs for mothers, and making artwork for their mums, and writing cards saying why they love their mum. They are expected to have a mother. It's the norm. It's the hardest part.' Adam worries that not having a mother is having a negative impact on Mike's behaviour. Sometimes he hits other children at school, and sometimes he is aggressive towards Lea. 'I think that Mike's anger stems from having several different nannies, and from not having the care of a mum to give him the love he needs,' said Adam. 'It's been an issue, and I've been talking to a counsellor about it. Hopefully, we'll be able to come to a solution.'

Now that the twins are four, their friends at pre-school have begun to ask questions about their mother. Adam finds this particularly challenging, 'The other day when I was picking them up, one of my son's friends asked me, "Where is Mike's mummy?" I was taken by surprise and didn't know what to say. I replied, "She's not here." Ever since, I've been thinking about what I should have said.'

Adam is also faced with the task of explaining to the twins why they don't have a mother: 'I tell them stories about somebody who didn't have kids and wanted to have children and went to somebody to help them to have children. As their understanding grows, I will tell them how it happened.' Lea is more interested than Mike in the story of their birth. 'Lea knows Kelley's special,' said Adam. 'She asked me specifically what Kelley is to her. I said that Kelley helped her come into the world. She asked, "Who gave birth to me? Did I come from your tummy?" I said, "No, you came from Jan, the surrogate's, tummy." She partly knows who Kelley is, but she doesn't have a clear understanding yet. Kelley comes and hugs them, and baths them, and stays a couple of days with them. They know that she's more than just a family friend. They love her.'

***

In 2010, lesbian couples began to have children through shared bio-logical parenting where one woman's egg is used to create an embryo with donated sperm, and the other woman carries the pregnancy. This enables both mothers to have a biological connection to their child; the mother who provides the egg has a genetic connection and the mother who goes through pregnancy has a gestational connection. Meg and Gail, who both work in a call centre, had their daughter, Lottie, this way, using Gail's egg. 'For straight couples, their babies are part of both of them. I didn't want our baby to come from just one of us, so we chose to do it this way,' said Meg. 'I didn't want Gail's family to think that she's not part of this child, and I didn't want my family to think that Gail's not part of this child, so it was really important to me that we did it this way. I'm Mamma and Gail's Mummy. This is the closest we could get to her physically being ours.'

The couple chose a sperm donor who looked like Meg in the hope that their child would resemble both mothers. 'Lottie is the spitting image of Gail,' said Meg. 'Physically she shouldn't be anything like me, but when I show people her photo, they all see a resemblance.' Because Meg was pregnant with Lottie, she took maternity leave while Gail continued to work. At first that was difficult for Gail because she didn't have much time to spend with Lottie. But now that Lottie is two, and Meg has returned to work, the couple play an equal role in Lottie's life, each working part-time and Lottie attending day-care. 'Now it's perfect because we share everything, we share responsibilities, we share decisions, we have a much more balanced life, all of us, instead of one being at home and one being at work.'

During the pregnancy, Gail thought that Meg had bonded more than she had with their unborn baby, but the moment Lottie entered the world, Gail felt the same, 'As soon as she came out, my love for her was unconditional. It's not that I didn't love her before, but my love was more for Meg carrying the baby. I hadn't connected until she came. I love her to bits. She's just amazing. Her sense of humour is the best thing. She's so funny. Even when she's naughty I can't help but love her.'

Meg and Gail have been very open about how Lottie was conceived, and plan to explain it to Lottie as soon as she begins to ask questions. Despite the positive reaction they have had from family and friends, they have encountered disapproval from members of their local community, which worries Meg. 'I see other people causing problems for Lottie. Those judgey people. Their children are going to repeat what they say at home. So if they say inappropriate things about us, their children are going to say them to my little Lottie. I don't think our family situation will cause the problem, I think other people will cause the problem.'

Meg and Gail are happy that they each have a biological connection to Lottie. As Meg put it, 'Because of what we've been through to have a baby, I think it's given us a greater appreciation of what we have. A lot of planning went into it, not just about how we'd have a baby, but also how we'd raise our baby, before the baby came. I think, for us, that's been a great advantage.' Gail concluded, 'It's quite a rollercoaster, but it's worth it. If everything goes right, the end is worth everything. You have to really want to do it because of everything you have to go through. It's hard, but it's completely worth it.'

***

Today, ever-changing technological advances in the field of reproduction are leading to new types of families, and new controversies over whether these emerging technologies should be permitted or banned. One example is mitochondrial donation, designed to prevent the transmission of incurable and life-threatening mitochondrial disease that is passed down through families from mother to child through the mitochondria in the mother's egg. Unlike the egg's nucleus, which contains the genes that influence our personal characteristics, the mitochondria that surround the nucleus provide less than one per cent of our genes. Rather than affecting who we are, the function of mitochondria is to provide energy for our cells. Although mitochondrial donation can be carried out in different ways, the end result is the same — the replacement of the faulty mitochondrial DNA in the mother's egg with healthy mitochondrial DNA from another woman. Although the scientific research that made mitochondrial donation possible was conducted in the United Kingdom by Sir Douglas Turnbull — who became interested in this issue when a woman, Sharon Bernardi, was referred to his clinic in Newcastle, England, because she had lost six new-born babies through mitochondrial disease — the first child conceived using this technique was born in Mexico in 2016.

Mitochondrial donation has sparked controversy because, for the first time, children have genetic material from three people; their mother, their father, and the woman who donated her mitochondrial DNA. It's for this reason that they are often referred to as 'three-parent babies'. The procedure has attracted criticism because of the potentially harmful effects on children's identity of knowing that someone other than their mother and father was involved in their conception. It is not yet known how children will feel about having two 'mothers' as they grow up — the mother who contributed their nuclear DNA, gave birth to them, and raised them, and the woman who contributed their mitochondrial DNA — as so few have yet been born. But given that fifty per cent of the genes of children born through egg donation come from a donor, and these children appear to be doing well, I think it's unlikely that having less than one per cent of one's genetic material from a donor will cause children psychological harm. We know that some children born from egg donation wish to find out about, and make contact with, the person who contributed half of their genetic make-up. Their primary motivation is curiosity — a wish to understand more about themselves and their ancestry. Some children born through mitochondrial donation may wish to do the same.

Scientific advances have also led to uterus transplants. In August 2019, when I was invited to speak at a meeting of the Nordic Fertility Society in Gothenburg, Sweden, I had the good fortune to meet Malin Stenberg, the first woman in the world to have a baby following a uterus transplant. Malin and Ewa Rosen, the woman who made it possible by donating her uterus, were there to talk about their experiences with the journalist, Henrietta Westman, who had documented their extraordinary story in her book, *The Way to Vincent: a story about a boy who became a worldwide sensation.*

It wasn't until 1995, when she was almost 17, that Malin discovered she had Rokitansky Syndrome, a rare condition that meant she had been born without a uterus. When her family doctor told her that she would never be able to have children, she was in shock. As she described it, everything went black. She felt ashamed to be different, and she questioned whether she was a real woman if she couldn't have children. As she grew older, her sadness grew, but she didn't want to talk about it. She had several boyfriends, but these relationships didn't last because of her condition. Malin focused on the advantages of a child-free life, and threw herself into sport and her career, convincing herself that she didn't want to be a mother. It was only when she met her future husband, Klaus, that everything changed, Malin told me. 'He said, "I don't believe you." He could see how much I loved kids. He said I was lying to myself. He was so right!'

The couple decided that they would try to find a way of having a family, but hit dead-ends with adoption and surrogacy, which is illegal in Sweden, and would have meant going abroad under uncertain circumstances which they were not keen to do. It was when Malin was invited to a meeting for women with Rokitansky Syndrome at the University Hospital in Gothenburg in 2010 that she first heard about uterus transplants. The team of doctors, led by Professor Mats Brännström, stressed that it was a risky procedure with no guarantee of success. The patient and the donor would both need to go through extensive surgery and take immunosuppressive medication to reduce the chance of the recipient's body rejecting a uterus from someone else. And perhaps the biggest hurdle of all, any woman who wished to try this procedure would be responsible for finding a donor. Malin's mother wanted to help, but her blood type didn't match, and her sister was too young As Malin pointed out, you can't just ring people up and say, 'Hey, can I have your uterus?'

The couple had given up hope when Ewa, the mother of Malin's husband's best friend, heard about the couple's plight from her daughter-in-law on Christmas Eve. 'They can have mine,' she said, 'I don't need it.' Ewa was 59. In February 2011, Ewa called Klaus with her exceptionally generous offer. She had nothing to gain personally — she simply wanted to help Malin and Klaus have the child they so desired. The surgery took place in February 2013. Ewa was nervous, but not as much as her husband and son. The surgery took many hours, first to remove Ewa's uterus while Malin and Klaus waited anxiously at home for the phone call to tell them it was time for Malin to come in for the transplant. The two women shared a room at the hospital during the recovery period, and they were back to normal within several weeks. But Malin had to wait for one year until it was deemed safe for her to try to get pregnant. The couple had 11 frozen embryos, but Malin became pregnant on the first attempt. Vincent entered the world at 5 am on 1 September 2014.

Today, Malin and Ewa are very close — the two families, and Malin and Klaus's parents, celebrate Christmas and Easter together, and

Ewa is Vincent's very special godmother. 'Vincent is a curious, active, sporty boy who loves horses and playing with his friends,' Malin told me. 'We fought so hard to have a child, we longed for it so much, every day we say how grateful we are. It means more that I can say.'

Before long, not only will children be conceived outside the body through IVF, but they will be gestated outside the body too. Artificial wombs that mimic the conditions of the human uterus are set to change the nature of reproduction. In the first instance, artificial wombs will be used to enable premature babies to continue to develop as if they are still in their mothers' bodies. In the future, artificial wombs may become an alternative to pregnancy. In 2017, it was reported that scientists at the University of Cambridge had kept a human embryo alive in an artificial womb until just before the legal limit of 14 days.

On the not-too-distant horizon, scientists believe it will be possible to make synthetic eggs and sperm, either from cells taken from male testes or female ovaries, from cells extracted from embryos at the earliest stage of development, or from non-reproductive tissue such as skin cells. This will be life-changing for men who can't produce sperm, and for women who can't produce eggs; they will be able to have genetically related children, obviating the need for sperm, egg, and embryo donation. It will also be transformative for same-sex couples. By enabling men and women to produce both eggs and sperm, this procedure will mean that gay and lesbian couples will be able to have children who are genetically related to both parents. Even more radical is the idea that single people will be able to have children conceived using synthetic eggs and sperm created from their own skin cells — children who are genetically related only to them. Although this may become technically possible in the future, the close similarity of the genes of these eggs and sperm would put the children at risk of being born with genetic disorders.

While these scientific advances have been met with opposition, none has triggered the wide-scale opprobrium sparked by the prospect of human germline genome editing. In November 2018, the announcement that Dr He Jiankui, a scientist from Shenzhen, China, had been responsible for the birth of the first genetically modified children shocked the scientific community and the world. He had used the gene editing technique known as CRISPR to alter the genetic make-up of twin girls when they were still embryos, with the aim of making them resistant to HIV. Although CRISPR is being used to study and treat genetic disease, never before had children been created from eggs, sperm, or embryos with edited genes — a procedure known as human germline genome editing — in which genetic alterations are passed from one generation to the next. While there may be potential benefits of being able to edit genes that are responsible for serious genetic disorders, and prevent these disorders being passed down the family line, the safety of the procedure has not been proven, the consequences not yet understood, and the social and ethical implications have not yet been properly addressed. In December 2019, Dr He was sentenced to three years in prison for conducting an 'illegal medical practice'.

What these future ways of forming families will mean for parents and children is hard to predict. They each raise complex social and ethical questions. Will the availability of womb transplants put pressure on women to undergo risky and invasive surgical procedures? Will artificial gametes mean that young children, or the very elderly, can have babies? Will gene editing be used to create 'designer babies', who are smarter and more attractive than they would otherwise have been? Will artificial wombs lead to the demise of surrogates, making it easier for infertile couples, gay couples, transgender people, and single men to become parents? For some, these emerging technologies bring to mind Aldous Huxley's dystopian vision of children conceived in the laboratory and gestated in artificial wombs topped up with hormones and chemicals to steer their development according to their future social roles. Others view them as scientific breakthroughs with the potential to benefit individuals and society. And yet others see them as ways of creating their own families that would not otherwise be possible for them.

***

Since the introduction of IVF in 1978, controversies have raged about which new reproductive procedures should and shouldn't be allowed, and IVF itself has gone from being a contentious and dangerous technology to a widely used and accepted fertility treatment. This is largely because regulation has been put in place to outlaw unsafe and unethical procedures, and professional bodies have issued strict guidelines on policy and practice. From our studies of new family forms that have emerged since the 1970s — families that were considered threatening and objectionable when they first appeared — it seems likely that many of the fears about future families will turn out to be unjustified; irrespective of the method of their conception and gestation, and providing that any new reproductive technologies are proven to be safe, considered to be ethical, and are properly regulated, children are likely to flourish as long as they have loving homes and a supportive social world.

Chapter 10

Conclusions

'For turning children into responsible and happy adults, there is absolutely nothing to beat the traditional family.'

DAILY MAIL NEWSPAPER, (1991).

'Queer families aren't that unusual from any other family really. Apart from the way we get treated, there's not really a big difference.'

JULIE, AGE 12, (2018).

In 2019, *BioNews,* a weekly online bulletin on what's new in genetics and reproduction, reported on a demographic study predicting that 3 per cent of the world's population — 400 million people — may result from assisted reproductive technologies by 2100, a figure that includes those conceived through assisted reproduction and their descendants. We have come a long way since *Nova* magazine claimed in 1972 that test-tube babies are 'the biggest threat since the atom bomb'. I was born in the post-war 'baby-boomer' years when the traditional family was at its peak. That's just how families were in the 1950s and 60s, and no one questioned it. Thinking back to 1976, when I began my first study of children with lesbian mothers, I am amazed by the changes to the family that have taken place since then. Who would have thought that same-sex marriage would be possible in almost 30 countries, and that more than eight million children would have been born by IVF?

Louise Brown, the first IVF baby, hadn't yet been conceived, and the idea that mothers could give birth to genetically unrelated children, that twins and triplets could be born years apart, or that donor-conceived half-siblings would be searching for each other over the Internet, was still the stuff of science fiction. Back then, we didn't have personal computers, let alone the Internet.

Is that the end of the story? Are there no longer concerns about children whose families don't fit the traditional family model? Sadly, the answer is no. In 2013, violence broke out in the streets of Paris when an estimated 150,000 people demonstrated against a new law allowing same-sex couples to marry and adopt children. Two years later, the Northern Ireland Health Minister was forced to resign after claiming that gay parents were likely to abuse their children. Since 2016, an increasing number of US states have introduced legislation to enable religiously affiliated adoption agencies to turn away prospective LGBTQ+ adoptive parents. And in 2019, protests broke out in Birmingham, England, against schools teaching children about families with same-sex parents. Amidst this growing backlash against non-traditional families, empirical evidence is more important than ever.

Since its heyday in the 1950s, the traditional family of married heterosexual parents with genetically related children has been in decline. By 2014, according to the Pew Research Center, less than half of children in the United States lived in a family with two married parents in their first marriage. But the traditional family is still held up as the ideal — the type of family we should all aspire to if we want to raise well-adjusted children. This is partly because families that are non-traditional are lumped together irrespective of whether they result from family breakdown or are created in new ways made possible by changing technologies and shifting social attitudes. The two are not the same and neither are the consequences for children. As we saw, children in single-parent families resulting from divorce, or born to single mothers from unplanned pregnancies, and children in stepfamilies who have to negotiate relationships with new family members, are more likely to face challenges than those whose parents stay together. By no means are all children affected. But the experience of their parents' separation and its aftermath, the financial hardship and lack of social support that often accompany single parenthood, and the transition to life in a stepfamily, for some, can take their toll.

The families in this book are different. Parents in LGBTQ+ families, and in families created by assisted reproduction, struggle to start a family. All are faced with infertility, or social disapproval, or both, in their quest for a child. Those who make it through are just as likely, and in some cases more likely, than parents in traditional families to have warm, close, and engaged relationships with their children. This doesn't mean that all children in new family forms flourish. But it does mean they have an equal chance of doing well.

Family means different things to different children. For Maria, family means one mum. For Nicholas it's two dads. For Gee it's her mum and dad, but she is also close to the surrogate who gave birth to her and who is also her genetic mother. Because modern families diverge from the traditional family in various ways — with one parent instead of two, male parents instead of female parents, same-sex parents instead of heterosexual parents, transgender parents instead of cisgender parents, and parents without a genetic or gestational connection to their children instead of biologically related parents — they separate aspects of family structure that usually go together, and help us understand how much they matter for all children, not just those in new family forms. What these families show us is that the make-up of families — the number, gender, sexual orientation, gender identity, and biological relatedness of parents — matters less for children than previously thought. The presence of a father, or even a mother, or two parents, is not essential for children to thrive. What matters most for children is the quality of relationships within their family, the support of their wider community, and the attitudes of the society in which they live.

***

So what exactly is it about family life that makes a difference to children's psychological wellbeing? This is a question that psychologists have been investigating for more than 50 years, and although families have been studied in different ways, there is a general consensus that the quality of parents' relationships with their children is key. Parents who are warm and affectionate towards their children, who are attentive and receptive to them, and who spend time interacting with and supporting them are more likely to have psychologically healthy children. In contrast, children of parents who are cold or rejecting, who are unreliable and inconsistent, and who are either too harsh or too lenient in disciplining them are more at risk of developing emotional and behavioural problems. Taken to its extreme, poor parenting becomes maltreatment — physical, sexual, and emotional abuse — which can have devastating and long-lasting consequences for children.

Research on children's relationships with their parents dates back to the middle of the 20th century, when the child psychiatrist and psychoanalyst, John Bowlby, and the psychologist, Mary Ainsworth, began to study infants' attachments to their mothers. It is no longer thought that children become attached only to their mothers; they usually become attached to the person most involved in looking after them, and they can form attachments to other people too, usually in a clear order of preference. Unless children experience severe neglect, such as those who were discovered in Romanian orphanages in 1989 after the fall of the Ceausescu regime, all children form attachments.

But children differ in how secure their attachments are. Some children become securely attached to their parents, and feel confident to explore the world around them and be comforted by them when they encounter stressful situations. Others, who are insecurely attached, respond less well to stress, either becoming extremely distressed and finding it difficult to take comfort from their parents, or showing little emotion and tending not to turn to them for solace. A minority of children, who may have experienced trauma or neglect in early childhood, show no clear approach to coping with stress. Children may be securely attached to both parents, insecurely attached to both parents, or securely attached to one parent and insecurely attached to the other parent. Those with single parents may be securely or insecurely attached to that parent. Research on why some children form secure attachments and others do not, shows that parents who are sensitive and responsive to their children's feelings are more likely to have secure children. But attachment is not set in stone. Secure children can become insecure, and vice versa, depending on the circumstances of their lives.

According to John Bowlby, as children grow older, they build up representations of their relationships with their parents in their minds that influence not only their expectations of how their parents will treat them, but also of how they come to see themselves. It's thought that secure children see their parents as available and helpful when they need them, and have a positive self-image, whereas insecure children see their parents as undependable and view themselves in a less positive light. How children think about their parents, and themselves, is believed to influence children's relationships with others as they grow up.

Children who are securely attached to at least one parent in infancy tend to do better emotionally and socially in their pre-school and early school years; high self-esteem, popularity with other children, and being independent at school are just some of the characteristics that are more typical of securely attached children. But it is not inevitable that securely attached infants will grow into well-adjusted children, or that children who have insecure attachments in the first years of life will experience psychological difficulties. What this research tells us is that secure attachment is more likely to result in positive outcomes for children, but other factors are involved.

Psychologists who have explored different ways in which parents influence their children have found that a good balance between warmth and affection on one hand, and control and discipline of children on the other, is important. Diane Baumrind examined how warmth and control intersect with each other, and identified four styles of parenting. Authoritarian parents are very controlling, expect their children to do as they say, and discipline them harshly. Permissive parents are loving parents, but exert little control over their children's behaviour and make few demands of them. Rejecting or neglecting parents are unsupportive and do not monitor what their children are doing. The most positive style of parenting is an authoritative style, combining warmth and affection with firm control. Authoritative parents monitor their children's activities and friendships, and control their children's behaviour through negotiation, rather than punishment, so that they still feel loved and accepted. Children of these parents are more likely to be self-controlled, responsible, cooperative, and self-reliant than children of the other types of parents, and less likely to develop emotional and behavioural problems.

It is not only parents' relationships with their children, but also with each other, that makes a difference to children's wellbeing. It's not so much dissatisfaction with their relationship, which children are not necessarily aware of, but outright conflict, that has the damaging effect. Research by the psychologist Mark Cummings has shown that children whose parents are hostile towards each other are more likely to be aggressive, disobedient, and difficult to control. Almost all children in two-parent families see their parents argue, and that's thought to be a good thing if they also see them make up. What seems to affect children is not whether their parents fight, but *how* they fight. If their parents' rows are frequent, severe — especially if they are physically violent — and don't resolve quickly, they are more likely to be damaging to children. It's especially upsetting for children if they are the subject of their parents' disputes, and also if they think that each argument between them is bringing them closer to splitting up. Witnessing their parents' hostility towards each other can cause children anguish. But that's not the only reason children are affected. It's hard for parents who are in conflict with each other to function as effective parents.

Parents' mental health problems can also affect their children. Children whose parents are depressed are not only more likely to show a wide range of psychological problems, but are also more likely to become depressed themselves. Although some children may inherit a susceptibility to depression, depression can interfere directly with parents' relationships with their children, making them less warm and responsive than they would normally be, which may have a knock-on effect on children's wellbeing. Parents' drug and alcohol dependence can also be damaging, not least because a high rate of neglect and abuse has been found among the children of alcoholic and drug-dependent parents.

It's not possible to understand the ways in which parents influence their children's wellbeing without taking account of the social circumstances of the family, one of the most damaging of which is poverty. Research by Vonnie McLoyd has clearly shown that children raised in poverty, in comparison with children from affluent backgrounds, are more likely to perform poorly at school, drop out of school early, become involved in antisocial behaviour, have unwanted pregnancies, and develop emotional problems in their teenage years. Poverty interferes with children's psychological development in many ways. Even before birth, children are at a disadvantage; they are more likely to be exposed to drugs, alcohol, and malnutrition in the womb, and to be born prematurely. Drug and alcohol dependence often go hand in hand with poverty. As they grow up, they are less likely to have access to toys and books at home and to attend high quality schools, both of which mitigate against academic achievement. Beyond that, poverty has a pervasive and deleterious effect on the quality of parenting that children receive. Parents who are faced with the pressures of making ends meet often lack support, become depressed, their relationships deteriorate, and the demands of their children become a further source of stress. It is now widely accepted that the link between poverty and children's difficulties stems, to a large extent, from the insidious effects of poverty on family relationships.

But not all children raised under even the most extreme conditions of social deprivation develop psychological problems. Why is it that some children are able to overcome hardship whereas others are affected throughout their lives? One reason is that some children are more resilient than others. These children seem to be much less affected by the kinds of stresses that, for other children, lead to psychological problems. They may be raised in poverty, or they may be victims of abuse, but however bad their experiences, they seem to bounce back.

Studies designed to find out what's different about resilient children have found that they stand out right from the start. As babies, they are more affectionate, more active, and have fewer eating and sleeping problems. At school, they are more independent, have higher self-esteem, and better relationships with their peers. But these children are set apart by more than just their characteristics. Resilient children are also more likely to have a close and affectionate relationship with at least one parent, and receive emotional support from someone outside the family, such as a teacher. A warm and supportive relationship with at least one person was found to be an important factor in protecting vulnerable children from the harmful effects of the stressors in their lives.

The quality of relationships between parents and their children is not simply down to parents; it goes both ways. From the day they are born, babies have distinct temperaments. Some cry more than others, some are more active than others, and some like being cuddled more than others. In the 1960s, the psychologists Stella Chess and Alexander Thomas were the first to study differences in the behaviour of newborn babies, classifying them as 'easy', 'difficult', or 'slow to warm up'. Since that time, other researchers have come up with a variety of ways in which infants differ from each other. These include how active the baby is, how easily the baby becomes distressed or frightened, how irritable the baby is, how sociable the baby is, and how quickly the baby responds to new situations. Babies' temperaments can have a profound effect on the behaviour of their parents towards them; parents may be more likely to pick up a crying baby who is easily soothed than a baby who is inconsolable no matter what they do. From birth, parents' behaviour towards their children is affected by their children's behaviour towards them.

As children grow older, they continue to influence their parents' behaviour. We often hear of parents treating their children differently; a mother or father may be more affectionate, or angry, towards one child than another, because of their different personalities. Evidence for this comes from studies by the psychologists Judy Dunn and Robert Plomin of brothers and sisters' perceptions of their relationships with their parents. Siblings often say that they are treated differently to each other by their parents, and it's not unusual for one child to be seen as 'the favourite'. This finding changed our understanding of how parents influence their children. We can no longer assume that just because children grow up in the same family, they have similar experiences.

Ethnicity and culture also play a role in parenting, and on the outcomes of different parenting practices for children. Being strict is one example. In cultures where strictness is the norm, it has a less negative effect on children than in cultures where it goes against the grain. In 2011, the publication of Amy Chua's book, *Battle of the Tiger Mother*, ignited a lively debate about the rights and wrongs of this Chinese American mother's controlling and demanding style of raising her two daughters. Such an approach was considered harsh by many western parents. What's acceptable in one culture isn't necessarily embraced by another.

Families are also shaped by the laws and social policies of the countries in which they live, with China providing a notable recent example. In 1979, China introduced a new policy to combat overpopulation; most families, especially those who were living in cities, were restricted to having only one child. Those who had more were fined by the authorities. As a consequence, many babies were abandoned by their parents or put up for adoption.

Lanfen Zhang was born near the Yellow River in 1976, in a small village where everyone had known each other for generations. Her father, Huan, was employed by a local brick factory, and her mother, Chengyi, worked in the fields growing wheat, peanuts, and corn. The family lived in a traditional house that wrapped around a central courtyard, with one building on the street, one more on either side, and the main building at the back for the most important people in the household, her grandparents. By the time Lanfen's sister, Ning, was born in 1982, the one-child policy had come into force. Her parents were fined more than ten times her father's monthly salary.

When Chengyi discovered she was pregnant for a third time, she knew she couldn't keep the baby. 'My youngest sister, Chen, was born in the summer of 1988,' Lanfen explained. 'The previous autumn, my mum told me that she was unwell, and needed to go to hospital in a different province for treatment. She was going to live in her sister's house in Lijiang, in south-west China, until the baby was born, but she didn't tell me the truth in case I couldn't keep the secret. She didn't want us to get into trouble with the authorities. One month after the birth, my mum left Chen in Lijiang with my auntie.'

It was through a letter from her mother to her grandmother that Lanfen discovered she had a second sister. 'I remember the afternoon in August 1988 like yesterday,' said Lanfen. 'We were in the small room. My grandma got out a letter and asked me to read it to her. She had learned some characters when she was younger, when they had a literacy programme, but she wasn't able to read the whole letter. It was then that I found out about the baby. I was told I must keep it secret, even from my younger sister.'

When Chen was born, a local couple who were unable to have children themselves, wanted to adopt her, and offered Chengyi and Huan a large amount of money. They refused, because a condition was that they couldn't see the child. But when a couple in their own family offered to adopt Chen, and promised that they would bring her to visit, they agreed to the arrangement. 'My sister is now 30, and they have never, ever visited my mum and dad with my sister.' said Lanfen. 'My mum was very hurt.' The two families did meet occasionally at family gatherings, but the adoptive parents were worried about losing Chen, were she to discover the truth. As tends to happen with family secrets, the story came out during an argument when Chen was ten.

Today, the three sisters are close. They are all married with children, and Chengyi and Huan were guests at Chen's wedding. At the time I spoke with Lanfen, they were planning a trip to Lijiang with Chengyi and Huan. 'It's just the five of us,' she told me. 'We have never been on a holiday on our own. For me, it's more like a ceremony, a family reunion. It's a way of showing our respect and gratitude to my auntie, and showing our youngest sister the place where she was born, and the people who looked after her. It's a happy ending!'

In 2013, China began to relax its one-child policy, and since January 2016, all couples have been allowed to have two children, with moves afoot to stop birth restrictions altogether, putting an end to the 'loneliest generation' of only children. Concerns about the increasingly ageing population and falling birth rates have led to the change in policy. By 2018, couples were being actively encouraged to have two children, but the nudging seems to be falling on deaf ears. As in other countries, many millennials are postponing starting a family until their thirties, to the disappointment of their parents. In 2016, the *China Daily* newspaper reported on the growing popularity of a matchmakers' market in People's Park in Shanghai, where elderly parents, keen to be grandparents, were looking for partners for their 30-something children.

An unintended consequence of the one-child policy is the higher proportion of men than women in today's Chinese population. Due to the cultural preference for sons, girls were more likely to be aborted, or put up for adoption, than boys under the one-child policy. If a couple could only have one child, they wanted that child to be male. Several decades on, Chinese men are having trouble finding female partners. The reversal of the one-child policy has also produced a boom in the fertility industry in China, not only because people are leaving it later to start a family, but also because couples who had their one permitted child in their twenties, find themselves unable to conceive because of their older age, now that they're free to have a second baby.

***

Just like children in traditional families, the psychological wellbeing of children who grow up in new family forms depends on the wellbeing of their parents, the quality of their relationships with their parents, and the social circumstances in which they grow up. But new family forms create additional issues for children, one of which is having a different pattern of genetic and gestational connections to people inside and outside their immediate family. For children born through egg, sperm, or embryo donation, or surrogacy, family can mean a wider array of people to whom they are biologically connected — donors, surrogates, and donor siblings — than it does for children in a traditional family unit. Some children have little interest in these people, others are curious and want to find out more, and some have a strong desire to meet them. Although most children don't see their donors or surrogates as parents, some do. This is more common among children of single parents. It's not surprising in a world where the traditional family reigns supreme — in the popular imagination, if not in reality — that some children of single mothers by choice wish for a dad.

Why is it that knowing about their donor or surrogate is important to some children and adults born through assisted reproduction? The reason is similar to that of adopted people who search for their birth parents — to gain a better understanding of who they are, where they come from, and where they fit in. Although egg and sperm donation are different from adoption in that the child has a genetic link to one parent, and embryo donation is different from adoption in that the parents experience the pregnancy and raise the child from birth — and in neither case is the child separated from their birth parents — egg, sperm, and embryo donation are like adoption to the extent that the children have a genetic connection to one or more people outside their nuclear family. Children born through surrogacy have a gestational connection to people outside their family, but unlike many adopted children, they are separated from the birth mother before they become attached. Finding out about the donors and surrogates who contributed to their birth fills a gap in knowledge about themselves. Seeing resemblances in physical and personality characteristics, learning about their ancestry, and being able to tell a more complete story of how they came to be — things that those of us who are the genetic children of their mothers and fathers take for granted — can give people born from donated eggs, sperm, embryos, or surrogacy a more secure sense of identity.

The separation of social, genetic, and gestational parenthood in new families produces new predicaments for parents, especially whether, what, and when to tell their children about their conception and birth. Research on families formed through adoption shows that parents who are open with their children, who acknowledge the differences between their family and other families, but don't over-emphasise them, and who convey this information in ways that are appropriate for their age, are more likely to have children who are accepting of how they came to be. Our own studies of families formed by assisted reproduction have led to the same conclusion. Not one set of parents who told their children about their origins at an early age regretted their decision to tell.

The huge popularity of televisions shows such as *Who Do You Think You Are?* which traces the ancestry of celebrities and the social history of their families, and the enormous number of people who are signed up to ancestry databases such as Ancestry.com and 23andMe to search their family tree, suggest that knowing where we come from is important to many people, not just to those who lack a genetic or gestational connection to their parents. I was interested to find out whether there are parallels between the experiences of the celebrities in the television show and those of donor-conceived people who search for their donor relations, so I asked Alex Graham, the creator of *Who Do You Think You Are?*, why he thinks the show is so successful. He replied, '*Who Do You Think You Are?* — like gravity — seems to operate at a distance, and at very great distances too, sometimes over many, many generations. The protagonists have testified to the strange connections they feel to relatives several generations removed — to a sense that they feel a link in a chain that goes back, sometimes many hundreds of years. I think the show resonates with a powerful desire to belong — to something or someone. To feel rooted somehow.' Alex Graham's reply clearly mirrors what many donor-conceived people who are curious about their origins tell us. The search for a sense of connection and belonging may be especially pertinent to people conceived by egg, sperm, or embryo donation, but ultimately resonates with us all.

It also works the other way. Increasingly, donors such as Jon and surrogates like Sarah are interested in knowing about, and sometimes knowing, the children born with their help. And some children's parents value contact too. Jenny and Pamela were surprised about the feelings of closeness they felt towards to their children's donor siblings and their parents. They hadn't expected it at all.

But sometimes the outcomes are more traumatic. Learning about one's donor conception later in life can be shocking and profoundly disturbing, as it was for Louise McLoughlin. On top of that, some people are discovering that they have large numbers of donor siblings, and some donors are discovering that they are responsible for the birth of large numbers of children, both of which can be overwhelming and distressing. Soon, the question of whether or not to tell children about their genetic origins may be irrelevant. As poignantly described in *The Guardian*, '"Your father's not your father": When DNA tests reveal more than you bargained for', and *The Atlantic*, 'When a DNA test shatters your identity', and in Dani Shapiro's moving and illuminating memoir, *Inheritance*, in 2019, today, people can find out that they have been conceived using donated eggs, sperm or embryos through genetic testing kits in combination with online genealogy databases such as 23andMe and AncestryDNA, reported to have more than 25 million DNA samples between them by 2019. All it can take is a saliva sample for someone to discover over the Internet whether they are the genetic child of their parents, and if not, who their genetic relatives are. Donor-conceived people, some of whom were unaware of their origins, are finding themselves matched with their donor and donor-siblings, and inadvertently discovering that their mother, their father, or both parents, are genetically unrelated to them. Sometimes children figure it out for themselves, from genetics lessons at school. Parents who are not open with children about their genetic origins from the start, run the risk of their children discovering this information for themselves. We have reached an age when secrecy about donor conception cannot be guaranteed, and that's just as true for donors who had been promised anonymity as it is for parents who decide not to tell. Even donors who don't sign up themselves may be identified by their donor offspring with a little detective work if others in the donor's family, even first or second cousins, have submitted DNA samples and their family tree. And it's not only donors who can be tracked down by curious donor offspring; a donor's own children, who may not have been told that their parent was a donor, can be identified in this way too, and may be shocked to be contacted by someone claiming to be their half-sibling.

***

Another challenge for parents and children in new family forms, particularly LGBTQ+ families, is stigmatisation. Stigma can affect parents' confidence in themselves, and can have a knock-on effect on their children. Although we often think of stigmatisation as something that occurs between people who are in contact with each other, as described by the school children who took part in our Stonewall study, it can happen at a global level, with a pernicious effect on social attitudes worldwide.

Frank Nelson and his husband, BJ Barone, both high-school teachers, were ecstatic following the birth of their baby boy, Milo, through surrogacy in Canada in June, 2014. With their attention focused on Milo, the couple didn't notice that a photo of them having skin-to-skin contact with their new-born baby by the birth photographer, a friend of the surrogate, had gone viral on Facebook. 'A friend of ours called the next day and she said, "There's about 50,000 Likes on it,"' Frank told me. 'And it just kept going up and up and up — to a couple of million by the end of the week. It happened to be World Pride in Toronto that weekend. Two days later, we were on the local news, and a week later we were on the news in Germany, Australia, and the UK.' The photo showed Frank and BJ, both naked to the waist, holding the baby against their bodies. 'The midwife wanted us both shirtless when the baby was born,' Frank explained. 'She told us that she wanted the baby to have skin-to-skin contact right away, to feel our heartbeat, and to bond with us. It was the midwife's suggestion.'

At first Frank and BJ were delighted by the positive reaction they received from people all around the world, and let the more hostile posts wash over them. 'We got so many beautiful messages from so many people that it seemed to outweigh it for me,' said Frank. 'We got a lot of lovely messages from people saying they had never seen two men with a baby like that before and it made them cry.'

But two years later they were shocked to find that the photo which had made them so proud, was being used by politicians in a smear campaign against gay parents. 'Mary FitzGibbons, an Irish politician running for election in 2016, who was against surrogacy and adoption for gay men, used that photo of us in her campaign,' said Frank. 'Around the same time, a Civil Unions bill was making its way through the Italian Senate. The Fratelli D'Italia, a nationalist conservative political party, used our photo on posters all over Italy in their campaign against the bill, and against surrogacy and adoption by LGBT people. Across our photo it said "This baby will never know its mother." As soon as the posters went up, we were inundated with messages from people on social media and from our family in Italy. It went against everything we stood for — parental rights for LBGT people and more favourable surrogacy laws in Europe. Now our photo was being used for the exact opposite.'

Many lawyers in Italy offered their services to help Frank and BJ fight this injustice to their family. The couple decided not to take it sitting down, and hired an Italian lawyer to file a lawsuit against the Fratelli D'Italia for copyright infringement and the illegal use of their image and that of their baby boy. When I spoke with Frank in July 2019, the lawsuit was making its way through the court system in Italy and he was hoping to receive positive news soon.

It's not just the parents, but also the children in LGBTQ+ families, who are faced with stigmatisation. We know that children's self-esteem and identity can be harmed by bullying and rejection. That can happen to any child. But not being accepted because of the make-up of their family can be particularly stressful. When children see prejudice and discrimination around them, they feel less able to be open about their own family. Stacey, 20, who took part in our Stonewall study of the school experiences of children with same-sex parents, explained, 'My brother and I knew some people in our school that had gay and lesbian parents and that did get bullied quite a lot and that scared us from telling people. So we never really told anyone. It was hard keeping secrets.'

The harmful effects of stigmatisation are sometimes held up as a reason to prevent LGBTQ+ people from adopting children, or having children through assisted reproduction. But the onus should be on schools and communities to combat prejudice and discrimination against children whose families don't fit the traditional family model. The children in the Stonewall study told us how to do it. They said that teachers shouldn't assume that everyone has a mum and dad; that families with same-sex parents should be talked about in school and included in lessons; and that schools should clamp down hard on homophobic bullying, something that doesn't always happen. The children want teachers to understand that having gay parents isn't a problem — it's other people's attitudes that can be the problem.

When schools create a positive and supportive environment for children with LGBTQ+ parents, and also for young people who identify as LGBTQ+, it can make all the difference. As Coral, 14, explained, 'In our school they have an equality group that deals with not very nice gay comments and saying the "gay" word all the time and sayings like that. They deal with it really well to be honest. Basically, they spread the word how it's not very good to say "oh this is so gay" "that's so gay" even though it's used as a different meaning. They tell them that's wrong and why you shouldn't say that.' For Mike, 17, simply seeing a poster on the wall was appreciated, 'Just this year a new English teacher joined who is gay, I think, and he has one of the Stonewall "Some People Are Gay Get Over It" posters in his classroom. Just seeing the poster in his room is really cool.'

**

Changes to the structure of the family in recent decades have led to the claim that the family is in decline. But families are changing, not disappearing. The Urban Dictionary, a dynamic online dictionary that reflects contemporary thinking, defines family as, 'A group of people, usually of the same blood (but do not have to be), who genuinely love, trust, care about, and look out for each other.' Gone is the notion that family means a mother and a father and their biological children. Today, family need not involve the presence of a mother, or a father, or genetic or gestational ties between children and their parents, and it may involve genetic and gestational connections between children and others outside their immediate family circle. For children, family usually means the parents who raise them, who share their daily lives, who love them, and who they love back, and the siblings who grow up with them, whether they are biologically connected or not. Some children born through assisted reproduction may get to know their donors and surrogates, their donors' and surrogates' own children, and the children their donors and surrogates helped create for others. New ways of having children are producing new connections between families that were impossible or unimaginable less than 50 years ago. Whether these connections with biological relatives in other families will stand the test of time, will depend on the social, and not the biological, relationships between them.

Knowing what to call each other can present complications for members of modern families. Kate Bourne, writing about her experiences at VARTA, evocatively described this problem in the 2014 book, *Relatedness in Assisted Reproduction: families, origins and identities*, 'What do I call my sperm donor? Donor, biological father, genetic father, father, real father, donor dad, progenitor, dad? What do I call people created with the same donor? Donor siblings, genetic half-siblings, half-brothers/sisters, brothers/sisters, sort of siblings, kind of cousins? How does a sperm donor describe a person conceived with his donated gametes? Biological son/daughter, donor son/daughter, offspring, child?' How does a donor-conceived person introduce their donor or half-sibling by donation to a stranger? Are we family, special friends or something in between?' In the absence of generally accepted terms for these new relationships, some children in our research made up their own; diblings [donor siblings], cousin-sister, and tummy-sister were a few of the labels that children used to describe the people they were connected to in other families through assisted reproduction. But the meaning they attached to these labels differed widely; just because they referred to someone born from the same donor as a sister or brother, or half-sister or half-brother, did not necessarily mean that they saw them in that way. Sometimes it just made life easier not to have to explain the relationship. Others deliberately avoided these terms because they did not see their genetic half-siblings as family. As Vasanti Jadva and Susan Imrie found out when they interviewed the children of surrogates, whether or not they felt close to the surrogacy child had little to do with the presence or absence of a genetic connection between them.

***

Creating families in novel ways brings new dilemmas. Following two surgeries, many rounds of timed intercourse and insemination with her husband's sperm, and eventually a successful IVF cycle that resulted in their son, and later their daughter, Gina and JP Davis were left with more embryos than they could use themselves. Unlike Jennifer and Tom, who had one embryo to think about, Gina and JP had 16, a very different proposition.

Gina worked as a genetic counsellor at a fertility clinic, but was surprised to find herself in the same situation as her patients. 'I'd been helping people with embryo donation for several years, and then suddenly I was on the other side,' she explained. 'I realised what a responsibility it is. I started thinking about how to find recipients for our embryos. We asked ourselves, "What are the qualities that are important to us? What are the qualities that would be best for the kids so that they all feel happy in their own families?" It was like playing God.' There were moments when the couple thought it was too difficult to donate their embryos: 'I thought to myself, "Is it selfish of me? Are they going to feel like they're guinea pigs in a science experiment of life?"' But the alternative was that the embryos didn't even have a chance.

The couple's biggest fear was that the children would be emotionally harmed, 'Even though they're in a lovely household with lovely parents, what if they feel a sense of loss? We wondered how they would feel, and if they could ever forgive us for making this decision for them.' Because of her work, Gina has a deep appreciation for what these embryos could mean for someone who wants a family, but also a profound feeling of responsibility to find them the best home. She explained, 'I know that DNA doesn't make a family but I also know that it is a critical piece in an identity story. I had to find a way to unite those two concepts. I had to feel I was doing my due diligence since I was responsible for creating these embryos.'

When we spoke in 2019, the couple had found their first recipients — Gina's Uncle Ted and his new wife, Lauren. At first they worried that donating embryos to someone in their family would make a difficult situation even more complicated than it need be, but they liked Ted and Lauren very much. That's what clinched it for them. 'We already know how his older kids turned out, so we already know what a great dad he is,' said Gina. But she was nervous. She worried about seeing their genetic children at family gatherings, and didn't know how she would respond.

Gina's fears turned out to be unfounded. 'They transferred one embryo and now they have a daughter, Alice, who is six months old,' said Gina. 'I get to see Alice's smile now; I get to see who she is and that she was meant to be here. It feels easier now. I see what wonderful

269

joy she has brought to her family. She's such a smiley, happy baby, and I look at her and think, "She's amazing!"' The two families have become close, especially Gina and Lauren. As Gina described it, 'I think they are comfortable with us being a bit closer than cousins might be, and they want her to know us and her whole story. They view it as the more family for Alice, the better. That will mean she is loved by even more people, and has a special place in people's hearts.' Today research on new family forms is not simply examining whether they match up to the traditional family, but in what ways they may be better.

Alice's birth solidified Gina and JP's decision to donate their embryos to other couples, but also showed them an ideal scenario that they know they can't necessarily replicate with future donations. They gave Ted and Lauren eight embryos and it worked with the first one. They still have eight left to donate, and an additional seven if Ted and Lauren decide not to transfer any more. Having worked with fertility patients for years, Gina worries about reaching out to someone, only to let them down if they don't seem right. She said, 'I just don't want to hurt people. I'd hate to drag people through yet another layer of heartbreak.' They hope to find some mixed-race couples to donate to, as JP has an African American father and a Filipino mother, but finding people like themselves has been hard. 'Both of us understand that feeling of not belonging,' said Gina. 'JP didn't feel totally accepted when he was growing up. For a long time, he felt displaced. And due to a complicated childhood and custody arrangement, I felt that too. That's the most painful part of this — that these children could feel the same way, and that we contributed to it. And that's scary because it's so the opposite of what we would ever want to do.'

***

Families have changed in form but not in function. They matter just as much for children as they ever did. Children are most likely to flourish in warm, supportive, stable families, whatever their structure, and are most likely to experience emotional and behavioural problems in hostile, unsupportive and unstable families, whatever their structure. Just because people become parents in non-conventional ways does not make them less capable parents or love their children less. It seems from our research that the opposite is true — those who have children against the odds become highly involved and committed parents.

But however connected children feel to their family, they must also function in the outside world. Children need to feel accepted, and that they belong, not only to their family, but also to their peer group and their wider community. One finding that stands out loud and clear, is that intolerance of their family can be hurtful and deeply distressing. It's not the make-up of their family, but other people's reaction to it, that is upsetting for children. That's why it's so important to include children's voices in our research, and essential that we listen, and respond, to what they tell us.

In October 2017, when Australia was conducting a postal survey on attitudes towards same-sex marriage, two teenage children with lesbian mothers made a film with young children about what they think about having same-sex parents. 'It makes me feel angry that people can't be together when they like each other,' says Azra, a lively seven-year-old. 'I just want to tell Australia that love makes a family.'

We can all learn from these children. They show us that what matters most for children is not the make-up of their family, but their parents' love.

Further Reading

Research cited

The following list of selected academic papers has been compiled from studies of new family forms conducted at the University of Cambridge Centre for Family Research, and previously at the Family and Child Psychology Research Centre, City University, London, and the Institute of Psychiatry, London. Papers that relate to more than one chapter are listed under the chapter to which they are most relevant. Many of the studies below are reviewed in *Modern Families: parents and children in new family forms* published by Cambridge University Press in 2015.

Chapter 1: Lesbian Mothers

Original longitudinal study of lesbian mother families

Golombok, S., Spencer, A., & Rutter, M. (1983) Children in lesbian and single parent households: Psychosexual and psychiatric appraisal. *Journal of Child Psychology and Psychiatry*, *24*, No 4, 551–572

Tasker, F. & Golombok, S. (1995) Adults raised as children in lesbian families. *American Journal of Orthopsychiatry*, *65*, No 2, 203–215.

Golombok, S. & Tasker, F. (1996) Do parents influence the sexual orientation of their children? Findings from a longitudinal study of lesbian families. *Developmental Psychology*, *32*, No 1, 3–11.

Longitudinal study of planned lesbian mother families

Golombok, S., Tasker, F., & Murray, C. (1997) Children raised in fatherless families from infancy: Family relationships and the socio-emotional development of children of lesbian and single heterosexual mothers. *Journal of Child Psychology and Psychiatry*, *38*, No 7, 783–792.

MacCallum, F. & Golombok, S. (2004) Children raised in fatherless families from infancy: A follow-up of children of lesbian and single heterosexual mothers at early adolescence. *Journal of Child Psychology and Psychiatry*, *45*, No 7, 1407–1419.

Golombok, S. & Badger, S. (2010) Children raised in fatherless families from infancy: A follow-up of children of lesbian and single heterosexual mothers in early adulthood. *Human Reproduction*, *25*, No 1, 150–157.

Study of general population sample of lesbian mother families

Golombok, S., Perry, B., Burston, A., Murray, C., Mooney-Somers, J., Stevens, M., & Golding, J. (2003) Children with lesbian parents: A community study. *Developmental Psychology*, *39*, No 1, 20–33.

Stonewall study of children with lesbian and gay parents

Guasp, A., Statham, H., & Jennings, S. (2010) Different Families: The experiences of children with lesbian and gay parents. London: Stonewall.

Chapter 2: Donor Conception Families

European study of assisted reproduction families

Golombok, S., Cook, R., Bish, A., & Murray, C. (1995) Families created by the new reproductive technologies: Quality of parenting and social and emotional development of the children. *Child Development*, *64*, No 2, 285–298.

Cook, R., Golombok, S., Bish, A., & Murray, C. (1995) Keeping secrets: A study of parental attitudes toward telling about donor insemination. *American Journal of Orthopsychiatry*, *65*, No 4, 549–559.

Golombok, S., Brewaeys, A., Cook, R., Giavazzi, M. T., Guerra, D., Mantovani, A., van Hall, E., Crosignani, P.G., & Dexeus, S. (1996) The European Study of Assisted Reproduction Families. *Human Reproduction*, *11*, No 10, 2324–2331.

Golombok, S., MacCallum, F., & Goodman, E. (2001) The 'test-tube' generation: Parent-child relationships and the psychological well-being of IVF children at adolescence. *Child Development*, *72*, No 2, 599–608.

Golombok, S., MacCallum, F., Goodman, E., & Rutter, M. (2002) Families with children conceived by donor insemination: A follow-up at age 12. *Child Development*, *73*, No 3, 952–968.

Golombok, S., Brewaeys, A., Giavazzi, M. T., Guerra, D. MacCallum, F., & Rust, J. (2002) The European Study of Assisted Reproduction Families: The transition to adolescence. *Human Reproduction*, *17*, No 3, 830–840.

Golombok, S., Owen, L., Blake, L., Murray, C., & Jadva, V. (2009) Parent-child relationships and the psychological well-being of 18-year-old adolescents conceived by *in vitro* fertilisation. *Human Fertility*, *12*, No 2, 63–72.

Owen, L. & Golombok, S. (2009) Families created by assisted reproduction: Parent-child relationships in late adolescence. *Journal of Adolescence*, *32*, 835–848.

Longitudinal study of families formed by egg and sperm donation

Golombok, S., Lycett, E., MacCallum, F., Jadva, V., Murray, C., Rust, J., Abdalla, H., Jenkins, J., & Margara, R. (2004) Parenting infants conceived by gamete donation. *Journal of Family Psychology*, *18*, No 3, 443–452.

Golombok, S., Jadva, V., Lycett, E., Murray, C., & MacCallum, F. (2005) Families created by gamete donation: Follow-up at age 2. *Human Reproduction*, *20*, No 1, 286–293.

Golombok, S., Murray, C., Jadva, V., Lycett, E., MacCallum, F., & Rust, J. (2006) Non-genetic and non-gestational parenthood: Consequences for parent-child relationships and the psychological well-being of mothers, fathers and children at age 3. *Human Reproduction*, *21*, 1918–1924.

Blake, L., Casey, P., Readings, J., Jadva, V., & Golombok, S. (2010) 'Daddy ran out of tadpoles': How parents tell their children that they are donor conceived, and what their 7-year olds understand. *Human Reproduction*, *25*, No 10, 2527–2534.

Golombok, S., Readings, J., Blake, L., Casey, P., Mellish, L., Marks, A., & Jadva, V. (2011) Children conceived by gamete donation: The impact of openness about donor conception on psychological adjustment and parent-child relationships at age 7. *Journal of Family Psychology*, *25*, No 2, 230–239.

Readings, J., Blake, L., Casey, P. Jadva, V., & Golombok, S. (2011) Secrecy, openness and everything in between: Decisions of parents of children conceived by donor insemination, egg donation and surrogacy. *Reproductive BioMedicine Online*, *22*, No 5, 485–495.

Jadva, V., Casey, P., Readings, J., Blake, L., & Golombok, S. (2011) A longitudinal study of recipients' views and experiences of intra-family egg donation. *Human Reproduction*, *26*, No 10, 2777–2782.

Blake, L., Casey, P., Jadva, V., & Golombok, S. (2013) 'I was quite amazed': Donor conception and parent-child relationships from the perspective of the child. *Children and Society*, 28, No 6, 425–437.

Casey, P, Jadva, V., Readings, J., Blake, L. & Golombok, S. (2013) Families created by donor insemination: Father-child relationships at age 7. *Journal of Marriage and Family*, *75*, 858–870.

Golombok, S., Blake, L., Casey, P., Roman, G., & Jadva, V. (2013) Children born through reproductive donation: A longitudinal study of child adjustment. *Journal of Child Psychology and Psychiatry*, *54*, 653–660.

Ilioi, E., Blake, L., Jadva, V., Roman, G., & Golombok, S. (2017) The role of age of disclosure of biological origins in the psychological wellbeing of adolescents conceived by reproductive donation: A longitudinal study from age 1 to age 14. *Journal of Child Psychology and Psychiatry*, *58*, No 3, 315–324.

Survey of donor siblings

Freeman, T., Jadva, V., Kramer, W., & Golombok, S. (2009) Gamete donation: Parents experiences of searching for their child's donor siblings and donor. *Human Reproduction*, *24*, No 3, 505–516.

Jadva, V., Freeman, T., Kramer, W., & Golombok, S. (2009) The experiences of adolescents and adults conceived by sperm donation: Comparisons by age of disclosure and family type. *Human Reproduction*, *24*, No 8, 1909–1919.

Jadva, V., Freeman, T., Kramer, W., & Golombok, S. (2010) Experiences of offspring searching for and contacting their donor siblings and donor. *Reproductive BioMedicine Online*, *20*, 523–532.

Study of adolescents who are aware of their donor conception

Slutsky, J., Jadva, V., Freeman, T., Persaud, S., Kramer, W., Steele, M., Steele, H., & Golombok, S. (2016) Integrating donor conception into identity: Parent-child relationships and identity development in donor-conceived adolescents. *Fertility and Sterility*, *106*, No 1, 202–208.

Persaud, S., Freeman, T., Jadva, V., Slutsky, J., Kramer, W., Steele, M., Steele, H., & Golombok, S. (2016) Adolescents conceived through donor insemination in mother-headed families: A qualitative study of motivations and experiences of contacting and meeting same-donor offspring. *Children and Society*, *31*, 13–22.

Study of families formed through embryo donation

MacCallum, F. & Golombok, S. (2007) Embryo donation families: mothers' decisions regarding disclosure of donor conception. *Human Reproduction*, *22*, No 11, 2888–2895.

MacCallum, F., Golombok, S., & Brinsden, P. (2007) Parenting and child development in families with a child conceived by embryo donation. *Journal of Family Psychology*, *21*, 278–287.

Study of families formed through identifiable egg donors

Imrie, S., Jadva, V., Fishel, S., & Golombok, S. (2019) Families created through egg donation: parent-child relationship quality in infancy. *Child Development*, *90*, No 4, 1333–1349.

Imrie, S., Jadva, V., & Golombok, S. (2020) 'Making the child mine': mothers' thoughts and feelings about the mother–infant relationship in egg donation families. *Journal of Family Psychology*. dx.doi.org/10.1037/fam0000619.

Chapter 3: Sperm, Egg, and Embryo Donors

Survey of UK sperm donors

Golombok, S. & Cook, R. (1994) A survey of sperm donation. Phase I: The view of UK licensed centres. *Human Reproduction*, *9*, No 5, 882–888.

Cook, R. & Golombok, S. (1995) A survey of sperm donation. Phase II: The view of donors. *Human Reproduction*, *10*, No 4, 951–959.

Survey of US sperm donors

Jadva, V., Freeman, T., Kramer, W., & Golombok, S. (2011) Sperm and egg donors' experiences of anonymous donation and subsequent contact with their donor offspring. *Human Reproduction*, *26*, No 3, 638–645.

Study of egg donors

Graham, S., Jadva, V., Freeman, T., Ahuja, K., & Golombok, S. (2016) Being an identity-release donor: a qualitative study exploring the motivations, experiences and future expectations of current UK egg donors. *Human Fertility*, *19*, No 4, 230–241.

Study of egg sharing

Gurtin, Z., Ahuja, K., & Golombok, S. (2012) Egg sharing, consent and exploitation: Examining egg-share donors' and recipients' circumstances and retrospective reflections. *Reproductive BioMedicine Online*, *24*, No 7, 698–708.

Gurtin, Z., Ahuja, K., & Golombok, S. (2012) Emotional and relational aspects of egg-sharing: Egg-share donors' and recipients' feelings about each other, each other's treatment outcome, and any resulting children. *Human Reproduction*, 1690–1701.

Gurtin, Z., Ahuja, K., & Golombok, S. (2013) Egg-share donors' and recipients' knowledge, motivations and concerns: Clinical and policy implications. *Clinical Ethics*, *7*, 183–192.

Survey of online sperm donation

Freeman, T., Jadva, V., Tranfield, E., & Golombok, S. (2016) Online sperm donation: A survey of the demographic characteristics, motivations, preferences and experiences of sperm donors on a connection website. *Human Reproduction*, *31*, No 9, 2082–2089.

Jadva, V., Freeman, T., Tranfield, E., & Golombok, S. (2017) Why search for a donor online? The experiences of those searching for and contacting sperm donors on the internet. *Human Fertility*, *21*, No 3, 112–119.

Chapter 4: Surrogates

Study of UK surrogates

Jadva, V., Murray, C., Lycett, E., MacCallum, F., & Golombok, S. (2003) Surrogacy: The experiences of surrogate mothers. *Human Reproduction*, *18*, No 10, 2196–2204.

Imrie, S., & Jadva, V. (2014) The long-term experiences of surrogates: Relationships and contact with surrogacy families in genetic and gestational surrogacy arrangements. *Reproductive BioMedicine Online*, 29, No 4, 424–35.

Jadva, V. & Imrie, S. (2014) Children of surrogate mothers: psychological well-being, family relationships and experiences of surrogacy. *Human Reproduction*, *29*, No 1, 90-96.

Jadva, V., Imrie, S., & Golombok, S. (2015) Surrogate mothers 10 years on: A longitudinal study of psychological well-being and relationships with the parents and child. *Human Reproduction*, *30*, No 2, 373–379.

Study of Indian surrogates

Lamba, N., Jadva, V., Kadum, K., & Golombok, S. (2018) The psychological well-being and maternal-foetal bonding of Indian surrogates: A longitudinal study. *Human Reproduction*, *33*, No 4, 646–653.

Chapter 5: Surrogacy Families

Longitudinal study of families formed through surrogacy

MacCallum, F., Lycett, E., Murray, C., Jadva, V. & Golombok, S. (2003) Surrogacy: The experience of commissioning couples. *Human Reproduction*, *18*, No 6, 1334–1342.

Golombok, S., Murray, C., Jadva, V., MacCallum, F., & Lycett, E. (2004) Families created through surrogacy arrangements: Parent-child relationships in the first year of life. *Developmental Psychology*, *40*, 400–411.

Golombok, S., MacCallum, F., Murray, C., Lycett, E., & Jadva, V. (2006) Surrogacy families: Parental functioning, parent-child relationships and children's psychological development at age 2. *Journal of Child Psychology and Psychiatry*, *47*, No 2, 213–222.

Golombok, S., Casey, P., Readings, J., Blake, L., Marks, A., & Jadva, V. (2011) Families created through surrogacy: Mother-child relationships and children's psychological adjustment at age 7. *Developmental Psychology*, *47*, No 6, 1579–1578.

Jadva, V., Casey, P., Blake, L., & Golombok, S. (2012) Surrogacy families 10 years on: Relationship with the surrogate, decisions over disclosure and children's understanding of their surrogacy origins. *Human Reproduction*, *27*, 3008–3014.

Golombok, S., Ilioi, E., Blake, L., Roman, G., & Jadva, V. (2017) A longitudinal study of families formed through reproductive donation: Parent-adolescent relationships and adolescent adjustment at age 14. *Developmental Psychology*, *53*, No 10, 1966–1977.

Zadeh, S., Illioi, E., Jadva, V., & Golombok, S. (2018) The perspectives of adolescents conceived using surrogacy, egg or sperm donation. *Human Reproduction*, *33*, No 6, 1099–1106.

Chapter 6: Gay Father Families

Longitudinal study of adoptive gay father families

Golombok, S., Mellish, L., Jennings, S., Casey, P., Tasker, F., & Lamb, M. (2014) Adoptive gay father families: Parent-child relationships and children's psychological adjustment. *Child Development, 85,* No 2, 456–468.

Jennings, S., Mellish, L., Casey, P., Tasker, F., Lamb, M., & Golombok, S. (2014) Why adoption? Gay, lesbian and heterosexual adoptive parents' reasons for adoptive parenthood. *Adoption Quarterly, 17,* 205–226.

McConnachie, A. L., Ayed, N., Jadva, V., Lamb, M. E., Tasker, F., & Golombok, S. (2019). Father-child attachment in adoptive gay father families. *Attachment and Human Development.* doi.org/10.1080/14616734.2019.1589067.

McConnachie, A. L., Ayed, N., Foley, S., Jadva, V., Lamb, M. E., Jadva, V., Tasker, F., & Golombok, S. (under review). Adoptive gay father families: A longitudinal study of children's adjustment at early adolescence. *Child Development.*

Study of gay father families formed through surrogacy

Golombok, S., Blake, L., Slutsky, J., Raffanello, E., Roman, G., & Ehrhardt, A. (2017) Parenting and the adjustment of children born to gay fathers through surrogacy. *Child Development, 89,* No 4, 1223–1233.

Blake, L., Carone, N., Raffanello, E., Slutsky, J., Ehrhardt, A., & Golombok, S. (2017) Gay fathers' motivations for and feelings about surrogacy as a path to parenthood. *Human Reproduction, 32,* No 4, 860–867.

Blake, L., Carone, N., Slutsky, J., Raffanello, E., Ehrhardt, A., & Golombok, S. (2016) Gay fathers through surrogacy: Relationships with surrogates and egg donors and parental disclosure of children's origins. *Fertility & Sterility, 106,* 1503–1509.

Chapter 7: Single Mothers by Choice

Survey of single mothers by choice

Jadva, V., Badger, S., Morrisette, M., & Golombok, S. (2009) 'Mom by choice, single by life's circumstance ...' Findings from a large-scale survey of the experiences of women who are 'single mothers by choice'. *Human Fertility*, *12*, 175–184.

Longitudinal study of single mothers by choice

Golombok, S., Zadeh, S., Imrie, S., Smith, V., & Freeman, T. (2016) Single mothers by choice: Mother-child relationships and children's psychological adjustment. *Journal of Family Psychology, 30*, No 4, 409–418.

Freeman, T., Zadeh, S., Smith, V., & Golombok, S. (2016) Disclosure of sperm donation: A comparison between solo mother and two-parent families with identity-release donors. *Reproductive BioMedicine Online, 33*, 592–600.

Zadeh, S., Freeman, T., & Golombok, S. (2016) 'What does donor mean to a four-year-old?' Initial insights into young children's perspectives in solo mother families. *Children and Society*, *31*, No 3, 194–205.

Zadeh, S., Jones, C., & Golombok, S. (2017) Children's thoughts and feelings about their donor and security of attachment to their solo mothers in middle childhood. *Human Reproduction*, *32*, No 4, 868–875.

Chapter 8: Trans Parent Families

Study of trans parent families

Zadeh, S., Imrie, S., & Golombok, S. (2019) Stories of sameness and difference: The views and experiences of children and adults with a trans* parent. *Journal of GLBT Family Studies*. DOI:10.1080/1550428X.2019.1683785.

Imrie, S., Zadeh, PS., Wylie, K., & Golombok, S. (under review) Children with trans parents: Parent-child relationship quality and psychological wellbeing. *Parenting: Science and Practice*.

Chapter 9: Future Families

Survey of people seeking co-parents

Jadva, V., Freeman, T., Tranfield, E., & Golombok, S. (2015) 'Friendly allies in raising a child': a survey of men and women seeking elective co-parenting arrangements via an online connection website. *Human Reproduction, 30,* No 8, 1896–1906.

Resources for children

During our research, something that came up again and again was that the families we spoke to don't see themselves represented in popular culture and this makes their children feel different to other children, which can cause distress.

There is still a long way to go before we reach true representation, but in the meantime, here is a list of children's books compiled by my publishers that celebrate different types of families:

And Tango Makes Three, Justin Richardson, Peter Parnell, and Henry Cole (Little Simon). A true story of two male penguins who create a non-traditional family. Ages 2–5.

Daddy, Papa and ME, Leslea Newman and Carol Thompson (Tricycle Press). Rhythmic text shows a toddler spending the day with their two daddies. Ages Baby–3.

Families, Families, Families, Suzanne Lang and Max Lang (Picture Corgi). Do you have two dads? Or one step mum? Or what about the world's biggest grandpa? Discover a whole host of silly animal families in this celebration of the love found in families big and small. Ages 3–5.

Love Makes a Family, Sophie Beer (Dial Books). Whether a child has two moms, two dads, one parent, or one of each, this simple preschool read-aloud demonstrates that what's most important in each family's life is the love the family members share. Ages Baby–3.

Mommy, Mama and ME, Leslea Newman and Carol Thompson (Tricycle Press). Rhythmic text shows a toddler spending the day with their two mummies. Ages Baby–3.

Our Story (Donor Conception Network). A series of illustrated books depicting different types of families. Ages 2–6.

Stella Brings the Family, Miriam B. Schiffer and Holly Clifton Brown (Chronicle Books). Stella's class is having a Mothers' Day celebration, but what's a girl with two daddies to do? A story about love, acceptance, and the true meaning of family. Ages 4–7.

The Extra Button, Jules Blundell (Michael Hanrahan Publishing). A sex-same gingerbread couple's journey to create a family using donor conception. Ages 3+.

The Family Book, Todd Parr (Little, Brown). Whether you have two mothers or two dads, a big family or a small family, a clean family or a messy one, Todd Parr assures readers that no matter what kind of family you have, every family is special in its own unique way. Ages 4–6.

The Girl with Two Dads, Mel Elliott (Egmont). Matilda is a new girl at Pearl's school, but there's something really different and cool about her family — she has TWO dads! Pearl is sure that Matilda's family must be very different to her own but, as they become friends, she starts to discover that maybe Matilda's family aren't so different after all … Ages 3–5.

The Lotterys Plus One, Emma Donoghue and Caroline Hadilaksono (Scholastic Inc.). What a family the Lotterys are: four parents, children both adopted and biological, and a menagerie of pets, all living and learning together in a sprawling house called Camelottery. Ages 8–12.

The Misadventures of the Family Fletcher, Dana Alison Levy (Yearling Books). A story about four adopted boys and their two fathers. Ages 9–12.

The Secrets of Sam and Sam, Susie Day and Max Kowalski (Puffin). The story of twins Sam and Sammie, who have two mums. Ages 8–11.

The Very Kind Koala, Kimberley Kluger-Bell (CreateSpace). A picture book for young children which provides an introduction to surrogacy. Ages 3+.

To Night Owl from Dogfish, Holly Goldberg-Sloan and Meg Wolitzer (Egmont). Avery (Night Owl) is bookish, intense, likes to plan ahead, and is afraid of many things. Bett (Dogfish) is fearless, outgoing, and lives in the moment. What they have in common is that they are both twelve years old, and their dads are dating each other. Ages 9+.

We Are Family, Patricia Hegarty and Ryan Wheatcroft (Caterpillar Books). Whether your family contains two dads or one mum; whether you're adopted or someone in your family is disabled; whether it's a big or small family – there's one thing that all families have in common, and that's love. Ages 3+.

What Makes a Baby, Cory Silverberg and Fiona Smyth (Seven Stories Press). A picture book about conception, gestation, and birth, which reflects the reality of the modern era. Ages 3–7.

Who's Your Real Mum?, Bernadette Green and Anna Zobel (Scribble). A story of a little girl with two mums that celebrates non-traditional families and captures exactly what lies at the heart of family life — love. Ages 3–6.

Acknowledgements

If it takes a village to raise a child, as the popular saying goes, it takes a whole other village to study how that child grows up. The research in this book would not have happened without the passion and commitment of an exceptional team of psychologists, sociologists, and other social scientists. I am deeply honoured to have had the opportunity to work with such a creative group of people. It has been exhilarating, sometimes difficult, but also full of fun.

At the Centre for Family Research in Cambridge, Vasanti Jadva has led our longitudinal investigation of families formed through egg donation, sperm donation and surrogacy, joined by others including Lucy Blake, Polly Casey, Jennifer Readings and Elena Ilioi. She also directed the follow-up study of UK surrogates with Susan Imrie, and the study of Indian surrogates with Nishtha Lamba. Tabitha Freeman and Vasanti Jadva initiated our research on donor siblings in the United States, and Sophie Zadeh and Tabitha Freeman designed and implemented the longitudinal study of single mothers by choice, carried out with the help of Jo Lysons and Kitty Jones. Susanna Graham also investigated single mothers by choice, as well as egg and sperm donors. Our UK study of adoptive gay father families was conducted by Anja McConnachie, Nadia Ayed, Laura Mellish and Sarah Jennings, and our US study of gay father families formed through surrogacy was led by Lucy Blake with the assistance of Jenna Slutsky and Elizabeth Raffanello. Susan Imrie and Sophie Zadeh pioneered the research on families with trans parents, and Susan Imrie spearheaded the study of families created with identifiable egg donors, in collaboration with Vasanti Jadva and Jo Lysons. The research on egg sharing was designed and carried out by Zeynep Gurtin. Most recently, investigations of co-parenting and single fathers by choice are being run by Sarah Foley and Sophie Zadeh, respectively, and Susie Bower-Brown is extending our work on trans parents. There are many others who have been involved along the way in Cambridge, London, and New York, including Fiona MacCallum, Emma Goodman, Claire Murray, Alison Bish, Emma Lycett, Beth Perry, Amanda Burston, Madeleine Stevens, Julie Mooney-Somers, Richard Harding, Margaret Pain, Larisa Villar-Hauser, Shirlene Badger, Sarah Evans, Humera Iqbal, John Appleby, Sherina Persaud, Gabriela Roman, Pamela Jiménez Etcheverria, Tatiana Visbol, Irenee Daly, Kate Shaw, Jess Grimmel, Niamh Chalmers, Georgie Jones, Poppy Hall, and the late Rachel Cook, as well as Diana Guerra in Barcelona, Maria Teresa Giavazzi in Milan, Anne Brewaeys in Leiden, and Francois Olivennes in Paris.

I can't imagine a more wonderful Administrator of the Centre for Family Research than Abby Scott. Her qualities are too many to list here so I would just like to say that working with her is a complete delight. I am also extremely grateful to Hannah Tigg, Administrative Assistant, for her huge contribution to the smooth running of the Centre and her amazing Friday cakes. My sincere thanks are due to my close colleagues Michael Lamb, Fiona Tasker, Anke Ehrhardt, Miriam Steele, Howard Steele, Melissa Hines, Claire Hughes, Helen Statham and Martin Richards, with whom I have collaborated over the years, and especially to Sir Michael Rutter, who supported the research in the early days when it was seen as too controversial by some, and uninteresting and pointless by others.

It goes without saying that the research would not have been possible without the many hundreds of families who have taken part, and who continue to welcome us into their homes. Thank you for trusting us with your personal stories, and for your unstinting kindness and hospitality, even in the face of our repeated visits as your children grow up. A big thank you to all the children who drew pictures for us, built houses from bricks, spoke to puppets and told us about their lives. A distinguished American psychologist once said to me that it's only longitudinal research that really tells us anything meaningful about child development, and I think there's a lot of truth in that. I am also deeply grateful to the parents and children who spoke to me for this book, sharing their most intimate thoughts, feelings, and experiences. Some wished me to change their names and identifying information, which I have done.

I am indebted to the Medical Research Council, the Economic and Social Research Council, the Nuffield Foundation, the European Commission, and the US National Institutes of Health, without whom the research described in this book would not have been possible. Special thanks are due to the Wellcome Trust who have gone above and beyond in supporting our work. I was awarded my first research grant from Wellcome in 1989, and they have provided the lion's share of our research funding since that time. I cannot thank them enough, not only for their financial support, but also for being such a far-sighted organisation, and for making their grant-holders feel valued, connected, and part of a much larger academic family. This book was set in motion by Kirty Topiwala, then Book Editor at Wellcome, who encouraged me to disseminate the findings of our research to a wider audience.

Carrie Plitt has been the best agent one could wish for. Thank you, Carrie, for championing this book and for teaching me about the importance of story-telling. My inspirational editor, Molly Slight, has nurtured this book from conception to birth. Thank you, Molly, and everyone at Scribe, including Philip Gwyn Jones and Adam Howard, for your enthusiasm and support. My heartfelt thanks to Susan Imrie, Vasanti Jadva and Sophie Zadeh for reading earlier versions and for their invaluable feedback, and to Andrew Solomon for reading early chapters. Thank you, Andrew, for your sharp insights, kind words, and generosity of spirit.

Finally, my fondest love goes to John, who has been there from the very start, and to Jamie, who arrived along the way.

Index

Credit: Suvi Roberts

Susan Golombok is one of the world's leading experts on new family forms. She is director of the Centre for Family Research at the University of Cambridge, a professorial fellow at Newnham College, Cambridge, and was a visiting professor at Columbia University in New York in 2005–2006 and retains an affiliation there. Golombok has often testified before governments, and her research was used as evidence in the US Supreme Court ruling on same-sex marriage in 2015. She lives in Cambridge, England.